GREAT PREACHING ON

THE RESURRECTION

GREAT PREACHING ON
THE RESURRECTION

COMPILED BY
CURTIS HUTSON

SWORD of the LORD
PUBLISHERS
P.O. BOX 1099, MURFREESBORO, TN 37133

ISBN 0-87398-319-X

Enlarged Edition: September, 1986

Printed and Bound in the United States of America

Preface

Here are nineteen sermons on the resurrection of Christ taken from the pages of THE SWORD OF THE LORD. These we feel were among the best sermons to be found on the subject.

The resurrection of Jesus Christ is the foundation for all Christian belief. It is the keystone in the arch which holds the other stones in place. Many other great doctrines stand or fall with the resurrection of Christ. The resurrection of Christ distinguishes Christianity from all other religions of the world. Every religion has a founder who lived, died and was buried; but Christianity has a Founder who lived, died, was buried, and after three days arose victoriously from the grave.

The resurrection of Christ is a fundamental of the Christian Faith. Paul said in Romans 10:9, "That if thou shalt confess with thy mouth the Lord Jesus, and shalt believe in thine heart that God hath raised him from the dead, thou shalt be saved." His resurrection is not only the proof of the work perfectly accomplished at the cross but also the pledge of the work yet to be done in those who believe. Our Lord's bodily resurrection insures the bodily resurrection of every believer. "But now is Christ risen from the dead, and become the firstfruits of them that slept" (I Cor. 15:20).

The Lord Jesus Christ arose to implement the most glorious plan, to assure us of the most important blessing, to impose upon us the most exalted duties, and to inspire us with the most elevated hopes.

Phillips Brooks, a prince of preachers of a generation past, is reported to have said that a sermon is the greatest of all forms of literature.

We think that a reading of this book of sermons will cause one to agree. The reader will be instructed and inspired as he reads these solid Bible messages on the greatest of all themes—the resurrection of Jesus Christ.

The Bible says of those early apostles, "And with great power gave the apostles witness of the resurrection of the Lord Jesus" (Acts 4:33).

Curtis Hutson
Editor, SWORD OF THE LORD

Table of Contents

I.   T. DeWITT TALMAGE
     Easter Joy 11

II. W. E. BIEDERWOLF
     Yes, He Arose 21

III. W. B. RILEY
     Jesus Christ Arose 35

IV. JOHN R. RICE
     The Importance of Christ's Resurrection
       in the Christian Faith 47

V.   CURTIS HUTSON
     Resurrection of Jesus Christ 71

VI. R. L. MOYER
     Supreme Importance of the Resurrection 87

VII. T. T. SHIELDS
     Testimony of the Resurrection 99

VIII. WILLIAM W. ORR
     I Believe It Is the Garden Tomb 109

IX. HYMAN APPELMAN
     Christ Is Risen 121

X.   D. L. MOODY
     Jesus Arose: So Shall We Rise 133

XI. H. A. IRONSIDE
     Implications of the Resurrection 147

XII. R. A. TORREY
     Up From the Grave He Arose! 155

XIII. CHARLES H. SPURGEON
    The Tomb of Jesus 169

XIV. B. H. CARROLL
    Infallible Proof of the Resurrection of Christ 185

XV. TOM MALONE
    The Biggest "IF" 201

XVI. SAM MORRIS
    "He Is Risen" 217

XVII. LOUIS T. TALBOT
    Christ Lives! 225

XVIII. JOHN R. RICE
    *Easter: Is It Wrong for Christians
    to Observe It?* 237

XIX. R. A. TORREY
    Christ's Crucifixion: Friday or Wednesday? 241

T. DeWITT TALMAGE
1832-1902

ABOUT THE MAN:

If Charles Spurgeon was the "Prince of Preachers," then T. DeWitt Talmage must be considered as one of the princes of the American pulpit. In fact, Spurgeon stated of Talmage's ministry: "His sermons take hold of my inmost soul. The Lord is with the mighty man. I am astonished when God blesses me but not surprised when He blesses him." He was probably the most spectacular pulpit orator of his time—and one of the most widely read.

Like Spurgeon, Talmage's ministry was multiplied not only from the pulpit to immense congregations, but in the printed pages of newspapers and in the making of many books. His sermons appeared in 3,000 newspapers and magazines a week, and he is said to have had 25 million readers.

And for 25 years, Talmage—a Presbyterian—filled the 4,000 to 5,000-seat auditorium of his Brooklyn church, as well as auditoriums across America and the British Isles. He counted converts to Christ in the thousands annually.

He was the founding editor of *Christian Herald,* and continued as editor of this widely circulated Protestant religious journal from 1877 until his death in 1902.

He had the face of a frontiersman and the voice of a golden bell; sonorous, dramatic, fluent, he was, first of all, an orator for God; few other evangelists had his speech. He poured forth torrents, deluges of words, flinging glory and singing phrases like a spendthrift; there was glow and warmth and color in every syllable. He played upon the heart-strings like an artist. One writer described him as the cultured Billy Sunday of his time. Many of his critics found fault with his methods; but they could not deny his mastery, nor could they successfully cloud his dynamic loyalty to his Saviour and Lord, Jesus Christ.

I.

Easter Joy

T. DeWITT TALMAGE

[The Brooklyn Tabernacle was elaborately decorated (April 25, 1886), both in platform and galleries. Within the church a scene of rare beauty was presented, the platform being covered with flowers arranged in various devices and breathing forth a delicate aroma. The building was so crowded that the doors were held open by the pressure, and many persons were turned away, being unable to get farther than the iron gate on the street.]

"But now is Christ risen from the dead, and become the firstfruits of them that slept." —I Cor. 15:20.

On this glorious Easter morning, amid the music and the flowers, I give you *Christian salutation.*

Hail! Easter morning. Flowers! flowers! All of them a-voice, all of them a-tongue, all of them full of speech today. I bend over one of the lilies and I hear it say: 'Consider the lilies of the field, how they grow; they toil not, neither do they spin, yet Solomon in all his glory was not arrayed like one of these.' I bend over a rose, and it seems to whisper: "I am the Rose of Sharon." And then I stand and listen. From all sides there comes the chorus of flowers, saying: "If God so clothe the grass of the field, which to day is, and to morrow is cast into the oven, shall he not much more clothe you, O ye of little faith?"

Flowers! Flowers! Braid them into the bride's hair. Flowers! Flowers! Strew them over the graves of the dead, sweet prophecy of the resurrection. Flowers! Flowers! Twist them into a garland for my Lord Jesus on Easter morning, and "Glory be to the Father, and to the Son, and to the Holy Ghost; as it was in the beginning, is now, and ever shall be."

Why, if a rainbow this morning had fallen and struck the platform, the scene could not have been more radiant. Oh, how bright and how beautiful the flowers, and how much they make me think of Christ and

His salvation that brightens everything it touches, brightens our life, brightens our character, brightens society, brightens the church, brightens everything! You who go with gloomy countenance pretending you are better than I am because of your lugubriousness, you cannot cheat. You old hypocrite! I know you. Pretty case you are for a man who professes to be more than conqueror! It is not religion that makes you gloomy, it is the lack of it. There is just as much religion in a wedding as in a burial, just as much religion in a smile as in a tear.

Those gloomy Christians we sometimes see are the people to whom I like to lend money, for I never see them again! The women came to the Saviour's tomb, and they dropped spices all around the tomb, and those spices were the seeds that began to grow, and from them came all the flowers of this Easter morn. The two angels robed in white took hold of the stone at the Saviour's tomb, and they hurled it with such force down the hill that it crushed in the door of the world's sepulchre, and the stark and the dead must come forth.

I care not how labyrinthine the mausoleum or how costly the sarcophagus or however beautifully parterred the family grounds, ye want them all broken up by the Lord of the resurrection. They must come out. Father and mother—they must come out. Husband and wife—they must come out. Brother and sister—they must come out. Our darling children—they must come out. The eyes that we close with such trembling fingers must open again in the radiance of that morn. The arms we folded in dust must join ours in an embrace of reunion. The voice that was hushed in our dwelling must be returned.

Oh, how long some of you seem to be waiting—waiting for the resurrection, waiting! And for those broken hearts today I make a soft, cool bandage out of Easter flowers.

Six years ago the night before Easter, I received an Easter card on which there was a representation of the exquisite flower, the trumpet creeper; and under it the words: "The trumpet shall sound and the dead shall rise." There was especial reason why at that time I should have that card sent me, and I present the same consolation today to all in this house, and who has escaped?

Christ in Rising From the Dead Conquered Death for All His Own

My friends, this morning I find in the risen Christ a prophecy of our own resurrection, my text setting forth the idea that as Christ has risen so His people will rise. He—the first sheaf of the resurrection harvest. He— "the firstfruits of them that slept." Before I get through this morning, I will walk through all the cemeteries of the dead, through all the country graveyards where your loved ones are buried; and I will pluck off these flowers, and I will drop a sweet promise of the Gospel—a rose of hope, a lily of joy on every tomb—the child's tomb, the husband's tomb, the wife's tomb, the father's grave, the mother's grave; and while we celebrate the resurrection of Christ, we will at the same time celebrate the resurrection of all the saved. "Christ the firstfruits of them that slept."

If I should come to you this morning and ask for the names of the great conquerors of the world, you would say Alexander, Caesar, Philip, Napoleon I. Ah! my friends, you have forgotten to mention the name of a greater conqueror than all these—a cruel, a ghastly conqueror. He rode on a black horse across Waterloo and Atlanta and Chalons, the bloody hoofs crushing the hearts of nations. It is the conqueror—Death.

He carries a black flag, and he takes no prisoners. He digs a trench across the hemispheres and fills it with the carcasses of nations. Fifty times the world would have been depopulated had not God kept making new generations. Fifty times the world would have swung lifeless through the air—no man on the mountain, no man on the sea, an abandoned ship ploughing through immensity. Again and again has he done his work with all generations. *He is a monarch* as well as a conqueror; his palace a sepulchre; his fountains the falling tears of a world.

Blessed be God, in the light of this Easter morning, I see the prophecy that his sceptre shall be broken and his palace be demolished. The hour is coming when all who are in their graves shall come forth. Christ risen, we shall rise. Jesus—"the firstfruits of them that slept."

Now, around this doctrine of the resurrection there are a great many mysteries.

No Trouble for a Miracle-Working God to Raise the Dead

You come to me this morning and say, "If the bodies of the dead are to be raised, how is this, and how is that?" and you ask me a thousand questions I am incompetent to answer; but there are a great many things *you believe* that you are not able to *explain*. You would be a very foolish man to say, "I won't believe anything I can't understand."

Why, putting down one kind of flower seed, comes there up this flower of this color? Why, putting down another flower seed, comes there up a flower of this color? One flower white, another flower yellow, another flower crimson. Why the difference when the seeds look to be very much alike—are very much alike? Explain these things.

Explain that wart on the finger. Explain the difference why the oak leaf is different from the leaf of the hickory. Tell me how the Lord Almighty can turn the chariot of His omnipotence on a rose leaf. You ask me questions about the resurrection I cannot answer. I will ask you a thousand questions about everyday life you cannot answer.

I find my strength in this passage: "All who are in their graves shall come forth." I do not pretend to make the explanation. You go on and say: "Suppose a returned missionary dies in Brooklyn; when he was in China, his foot was amputated; he lived years after in England, and there he had an arm amputated; he is buried today in Greenwood; in the resurrection will the foot come from China, will the arm come from England, and will the different parts of the body be reconstructed in the resurrection? How is that possible?"

You say, "The human body changes every seven years, and by seventy years of age a man has had ten bodies; in the resurrection which will come up?" You say, "A man will die and his body crumble into the dust, and that dust be taken up into the life of the vegetable; an animal may eat the vegetable; men eat the animal. In the resurrection, that body, distributed in so many directions, how shall it be gathered up?" Have you any more questions of this style to ask? Come on and ask them. I do not pretend to answer them. I fall back upon the announcement of God's Word: "All who are in their graves shall come forth."

You have noticed, I suppose, in reading the story of the resurrection, that almost every account of it in the Bible gives the idea that the characteristic of that day will be a great sound. I do not know that it will be very loud, but I know it will be very penetrating. In the mausoleum where silence has reigned a thousand years, that voice must penetrate. Millions of spirits will come through the gates of eternity, and they will come to the tombs of the earth, and they will cry: "Give us back our bodies; we gave them to you in corruption; surrender them now in incorruption." Hundreds of spirits hovering about the crags of Gettysburg, for there the bodies are buried. A hundred thousand spirits coming to Greenwood, for there the bodies are buried, waiting for the reunion of body and soul.

All along the sea route from New York to Liverpool, at every few miles where a steamer went down, departed spirits coming back, hovering over the wave. There is where the *City of Boston* perished—found at last. There is where the *President* perished. Steamer found at last. There is where the *Central America* went down. Spirits hovering—hundreds of spirits hovering, *waiting for the reunion of body and soul.* Out on the prairie a spirit alights. There is where a traveler died in the snow. Crash goes Westminster Abbey, and the poets and orators come forth.

Who can sketch the scene? I suppose that one moment before that rising there will be an entire silence, save as you hear the grinding of a wheel, or the clatter of the hooves of a procession passing into the cemetery. Silence in all the caves of the earth. Silence on the side of the mountain. Silence down in the valleys and far out into the sea. Silence!

But in a moment, in the twinkling of an eye, as the archangel's trumpet comes pealing, rolling, crashing across the mountain and sea, the earth will give a terrific shudder; and the graves of the dead will heave like the waves of the sea. The drowned will come up and lift up their wet locks above the billow; and all the land and all the sea become *one moving mass of life*—all faces, all ages, all conditions gazing in one direction and upon one throne—the throne of resurrection. "All who are in their graves shall come forth."

"But," you say, "if this doctrine of the resurrection is true, as prefigured by this Easter morning, Christ, 'the firstfruits of them that slept,' Christ's rising a promise and a prophecy of the rising of all His people, can you tell us something about the resurrected body?"

I can. There are mysteries about that, but I shall tell you three or four things in regard to the resurrected body that are beyond guessing and beyond mistake.

I. RESURRECTION BODY—A GLORIOUS BODY

In the first place, I remark in regard to your resurrected body: *it will be a glorious body.* The body we have now is a mere skeleton of what it would have been if sin had not marred and defaced it.

Take the most exquisite statue that was ever made by an artist, and chip it here and chip it there with a chisel, and batter and bruise it here and there, and then stand it out in the storms of a hundred years, and the beauty would be gone. Well, the human body has been chipped and battered and bruised and damaged with the storms of thousands of years—the physical defects of other generations coming down from generation to generation. We inherit the infelicities of past generations;

but in the morning of the resurrection, the body will be adorned and beautified according to the original model. And there is not so much difference between a gymnast and an emaciated wretch in a lazaretto, as there will be a difference between our bodies as they are now and our resurrected forms.

There you will see the perfect eye after the waters of death have washed out the stains of tears and study. There you will see the perfect hand after the knots of toil have been untied from the knuckles. There you will see the form erect and elastic after the burdens have gone off the shoulder—the very life of God in the body.

In this world, the most impressive thing, the most expressive thing, is the human face; but that face is veiled with the griefs of a thousand years; but in the resurrection morn *that veil will be taken away* from the face, and the noonday sun is dull and dim and stupid compared with the outflaming glories of the countenances of the saved. When those faces of the righteous, those resurrected faces, turn toward the gate or look up toward the throne, it will be like the dawning of a new morning on the bosom of everlasting day! O glorious, resurrected body!

II. RESURRECTION BODY—AN IMMORTAL BODY

But I remark also in regard to that body, which you are to get in the resurrection, it will be an immortal body. These bodies are wasting away. Somebody has said that as soon as we begin to live, we begin to die. Unless we keep putting the fuel into the furnace, the furnace dies out. The blood vessels are canals taking the breadstuffs to all parts of the system. We must be reconstructed hour by hour, day by day. Sickness and death are all the time trying to get their prey under the tenement or to push us off the embankment of the grave. But, blessed be God, in the resurrection we will get a body immortal. No malaria in the air, no cough, no neuralgic twinge, no rheumatic pang, no fluttering of the heart, no shortness of breath, no ambulance, no dispensary, no hospital, no invalid's chair, no spectacles to improve the dim vision; but health, immortal health! O ye who have aches and pains indescribable this morning—O ye who are never well—O ye who are lacerated with physical distresses, let me tell you of the resurrected body, *free from all disease.* Immortal! Immortal!

III. RESURRECTION BODY—A POWERFUL BODY

I go further and say in regard to that body which you are to get in the resurrection, it will be a powerful body. We walk now eight or ten miles, and we are fatigued. We lift a few hundred pounds, and we are exhausted. Unarmed, we meet a wild beast; and we must run or fly or climb or dodge because we are incompetent to meet it. We toil eight or ten hours vigorously, and then we are weary. But in the resurrection we are to have a body that *never gets tired.* Is it not a glorious thought?

Plenty of occupation in Heaven. I suppose Broadway, New York, in the busiest season of the year, at noonday, is not so busy as Heaven is all the time. Grand projects of mercy. Victories to be celebrated. The downfall of despotisms on earth to be announced. Great expeditions on which God shall send forth His children. *Plenty to do, but no fatigue.* If you are seated under the tree of life, it will not be to rest but to talk over with some old comrade old times—the battles where you fought shoulder to shoulder.

Sometimes in this world we feel we would like to have such a body as that. There is so much work to be done for Christ, so many tears to be wiped away, so many burdens to lift, so much to be achieved for Christ, we sometimes wish that from the first of January to the last of December we could toil on without stopping to sleep or take any recreation or to rest or even to take food—that we could toil right on without stopping a moment in our work of commending Christ and Heaven to all the people. But we all get tired.

It is a characteristic of the human body in this condition: we must get tired. Is it not a glorious thought that after a while, after the service of God, we are going to have a body that will never get weary? O glorious resurrection day! Gladly will I fling aside this poor body of sin and fling it into the tomb, if at Thy bidding I shall have a body that never wearies.

That was a splendid resurrection hymn that was sung at my father's burial:

> **So Jesus slept, God's dying Son**
> **Passed through the grave and blessed the bed.**
> **Rest here, blest saint, till from His throne**
> **The morning breaks to pierce the shade.**

O blessed resurrection! Speak out sweet flowers, beautiful flowers. While you tell of a risen Christ, tell of the righteous who shall rise. May God fill you this morning with anticipation!

We Will Meet Our Christian Loved Ones in the Resurrection

I heard of a father and son who, among others, were shipwrecked at sea. Father and son climbed onto the rigging. The father held on, but the son after a while lost his hold on the rigging and was dashed down. The father supposed he had gone hopelessly under the wave. The next day the father was brought ashore from the rigging in an exhausted state and laid in a bed in a fisherman's hut. After many hours had passed, he came to consciousness and saw lying beside him on the same bed his boy.

Oh, my friends! what a glorious thing it will be if we wake up at last to find our loved ones beside us—coming up from the same plot in the graveyard, coming up in the same morning light. The father and son alive forever, all the loved ones alive forever, nevermore to weep, nevermore to part, nevermore to die.

May the God of peace, that brought again from the dead our Lord Jesus, the great Shepherd of the sheep, through the blood of that everlasting covenant, make you perfect in every good work, to do His will; and let this brilliant scene of the morning transport our thoughts to the grander assemblage before the throne. This august assemblage is nothing compared with it. The one hundred and forty and four thousand, and the "great multitude that no man can number," some of our best friends among them, we, after a while, to join the multitude. Blessed anticipation.

> **Blest are the saints beloved of God,**
> **Washed are their robes in Jesus' blood,**
> **Brighter than angels, lo! they shine,**
> **Their wonders splendid and sublime.**
>
> **My soul anticipates the day,**
> **Would stretch her wings and soar away,**
> **To aid the son, the palm to bear,**
> **And bow, the chief of sinners, there.**

WILLIAM EDWARD BIEDERWOLF
1867-1934

ABOUT THE MAN:

Presbyterians produced some of the most noteworthy evangelists of the late 1800's and early 1900's—and a notable among them was William E. Biederwolf.

After his conversion, he continued his education at Princeton, Erlangen and Berlin universities, and at the Sorbonne in Paris.

Biederwolf's first church was the Broadway Presbyterian Church of Logansport, Indiana, the state where he was born. Then he became a chaplain in the Spanish-American War and then entered evangelism—a ministry he was to serve for 35 years.

In conjunction with his evangelism, Dr. Biederwolf was associated with the world-renowned Winona Lake Bible Conference for 40 years.

In 1929, he became pastor at the storied Royal Poinciana Chapel in Palm Beach, Florida, a position he held until his death.

Biederwolf's ministry was mighty. Perhaps his greatest campaign was in Oil City, Pennsylvania, in the bitter winter of 1914. Thousands thronged the tabernacle. Twice it was enlarged. His messages were pungent and powerful.

His kind of preaching brought men and women from every walk in life coming in deep contrition for their sins—the mayor of the city, physicians, lawyers, and men from the factories, young people from the schools; and the whole city and county were mightily stirred in deep concern about the things of God.

He was the author of several books.

II.

Yes, He Arose

WILLIAM EDWARD BIEDERWOLF

"If Christ be not risen, then is our preaching vain, and your faith is also vain." —I Cor. 15:14.

I always feel when I approach the subject of the resurrection as though God were saying, "Take off thy shoes from off thy feet, for the ground whereon thou standest is holy ground," and I bow with uncovered head in the presence of a subject wrapped round about with such divine glory, awful majesty and solemn, soul-moving awe as this one.

There are interesting subjects connected with the Christian religion, but there are none more interesting than the resurrection. There are other important subjects, but hardly any so important as this one, for, "If Christ be not risen, then is our preaching vain, and your faith is also vain," and, "If in this life only we have hope in Christ, we are of all men most miserable," and this Gospel I preach is a fake and it isn't worth a half a hallelujah more than Buddhism or Theosophy or Unitarianism or Christian Science or any other system of ethics as a religion to save your soul and keep it out of Hell.

You know Renan, the old French infidel, wrote up the life of Jesus; and when he had brought it along as far as the cross where Jesus died, Renan wrote the word, *Finis,* as if that were the end of it all. The fellow who printed the book, his publisher, as unbelieving and even more bigoted than Renan himself, put on the fly-leaf after that lying, dismal word, *Finis,* a woodcut of the crucified Saviour. There He was, hanging on the cross with drooping head, matted hair and pale, blood-streaked face. Everybody had deserted Him; the storm clouds had gathered in the sky, and black-pinioned birds were circling through the gloom. Everything about the scene spelled defeat.

Well, Jesus did die that way. But He didn't have to. One word from those silent lips of His and all Heaven would have rushed to His rescue. I think it was all God could do to keep them back anyhow. I think Michael pulled his sword and wanted to lead them on. I can almost see him and hear him. I can see him hang out over the ramparts of Heaven and shout, "O Jesus, if you want us to come, just lift your hand and wave it; you can do it as easy as if it weren't nailed. Nod your head, Jesus; just make some sign and there'll be something doing the world will never forget."

But Jesus said, "No, Michael, I can't do it; the Father and I know why I am here, and it is best for Me to die." Then He bowed His head and cried, "It is finished," and He was dead.

Yes, it was finished. But what was finished? The redemption of the world! And when Renan wrote that word, *Finis,* he bore witness to a mightier truth than ever he dreamed. But he didn't mean it that way. He meant the thing was all up and that when they laid Jesus away in the tomb of Joseph of Arimathaea, He rotted away like any other dead Jew.

And yet it was not finished. They laid Him in the tomb and said, "We'll seal it and put a Roman guard about it because He said He would rise. We will fix Him and show the world He was a faker." That's what they said, and that's what they did.

But do you remember about old King Chanute's going down to the beach and commanding the tide not to roll in? Well, that was a dead easy thing to expect compared with expecting that Jesus would stay in the grave when He had said He would rise! For the bars of death could not hold Him.

Renan said the resurrection of Jesus was a myth and that the theory of a resurrected God came out of the passion and strong imagination of Mary Magdalene, an hallucinated woman. And Strauss and Weissaker and Haechel and a lot of other infidels and Christless unbelievers have said other things and done everything under God's Heaven to get rid of this fundamental thing upon which the whole superstructure of the Christian faith is reared.

No wonder the old Devil has trained all the heavy artillery of Hell against this great fortress; for when it goes, the throne of God must fall, all Heaven must capitulate, and it's all off with religion; and that would make Hell howl with delight.

Now there are three questions I want to ask and answer about the resurrection.

First—Could God raise Jesus from the dead?

Second—Did God raise Jesus from the dead?

Third—Why did God raise Jesus from the dead?

I. COULD GOD RAISE JESUS FROM THE DEAD?

When Paul preached the resurrection, those old Epicurean and Stoic philosophers up in Athens called him a "babbler" and a "setter forth of strange doctrines." But Paul said, "Why should it be thought a thing incredible that God should raise the dead?"

Now I am not going to waste any time with the so-called scientific arguments against the possibility of this thing. Admit God, and impossibility must throw up its hands.

Most of the scientific objections to Christianity are born out of unbelief anyhow; and when they are not, it is amusing to see how quickly unthinking unbelief makes an idiot out of itself by using them to knife religion, until some old tablet is dug up or something turns up and tells science where to get off.

You know the science of chemistry once analyzed man and found that the brain in its final analysis culminated in phosphorus. My, how the discovery startled us! Phosphorus composed the "Hallelujah Chorus," painted the Sistine Madonna and wrote Tennyson's *In Memoriam!* And then the wiseacres went on and had it doped out for us that phosphorus was the basis of everything.

It was about this time that an old skeptic, who always took great delight in trying to argue his old black neighbor out of his faith, thought he had him cornered at last and said to him, "Mose, it's all up with your religion now."

"How do you make dat out?" said Mose.

"Well, you say the Bible teaches that all the dead shall be resurrected, and we have just found out that everything is made out of phosphorus. Now if all the millions and millions who have died and who are to die are to be given resurrection bodies, there won't be enough phosphorus to go around."

"Oh," said Mose, "der's no difficulty 'bout dat. Don't de Bible say de dead in Christ shall rise fust? Dey'll be plenty phosphorus for dem what rises fust, but you and de oders like you will have to scratch 'round for your phosphorus."

I like that simple sort of faith in the Word of God!

I like what Kuyper, that great and learned Dutch statesman, said:

> If then, after all legitimate examination and explanation there still remains (in the test) seeming inexplicables, *cruces interpretum,* before

which not I—for that implies nothing—but all confessing theologians stand, even then I do not hesitate a moment to say in the hearing of the whole scientific world, that facing the choice between leaving this question unanswered, and with the simple-minded people of God confessing my ignorance, or with the learned ethical brethren from scientific logicalness rejecting the infallibility of Scripture, I firmly choose the first, and with my whole soul shrink back from the last.

No, my friends, the possibility of this thing we are not going to argue. Admit God and incredulity will vanish into thin air. Do you expect to limit the God who out of nothing created the heavens and the earth! the God who hung the planets upon the air and sent them whirling and whizzing along their courses crossing a thousand tracks of other worlds with minute precision! the God who flashed a ray of created light through a waterdrop sparkling with His glory and left it upon Heaven's transparent curtain half circled in all the bewildering colors of the rainbow! the God who made the inanimate animate and called into being every living thing, the author of life Himself!?

"Why," said Paul, "should it be thought a thing incredible that God should raise the dead?" Of course He could do it. And if He couldn't do it, then we haven't any God and that's all there is to it.

II. DID GOD RAISE JESUS FROM THE DEAD?

DeWette, one of the great leaders of Rationalism, labored on this thing with the most precise and scientific investigation; and he said, "The resurrection of Jesus Christ cannot be called into doubt any more than the historical certainty of the assassination of Caesar." This is the statement that made Neander, the great church historian, shed tears when he read it.

The Old Testament prophesied the resurrection of Jesus. Jesus said He would rise. But did He rise?

1. There was an angel there who said He did. He said to the women on Easter morning, "I know that ye seek Jesus who was crucified. He is not here. He is risen. Come and see the place where they laid him."

"Oh," you say, "that's all a lie worked up by the writers to pull the wool over our eyes."

All right; it takes more than an angel to make some people come across.

2. Jesus appeared eleven times after His resurrection. You say, "How do we know?"

I say, "The Bible says so."

You say, "The whole thing is a fabrication, and the writers lied."

I say, "You belittle yourself for the want of good judgment."

Examine the account with a microscope and you can tell mighty quick that it is not a fabrication. Why did they represent a weak woman offering to carry away the body of a full-grown man? If it were a lie that was to be manufactured and I had written it, I would have made her say, "Tell me where you have laid him and I will get a dray and haul Him away."

Why did they make Christ fold up that napkin so carefully? I would have made Him tear it from His face, slam it into a corner and jump out on the run.

And in a dozen other ways it's a mighty poor story if they made it up. Why did they write it up that way? Because that is just the way it happened.

3. The disciples said He did. You say, "The disciples lied and knew they were lying when they said it."

Well, but the disciples died for it, and it is strange they would die for what they knew was a lie.

4. The enemies of His resurrection have never been able to present one iota of evidence that He did not rise. When the apostles went up and down the land and hurled this doctrine into their very teeth, His enemies never peeped except to say the disciples stole the body. And that's a fool thing to say, as I'll show you.

5. Now, if Jesus did not rise from the dead, how are you going to account for the empty grave? If all the infidels on this side of Hell were to go into session for the purpose of exploding and overthrowing the resurrection of Jesus, I could hurl the empty sepulchre into the midst of their diabolical deliberations and utterly confound and confuse them.

The empty grave! Say that, and you have them going. For they all have to admit it. The most bitter opponent does. Even old infidel Schenkel says, "It is an indisputable fact in the early morning of the first day of the week following the crucifixion, the grave of Jesus was found empty."

Well, then, if the grave was empty and there was no resurrection, either His friends or His foes took the body away.

Of course, His enemies didn't take it away; for if they had, they would have produced it as the most effectual way of shutting the mouths of the disciples who were preaching everywhere that God had raised Him from the dead.

Let us look, then, at some of the theories the infidels advance to get rid of the resurrection. There are three of them.

A. Some of the infidels and critics of the resurrection say the disciples stole the body, then deliberately tried to deceive the world. That is the bluff the Jews tried to get away with. "They gave large money to the soldiers, saying, Say ye, His disciples came by night and stole him away while we slept."

But that is a fool's argument. These disciples laid down their lives for this thing, and no man would die for what he knew was a lie. Men will die for error, but not for what they know is a fake. Men lay down their lives for what they believe. Even old Strauss says, "This much must be acknowledged, that the apostles firmly believed that Jesus had risen."

Come again, Mr. Infidel.

B. Some of them say He never died — He was just in a swoon. The odor of the spices and the cool air of the tomb revived Him — He came back, got up and left the tomb.

But there are four arguments that knock this old swoon theory into a cocked hat.

It makes a history out a joke. In the first place, old Strauss put it right when he said that a man who crept forth half dead from the grave and crawled about, a fit subject for a hospital, could never have so impressed His disciples that He was the conqueror of death and the grave as to have made their moral transformation one of the marvels of the world.

It makes the disciples out a set of consummate fools. They recorded all sorts of things about Him after His resurrection that couldn't be true of Him if He came out of the tomb with the same physical body He had when He entered it.

It makes Jesus out a fool. Do you suppose for one minute that Jesus would risk the founding of a religion which He expected to sweep around the world and which He knew would arouse the keenest antagonism of those hard-headed Jews and the criticism of Gentile philosophy and challenge the dictum of Science, upon a statement so flimsy and so easy to have a hole knocked through it as that? Give Him credit for a little sense anyhow.

It makes Jesus out an unprincipled monster. The disciples thought He had died, but He knew He hadn't. And yet this thing that remolded their lives, this thing that furnished them the ground of their hopes, this thing they depended upon to convert the world, this thing for which they laid down their lives, He knew was a lie; and yet He never told them. You can't put anything over on Jesus like that. You must admit He was decent, if nothing else.

Come again, Mr. Infidel.

C. Well, some of them say the disciples had a brainstorm. They were hallucinated. They thought they saw Him, but they never did. This is the famous Vision Theory. The Hallucination Theory is a better name for it. Old Renan and Strauss are the biggest guns back of this theory.

Well, when you're talking about absurdity, you've got to go some to beat that. It is the limit. You can prove its absurdity in a dozen different ways.

If it were only a vision, how did it happen at times to last so long? Visions are usually over in a minute and at most a few minutes, but the walk to Emmaus and other appearances lasted for hours. The theory's absurd.

He appeared to the disciples at the same instant, and five hundred saw Him on one occasion. Who ever heard of this many people having the same vision at the same time? These old infidels deny one miracle and want us to substitute five hundred miracles in its place. The theory is foolish.

If they were visions, how did they happen to end so suddenly? Hallucinated enthusiasm doesn't usually work that way. You would expect more glorious visions and more frequent ones as the time went on, especially round about the time of Pentecost when people were so wrought up and in the days of persecution when they especially felt the need of His presence. But at the end of forty days they suddenly stopped. The theory is silly.

After the disciples found out He had really risen, they expected Him to appear in Galilee. The angel and Jesus Himself said He would, yet that very night He appeared to them at Jerusalem. If the so-called appearances were only visions and so depended on the mental state of the disciples, how are you going to explain this? It's up to you. The theory is nonsensical.

Any one of these arguments blows your Hallucination Theory into smithereens, knocks it into a cocked hat, whips it to a frazzle, puts it out of commission.

But say, Mr. Skeptic, here is one that will get you. If, as Renan says, the hallucinated imagination of Mary and the disciples gave to the world a resurrected God, how are you going to account for the fact that in spite of what Jesus said about His resurrection, they were not expecting Him to rise?

They went on the third morning to the tomb to anoint a dead body, not to behold a risen Lord. When they found Him gone, they did not even think of Him as risen; and Mary said to the disciples, "Someone has taken him away, and we know not where they have laid him."

When the disciples were told of His resurrection, it is said, "They believed not."

After the two disciples on the way to Emmaus had been told of His resurrection, they told Christ all that had happened but said they did not know what had become of Jesus.

And finally when He did appear, instead of grasping at the fulfillment of their so-called dream and hallucination, it says, "they were terrified and affrighted and supposed that they had seen a spirit."

Hallucination, nothing! The theory is a joke. The trouble is with the fellow who got it up. He had something worse than hallucination of the brain. And yet you will find a lot of little cap-and-gown professors in our universities today, and colleges and schools, and, alas, in some places of ecclesiastical learning who, in their inordinate desire to get rid of the supernatural, will pump that stuff into their students as the brilliant conclusion of their own self-estimated colossal and stupendous intellect.

Talk about being progressive! They're nothing but theological crawfish, crawling back to Renan and Strauss and back to Porphry and Celsus and other old destructive critics of ten centuries ago. There is nothing to it. Jesus did rise from the dead. Mrs. Eddy says He didn't die, but was alive in the tomb demonstrating the truth of Christian Science.

I suppose that's what she is doing now. But she is not getting there quite as fast as He did. Some of her followers said she would rise, but you know what Billy Sunday said he would do if she did.

III. IF GOD COULD AND DID RAISE HIM, WHY DID HE?

For four reasons.

1. He did it to make good the word of His blessed Son and to establish once for all and beyond all doubt the truth of His glorious divinity. I read in Romans 1:4 that Christ was "declared to be the Son of God with power . . . by the resurrection from the dead."

If, as the English poet says, the Syrian stars look down every night upon His grave, how are you going to explain His repeated claim that He would rise on the third day, except that He was a liar or a lunatic?

He asked the Jews why they were stoning Him and they said, "Because you, being a man, claim to be God, and you are a blasphemer." Well, He did claim it; and if He was in His right mind, it was either so or it was the rankest blasphemy. Jesus said He would prove it by His resurrection, and God had to raise Him to make good His word and so prove Him to be what He claimed He was. Where does Unitarianism get off in the light of the resurrection? To perdition with the idea that Jesus Christ was only a good man.

2. He did it to furnish every believer the God-given assurance that he is justified in Christ Jesus. Romans 4:25 says that Jesus "was raised again for our justification." You know Jesus said He came to "offer his life a ransom for many" (Matt. 20:28), that He would die to make atonement. And He did. But if God hadn't raised Him from the dead, we never would have known that the atonement was accepted; so "He was raised again for our justification." It makes no difference how much you have sinned in the past; God will count you righteous for Christ's sake if you want Him to. But there is no way to escape the damnation of Hell if you turn your back on Jesus Christ.

3. He did it to let men know that there isn't any doubt about the judgment to come. Paul said, "[God] hath appointed a day, in the which he will judge the world in righteousness by [Jesus Christ] . . . wherefore he hath given assurance unto all men, in that he hath raised him from the dead" (Acts 17:31).

Jesus said the hour was coming when the dead would hear His voice and rise, "they that have done good, unto the resurrection of life; and they that have done evil, unto the resurrection of damnation [judgment]." When they laughed and called Him a fool, God put His own seal on the claim by raising Him from the dead. Nothing is more certain in God's universe than that there is a judgment day coming.

Oh, you say you don't care for the judgment! No! But you won't be in it two minutes until you will change your mind so quick it will make your head swim.

Oh, no, you wouldn't care for judgment? You're a brave one—you are!

4. He did it so everyone united to Jesus Christ by faith may know that they also are going to be raised from the dead. Do you remember what Paul said about the resurrection? "Christ the firstfruits; afterwards they that are Christ's at his coming."

I know the Devil sometimes gives you a good run for your faith, and maybe you begin to doubt a little. You go and stand by the grave and see the coffin go down and something seems to say, "Will I ever see the dear one again?" And your own heart says, *No.* Everything around you says, *No.* Then you think of the words of Paul, "If we believe that Jesus died and rose again, even so them also which sleep in Jesus will God bring with him" when He comes. You brush away your tears and hear the voice of Jesus say, "I am the resurrection, and the life: he that believeth in me, though he were dead, yet shall he live," and, "Thy father shall rise again"; and, "Thy mother shall rise again"; and, "Thy sister shall rise again." You thank God and sorrow not as others who have no hope.

Everything depends on the resurrection of Jesus Christ. That's the cornerstone upon which the whole superstructure of Christianity rests; undermine it, and the whole business drops. It is the keystone of the arch; knock it out, and the whole thing falls with a crash.

If Jesus Christ did not rise from the dead, how do I know that He is the Way, the Truth and the Life?

How do I know that He that believeth on the Lord Jesus Christ shall be saved?

How do I know that the blood of Jesus Christ cleanseth from all sin?

How do I know that He has gone to prepare a place for me and that He will come again and receive me unto Himself?

How do I know that death has lost its sting and the grave has been swallowed up in victory?

How do I know that the Spirit of God who raised Jesus Christ from the dead shall also quicken my mortal body?

How do I know that when He shall appear I shall be like Him?

How do I know that "the sufferings of this present time are not worthy to be compared with the glory which shall be revealed in me"?

How do I know that the promises of this Book are worth any more than the ink it took to print them or the paper it takes to hold them?

I don't know. There is no way to know. If Jesus Christ did not rise from the dead, then I have nothing to do but to take a chisel and hammer and go out to the grave of my loved ones and chisel away the beautiful words, "I am the resurrection and the life," and cut in their place the cold, icy and heart-breaking words, "I do not know; I have no way to tell."

"If Christ be not risen," Paul says, "our preaching is in vain, and your faith is vain also," and "of all men we are most miserable."

But, thank God, He did rise! They sealed His tomb, but it couldn't hold Him. He lay there cold and dead in the grave. All earth had given up hope, but all Heaven knew better. I think Gabriel must have said to the celestial choir, "Hold your breath a minute now, for you'll need it"; and as the minute of the world's mightiest miracle ticked off, the breath of God swept through the sleeping clay; and like a flash of light, His glorious Son was on His feet again, while Heaven's angelic choir rose tier upon tier and row upon row and shouted, "Hallelujah! Hallelujah! Hallelujah! Christ is risen! The Son of God is alive!"

Glory to Jesus!

> **Up from the grave He arose,**
> **With a mighty triumph o'er His foes.**
> **He arose a victor from the dark domain,**
> **And He lives forever with His saints to reign.**
> **He arose! He arose!**
> **Hallelujah, Christ arose.**

He is up there now at the right hand of God pleading His atoning death for you and me. Don't you feel like waving Him a Chautauqua salute and saying, "Hurry, Jesus, and come back again"? For when He comes again, even those also who are asleep in Him will He bring with Him. What a day that will be!

Excuse the personal reference, but I can't help it. I saw the place where they laid Him. All four of the Gospels say it was a new tomb, and it was. In fact, it was unfinished.

The golden sunlight was streaming in through the open door, for the stone was not there. The Bible says Peter stooped down and went in. So would you have to stoop if you entered. I saw four niches for members of Joseph's family that had never been occupied and one commenced but never finished. Then I looked into the place where I believed my Saviour to have been laid. But, Hallelujah! He was not there! He had risen! I can seem to feel the tears running down my cheeks now as they did then in the solemn presence. I bowed myself, and how long I stayed I do not know. But I said, "O empty tomb of Christ, tell me something of that strange morning." And it said:

"Biederwolf, it was strange indeed. Outside the birds were singing their morning carols and the sun was just shooting his silver arrows through the gates of the eastern skies, but in here it was all dark and quiet. Then suddenly it seemed as if the blazing sun itself had dropped into the tomb, and two angels appeared.

"One sat down quietly at my head and the other at my foot. Then the earth shook and I heard something snap like the breaking of a seal. The stone commenced to roll back. Jesus, who had been lying here cold and dead for three days and nights, stirred and stood up. He didn't make any fuss about it. He first took the napkin off His face and said, 'Good morning, Gabriel. Good morning, Michael.' He folded the napkin and laid it by itself, then took off the linen graveclothes. He said, 'Gabriel, stay here. Michael, stay here. Tell the women when they come to anoint My body what has taken place. I'll see you a little later in the Father's house.' And just as He started through the door, He disappeared. It certainly was a strange morning. When they hewed me out of this old rock, I never expected anything like that."

I said, "Thank you, old tomb." And after I had waited long enough to ask God to help me be a better man, I stooped through the door and walked away; and I thought, *God pity a man who has no resurrected Saviour; God pity a man who has no living hope and no faith.*

I've been living for Him now for thirty years in my faltering, stumbling way, but I am walking with my face toward Heaven where I shall one day see Him. I want you to come and put your hand in mine and promise God you will walk with me until our journey ends in the glory-lit presence of the throne of God.

W. B. RILEY
1861-1947

ABOUT THE MAN:

Dr. W. B. Riley was for 45 years pastor of First Baptist Church, Minneapolis, and pastor emeritus three years. His ministry there built this church to the largest membership in the Northern Baptist Convention.

But all over America Dr. Riley moved and swayed audiences. Thousands were won to Christ in great campaigns.

Riley's ministry was one of preaching the Gospel as well as fighting foes of the Gospel. He sometimes prefaced what he wrote with: *"As one who has given his life to the defense and propagation of fundamentalism."*

William Jennings Bryan once called him *"the greatest Christian statesman in the American pulpit."*

The teaching of evolution was a hot issue in his day, so his debates became another phase of his ministry. Bryan had died in 1925, so the mantle for fighting evolution passed to Riley.

One can well compare Dr. Riley with Charles Spurgeon in the largeness of his work: 1. Like that prince of preachers in London, the Minneapolis pastor-evangelist-crusader carried on for several decades an effective ministry; his church grew about as large as Spurgeon's. 2. Like Spurgeon, he turned out many books, including a 40-volume sermon-commentary. 3. Even as Spurgeon, he was a prophet to a whole nation of moral decline and infidelity in the church. 4. As Spurgeon withdrew from the Baptist Union, so Riley withdrew from the Northern Baptist Convention. 5. Like Spurgeon, he founded a growing training college and seminary. 6. Like Spurgeon, he was an editor, editing *The Christian Fundamentalist* and *The Northwestern Pilot.*

Truly, in the days of his strength, Dr. Riley was one of America's greatest preachers.

III.

Jesus Christ Arose

W. B. RILEY

"And he said unto them, Why are ye troubled? and wherefore do questionings arise in your heart? See my hands and my feet, that it is I myself: handle me, and see; for a spirit hath not flesh and bones, as ye behold me having. And when he had said this, he showed them his hands and his feet. And while they still disbelieved for joy, and wondered, he said unto them, Have ye here anything to eat? And they gave him a piece of broiled fish. And he took it, and ate before them."— Luke 24:38-43, American Standard Version.

The questioning of the resurrection of Jesus did not originate with any modern conservative. The disciples of Jesus were the first to doubt His triumph over the grave, and Jesus Himself delivered the original and sufficient answer to that skepticism. Infidelity in its every phase is ancient, and God's answer to it is both ancient and adequate.

The above text is a marvelous putting of both of these points. It anticipates the questionings of the twentieth century; it supplies a scientific answer to the same. These are days when certain teachers in scientific circles boast the fact that they depend not upon hearsay, but demand a demonstration; they proceed not upon the basis of credulity, but rather upon the plane of positive proofs. And they propose to bring the whole history of the Christ and the whole claim of the Bible to the same process, by which, as one suggests, they "analyze salt, examine a rock, or observe a star."

Who objects? The resurrection of Jesus invites exactly such examination, and the record of it involves the most scientific process.

I. PROOF OF THE RESURRECTION

Attorney Francis J. Lamb of Madison, Wisconsin, brought from the Oberlin Press a book entitled, *The Miracle and Science,* in which he subjected the New Testament evidences to the jural tests, questioning each statement exactly as would be done in a court of justice where human life was at stake, and judge and jury were alike determined to discover the absolute truth involved in the procedure. After 284 pages of investigation, he affirms:

> Tested by the standards and ordeals of jural science, by which questions of fact are ascertained and demonstrated in contested questions of right between man and man, in courts of justice, the resurrection of Jesus stands a demonstrated fact.

Subjected to all the tests known to the natural sciences, this record will stand with equal solidity. Its proofs appeal to every one of the physical senses.

The empty tomb affirmed His physical resurrection. When, on the report of Mary Magdalene, Peter and John visited the tomb, John outran Peter, and coming first to the sepulchre, stooped down and, "looking in, saw the linen clothes lying." But the impetuous Peter who went into the sepulchre "saw the linen clothes lying, and the napkin that was about his head, not lying with the linen clothes, but wrapped together in a place by itself"; but, as Luke's Gospel adds in this connection, "the women which were early at the sepulchre found not his body."

Various, and even curious, have been the attempts to account for the empty tomb. Dr. Hooykaas suggests that "in the faith and preaching of the Apostles, the term 'resurrection' simply denoted the Saviour's ascension from the underworld, into which the Jews believed the purest and most holy, without exception, must descend to the heavenly glory," and that this was the reason why the Jews never said "Jesus rose from the dead, but from the place where the shades of the departed abide." Gunkel adopts this idea, and adds, "Faith in the death and resurrection of the gods was an important part of the mythology of the Orient."

But neither of them tell us whatever became of the body of Jesus; nor do they explain why it should be spoken of as resurrection at all, since the same Jews believed that every good man was immortal and his spirit would go to Glory. Gunkel admits that "the official faith of the Jews at the time of Christ knew nothing of the physical resurrection." Renan claims that Mary Magdalene, who had been once possessed with devils, was capable of vivid imagination and, in her affection and love for the Lord, believed He had risen from the tomb. And Renan exclaims, "O Divine power of love; sacred moments, in which the passion of one whose senses were deceived, gives to the world a God risen from the dead."

A very pretty speech, and its eloquence and enthusiasm have carried the thoughtless to a like conclusion. But a few questions fling the whole argument into confusion and despoil the skeptical plea. Was Mary Magdalene also capable of hypnotizing the Roman soldiers and either rendering them helpless or else leading them captive at will? Did she compel them to release their solemn charge of guarding the tomb and risk the discipline of the most imperious government that ever appointed a watch? Did she so far hypnotize the Jews whose fury had affected the crucifixion of Jesus as to silence their testimony regarding what actually transpired? Did she accomplish the even more difficult task of hypnotizing the disciples to the extent of making them willing to live on a piece of imagination, and finally to die in its defense? Even if all these questions were answered in the affirmative, the solution is not yet.

The sight of sane men attest the truth of His physical resurrection. How many witnesses of unimpeached character, exceptional intelligence and splendid mental balance must be brought into court to make out a case? When Paul comes to give a reason for the faith that is in him, he never mentions the testimony of any one of the women. Whether that was because, writing by inspiration, the Spirit anticipated the modern heresy that would seek to make the risen Christ a mere creation of an hysterical woman's fancy and affection, we do not know. But Paul says,

"He appeared to Cephas; then to the twelve; then he appeared to above five hundred brethren at once, of whom the greater part remain until now, but some are fallen asleep; then he appeared to James; then to all the apostles; and last of all . . . to me also."—I Cor. 15:5-8, A.S.V.

The lives of these men, as recorded in the New Testament, show them extremely sane, marvelously well-balanced, most strangely free from sensational speech or conduct. Happy the man on trial for his life who could have witnesses of such character and balance appear in his behalf.

They put the risen Christ to *the test of touch*—"Handle me and see, a spirit hath not flesh and bones as ye see me have."

They put Him to *the test of sight*—"When he had thus spoken he showed them his hands and his feet."

They put Him to *the test of taste*, for they gave Him a piece of broiled fish, and He ate it before them.

They put Him to *the test of hearing,* for it was when He called Mary's name that she recognized Him.

They put Him to *the test of former fellowship,* for it was when He "broke bread" at Emmaus that the two knew Him.

By what possible mental processes do men ask us to accept the theory of evolution on the word of a Darwin, the opinion of a Huxley, the suggestion of a Spencer, apart from proofs, and yet reject the record of the resurrection in the face of every physical test to which the same could be subjected?

To be sure, we are told that these men were hoping to see Jesus raised from the dead, and it is a common psychological experience to see the thing for which one is waiting and watching. But the fact is, they were not hoping to see this. Hope had died out of their bosoms. The women did not seek the sepulchre in the early morning expecting to see a risen Jesus; they bore their spices "to embalm the dead." Peter and John did not go there to keep an appointment made before His crucifixion; they went merely to investigate an unbelievable report that the tomb was empty. Cleophas voiced the despair that had settled upon them all, when, not knowing to whom he was speaking, he said to Jesus, "We trusted that it **had been** he which should have redeemed Israel." Mark the tense! It is a past hope to which he refers—"We trusted that it **had been** he which should have redeemed Israel." It is a pluperfect affair; it lives no more! Thomas would not even believe it on the testimony of his well-known and dearly loved brethren, and demanded the scientific test of sight and touch and was never convinced until both had been provided him. Renan attempts to parallel the opinion of the disciples by saying, "At the moment in which Mahomet expired, Omar rushed from the tent, sword in hand, and declared that he would hew down anyone who should dare to say that the prophet was no more."

But the parallelism fails to apply to the disciples. They never denied His death, and they never conceded His resurrection until the physical evidences convinced them. Even Mary Magdalene, dubbed "the imaginative one," did not believe until she saw Him; and not even then until He spoke to her. And there is no hint that Peter ever recovered his faith until he found his living Lord. Paul was not only nonconvinced, but determined that it should not be so; hence the great value of his testimony.

Is Voltaire right in saying, "When one has a great number of very sensible witnesses who agree in having seen all, who are sane bodily and mentally and who are impartial and disinterested and who solemnly certify to the fact, he then has proof"? If so, then the resurrection of Jesus Christ is put forever past dispute.

Gunkel tells us that they claimed an empty grave for Zeus in Crete. What if they did? What came of it? Who became apostles of that faith? What proof of their position did they present? What movement dominating the centuries did they originate?

Rudolph Schmid has a book entitled, *The Scientific Creed of a Theologian*—a volume that voices "New Theology" with such a vengeance as to leave little place in it for either science or Scripture; and yet, at the conclusion of the entire work, Schmid is compelled to admit the proofs of the physical resurrection and declares that the faith of the present is returning "to the affirmation of the Easter message in the full sense in which it has been proclaimed and believed from the beginning."

> **Christ the Lord is risen today,**
> **Sons of men and angels say:**
> **Raise your joys and triumphs high,**
> **Sing, ye heavens, and earth reply.**
>
> **Love's redeeming work is done,**
> **Fought the fight, the battle won;**
> **Lo! our Son's eclipse is o'er;**
> **Lo! He sets in blood no more.**

II. PERSON OF THE RESURRECTION

"Behold my hands and my feet, that it is I myself."—Luke 24:39.

His physical identity was preserved. The body that was missing at the tomb was found by Mary Magdalene and recognized; by the two on the way to Emmaus, and recognized; by James, who had known Him in the flesh, and recognized; by the apostles, who had had years of fellowship with Him, Thomas being absent, and recognized; by the same apostles, Thomas being present, and recognized; yea even by above five hundred brethren at once, and recognized.

The body He has now is the body that was buried in Joseph's tomb. To be sure, it may be wrapped in the glory in which He lives at the right hand of God, and yet the tabernacle is the same, only the shekinah has covered it.

A writer to the *Baptist Standard* of March 26, 1910, says,

After His resurrection He ate physical food, or seemed to do so;

and possessed flesh and bones, but we are not to suppose that with these He passed into Heaven.

Why not? It was promised that His body should not see corruption, and glorification is not displacement. The disciples saw Him ascend into Heaven. Certainly the faith of Charles Wesley was in the Christ who took a body from the tomb to Heaven; and he set that faith to music:

> **Arise my soul, arise;**
> **Shake off thy guilty fears;**
> **The bleeding Sacrifice**
> **In my behalf appears:**
> **Before the throne my Surety stands,**
> **My name is written on His hands.**
>
> **Five bleeding wounds He bears,**
> **Received on Calvary;**
> **They pour effectual prayers,**
> **They strongly plead for me;**
> **"Forgive him, O forgive," they cry,**
> **"Nor let that ransomed sinner die!"**

Fanny Crosby, who lived close to Christ and, after many years of communion, entertained the hope of seeing the very Saviour who walked the Judean hills and ascended from the Mount, wrote:

> **When my life-work is ended,**
> **And I cross the swelling tide,**
> **When the bright and glorious morning I shall see;**
> **I shall know my Redeemer**
> **When I reach the other side,**
> **And His smile will be the first to welcome me.**
>
> **I shall know Him, I shall know Him,**
> **And redeem'd by His side, I shall stand.**
> **I shall know Him, I shall know Him,**
> **By the print of the nails in His hand.**

He came from the grave unchanged in intellect. Before He went into it, it was His custom to appeal to the sacred Scriptures. "It is written" was His support and defense. As he walked with the two on the way to Emmaus, He renewed this custom, quoting from the Old Testament prophecies to show that Christ had to suffer and to enter into His glory; and "beginning at Moses and all the prophets, he expounded unto them in all the scriptures the things concerning himself."

The break, therefore, in His thinking, caused by this burial, seemed to have been no greater than such as characterizes us when we sleep and wake again. Waking out of death, His mind ran on with the same problems that concerned Him before His crucifixion, for the simple reason that He is the same Christ.

Years ago, the Easter number of *The Ladies Home Journal* had in it a remarkable article written by that most remarkable girl Helen Keller who, though blind, deaf and dumb, secured an education that has released her wonderful intellect. She told the story of her long sickness that resulted in a paralysis to so many of her powers. It came upon her when she was a little child of nineteen months, and we see her meaning when she says,

> During the first nineteen months of my life, I had caught glimpses of broad green fields, a luminous sky, trees and flowers, which the darkness that followed could not wholly blot out. If we have once seen, the day is ours, and what the day has shown.

Ah, truly, the grave in no wise obscured the vision of Jesus Christ. He walked in "the day" before He went to the grave; when He came from it, "the day" was continued for Him.

Before He went to the grave, He outlined His post-burial plans; when He came out of it, He took up the thread of life at the very point where the crucifixion had broken it.

He was the same in spirit as before His decease! His devotion to God abated in nothing; His love to men suffered no decline; His commission to the world and His plans for the church changed not a whit. The Great Commission,

"Go ye therefore, and teach all nations, baptizing them in the name of the Father, and of the Son, and of the Holy Ghost: Teaching them to observe all things whatsoever I have commanded you: and, lo, I am with you alway, even unto the end of the world. Amen."—Matt. 28:19,20,

He has not forgotten! On the contrary, He promises the power for its fulfillment.

"Ye shall receive power, after that the Holy Ghost is come upon you: and ye shall be witnesses unto me both in Jerusalem, and in all Judaea, and in Samaria, and unto the uttermost part of the earth."

The continuity of the Christ-life, which made the grave seem but a shadow through which He walked, gives a sweet meaning to the Christian's conception of the present Christ—He is "the same yesterday and to day and for ever."

III. PROMISES OF THE RESURRECTION

As Christ escaped corruption, Christians shall conquer against it. The body that was put into the grave was capable of decay, but God saw to it that His glorious One "should not see corruption." His resurrection brought Him up to "life for evermore." Lazarus might die, having been once raised from the dead! Not so with the Christ! He had conquered death!

They can bring up the ashes of Wycliffe and fling them to the brook, and the brook carry them to the Avon, and the Avon to the seas; but the Son could not be touched by death again, nor by corruption. Herein is the pledge of our victory: We may be sown in corruption, but we have the promise that we shall be raised in incorruption. Through Christ the Conqueror we shall have our victory over the grave and death. Paul fairly gloats over the prospect, saying,

"So also is the resurrection of the dead. It is sown in corruption; it is raised in incorruption: It is sown in dishonour; it is raised in glory: it is sown in weakness; it is raised in power: It is sown a natural body; it is raised a spiritual body. There is a natural body, and there is a spiritual body."—I Col. 15:42-44.

And he tells the very process by which it shall come to pass: "For this corruptible must put on incorruption, and this mortal must put on immortality" (vs. 53).

Blessed prospect it is! John had it in view when he wrote,

"Beloved, now are we the sons of God, and it doth not yet appear what we shall be: but we know that, when he shall appear, we shall be like him; for we shall see him as he is."—I John 3:2.

When I recall the true words of Campbell Morgan,

> Upon the fact of the historical resurrection stands or falls the whole fabric of Christianity. Unless Jesus of Nazareth actually came back from the grave, then indeed have "we followed cunningly devised fables," and have been hopelessly deceived,

I thank God for the certainties that support this event of the centuries. Dr. John McDowell Leavitt said:

> Once I stood on the Jura to see Mont Blanc. Forty miles away the monarch seemed rising from Lake Geneva. His sublime summit glittered in the sun. Each peak about him I have forgotten. But he, the mountain-king, will live in my memory forever. Only as they

added to his glory did I feel interest in lake, or hill, or vale, or cloud, or snow, or sunshine. Earth and sky were servants of his majesty.

As Mont Blanc amid mountains, the resurrection of Christ amid proofs! Subserving it—type and prophecy and probability—all other inferior arguments. In it they find their place and power. Resurrection proved is Christianity proved. Resurrection believed is Christianity believed.

Yes, that is the remorseless logic of it all! Paul, the logician of the centuries, has pushed it to its legitimate limits,

"If Christ hath not been raised, then is our preaching vain, your faith also is vain . . . ye are yet in your sins. Then they also that are fallen asleep in Christ have perished . . . But now hath Christ been raised from the dead, the firstfruits of them that are asleep. For since by man came death, by man came also the resurrection of the dead. For as in Adam all die, so also in Christ shall all be made alive."—I Cor. 15:14, 17, 18, 20-22, A.S.V.

Glorious prospect!

> **He lives! the great Redeemer lives!**
> **What joy the blest assurance gives!**
> **And now, before His Father, God,**
> **He pleads the merits of His blood.**
>
> **Away, ye dark, despairing thoughts;**
> **Above our fears, above our faults,**
> **His powerful intercessions rise;**
> **And guilt recedes, and terror dies.**
>
> **Great Advocate, almighty Friend,**
> **On Thee our humble hopes depend!**
> **Our cause can never, never fail,**
> **For Thou dost plead, and must prevail.**

But the apostle makes one remark more; with that, I conclude. "But each in his own order: Christ the firstfruits; then they that are Christ's, at his coming." The fruition of His resurrection will be found when He descends "from heaven with a shout, and with the voice of the archangel, and with the trump of God: and the dead in Christ shall rise first." It was to that blessed thought that John referred when he wrote, "Beloved . . . it doth not yet appear what we shall be: but we know that, when he shall appear, we shall be like him; for we shall see him as he is."

It is a glorious hope to entertain; it is a blessed Gospel to preach. It means more than a mere resurrection; it means a resurrection to behold the *King* in His glory; to see Him with the scepter in hand—Satan overthrown—and to enter with Him upon the government of the world in righteousness. The saintly Gordon said,

> The resurrection of our Lord, then, is not merely a pledge of our own; it is our own, if we are His, for the Lord who loved us, even when we were dead in sins, hath quickened us together with Christ, and hath raised us up together, and hath made us sit together in heavenly places in Christ Jesus.

George Herbert made a proper appeal to that man with the sad heart, who would know the resurrection, when he said:

> **Arise sad heart; if thou dost not withstand**
> **Christ's resurrection, thine may be;**
> **Do not by hanging down break from the hand,**
> **Which, as it riseth, raiseth thee.**

And yet, let us conclude with this statement, that the so-called scientific world, which gropes its way in skepticism, will never be converted by the historical evidences of a risen Christ! The resurrection life, lived by the present-day Christians, is the additional proof God needs to convince the world of "sin, and of righteousness, and of judgment" to come. It will believe in a Saviour at the right hand of God only as it sees Him formed in our hearts "the hope of glory" and revealed in our lives as "the power of righteousness."

JOHN R. RICE
1895-1980

ABOUT THE MAN:

Preacher . . . evangelist . . . revivalist . . . editor . . . counsellor to thousands . . . friend to millions—that was Dr. John R. Rice, whose accomplishments were nothing short of miraculous. Known as "America's Dean of Evangelists," Dr. Rice made a mighty impact upon the nation's religious life for some sixty years, in great citywide campaigns and in Sword of the Lord Conferences.

At age nine, after hearing a sermon on "The Prodigal Son," John went forward to claim Christ as Saviour. In 1916, with only $9.35 in his pocket, he rode off on his cowpony toward Decatur Baptist College. He was now on the road to becoming a world-renowned evangelist, although he was then totally unaware of God's will for his life.

There was many a twist and turn before Rice rode through the open door into full-time preaching—the army, marriage, graduate work, more seminary, assistant pastor, pastor—then FINALLY, where God planned to use him most—in full-time evangelism.

Dr. Rice and his ministry were always colorful (born in Cooke county, in Texas, December 11, 1895, and often called "Will Rogers of the Pulpit" because of their likeness and mannerisms)—and controversial. CONTROVERSIAL—and correctly so—because of his intense stand against modernism and infidelity and his fight for the Fundamentals.

Dr. Rice lived and died a man of convictions—intense convictions. But, like many other strong fighters for the Faith, Rice was also marked with a sincere spirit of compassion. Those who knew him best knew a man who loved them. In preaching, in prayer, and in personal life, Rice wept over sinners and with saints. But there is more . . .

Less than seventy-one hours before the dawning of 1981, one of the most prolific pens in all Christendom was stilled. Dr. John R. Rice left behind a legacy in writing of more than 200 titles, with a combined circulation of over 61 million copies. And through October of 1981, a total of 24,058 precious souls reported trusting Christ through his ministries, not counting those saved in his crusades nor in foreign countries where his literature has been translated.

And who but God knows the influence of THE SWORD OF THE LORD magazine which he started and edited for forty-six years!

And while "Twentieth Century's Mightiest Pen"—and man—has been stilled, thank God, the fruit remains! Though dead, he continues to speak.

IV.

The Importance of Christ's Resurrection in the Christian Faith

JOHN R. RICE

"And if Christ be not risen, then is our preaching vain, and your faith is also vain. Yea, and we are found false witnesses of God; because we have testified of God that he raised up Christ: whom he raised not up, if so be that the dead rise not. For if the dead rise not, then is not Christ raised: And if Christ be not raised, your faith is vain; ye are yet in your sins. Then they also which are fallen asleep in Christ are perished. If in this life only we have hope in Christ, we are of all men most miserable. But now is Christ risen from the dead, and become the firstfruits of them that slept."—I Cor. 15:14-20.

"Therefore my heart is glad, and my glory rejoiceth: my flesh also shall rest in hope. For thou wilt not leave my soul in hell; neither wilt thou suffer thine Holy One to see corruption."—Ps. 16:9,10.

"For as Jonas was three days and three nights in the whale's belly; so shall the Son of man be three days and three nights in the heart of the earth."—Matt. 12:40.

". . .and the third day he shall rise again."—Matt. 20:19.

Jesus Christ is alive today! He was crucified and buried, and three days later arose bodily from the grave. Joseph's new tomb, where Jesus had been buried, was left empty save for the burial garments.

He straightway appeared to hundreds of people. First, to Mary Magdalene and "the other Mary." Then to Peter, then to the rest of the twelve, then in Galilee to a great gathering of over five hundred Christians. Then again James and all the apostles saw Him. Finally He was seen by Paul on the road to Damascus.

Forty days Jesus went among the disciples, teaching and strengthening them. They felt of His body, handled the hands with the wounds, and were convinced. They saw Him eat and drink. He taught and explained the Scriptures. Every doubt was brushed away by the evidence which the Bible calls "many infallible proofs" (Acts 1:3).

The twelve saw Him ascend bodily to Heaven. Later He appeared to Paul on the road to Damascus. Later still to John the Beloved on the Isle of Patmos.

One cannot find a record of a single New Testament Christian who doubted the personal, bodily resurrection of Jesus Christ. The Apostles' Creed affirms, "*The third day he rose again from the dead.*"

His resurrection has thus been everywhere recognized as a cardinal doctrine of Christianity. The old Catholic church believed in the resurrection of Christ. Today the Roman Catholic church believes it firmly. The Greek Catholic church has always declared it.

All the historic **Protestant** creeds affirm the resurrection of Christ. Not one historic denomination claiming to be Christian has denied the resurrection, save Unitarians alone. Intelligent leaders of Unitarianism do not claim to be specifically and exclusively Christian. They do not acknowledge Christ as God and so have not been historically recognized as Christian. Historic Christianity is based on the doctrine that Christ died for our sins and rose again bodily from the grave.

By the resurrection, of course, we mean His bodily resurrection. There is no other kind. Those who say that they believe in a spiritual resurrection are parrots quoting, without thinking, some deceiving infidel; or they themselves are willfully trying to deceive.

No one ever taught that the spirit of Jesus was buried in Joseph's grave. No one ever taught that the spirit of Jesus died. His resurrection from the dead always refers to the body. When He said, "Father, into thy hands I commend my spirit" (Luke 23:46), He made it plain it was His body that would die.

It was the body that they anointed with spices and wrapped in linen after they had taken it down from the cross. It was that body, with wounds in the hands and feet and a great hole in the side, which they laid in Joseph's tomb. It was that body that the soldiers guarded, with a great stone rolled against the door and sealed with a Roman seal. It was that body that rose from the dead.

It is the talk of a thoughtless ignoramus who says, "I believe in a spiritual resurrection." The only kind of resurrection is a bodily resurrection. And the Bible teaches that Christ rose bodily from the grave.

Before His death, Jesus said to the dying thief, "To day shalt thou be with me in paradise" (Luke 23:43). Christ's spirit went at once to be with the Heavenly Father. Since only the body of Jesus was buried, then only the body of Jesus could be resurrected. There is no resurrection except the bodily resurrection.

To deny the resurrection of Christ is to deny His deity. To deny the resurrection of Christ is to deny historic Christianity. To deny the resurrection of Christ is to deny the Bible. To deny the resurrection is to place oneself beside infidels and scoffers.

If Bob Ingersoll and Tom Paine were to join a church and put on clerical robes, yet believe and preach their infidelity, that would not make them Christians. Today, neither are infidels in the church Christians. Those who deny the resurrection of Jesus Christ deny Christ and Christianity.

It would be almost impossible to overestimate the importance of the Bible doctrine of the resurrection of Christ. Consider the evidence of its importance.

I. RESURRECTION OF CHRIST PART OF THE SAVING GOSPEL

In I Corinthians 15:1-4, Paul, by divine inspiration, tells us that the Gospel "by which also ye are saved" is "that Christ died for our sins according to the scriptures; And that he was buried, and that he rose again the third day according to the scriptures."

There are two elements in this "gospel," as stated here. First, Christ died. Second, He rose again from the dead the third day. But both happened exactly "according to the scriptures." Both His death and His resurrection were in literal fulfillment of the Old Testament prophecies and types and promises.

Read the two introductory verses again in I Corinthians 15:1,2.

"Moreover, brethren, I declare unto you the gospel which I preached unto you, which also ye have received, and wherein ye stand; By which also ye are saved, if ye keep in memory what I preached unto you, unless ye have believed in vain."

This is the Gospel which Paul preached, the Gospel that sinners believed and received, the Gospel by which they were saved. Then verses 3 and 4 define this Gospel that Paul preached and by which people were saved.

Note the strange statement in verse 2, saying that the Corinthians were saved by this Gospel, "unless ye have believed in vain." That is explained by verse 14, "And if Christ be not risen, then is our preaching vain, and your faith is also vain." That is, the Gospel itself is a vain gospel unless Christ be risen from the dead. Any gospel without a resurrected Saviour is a vain gospel that could save nobody. Any such preaching is vain, says the Spirit, speaking through Paul.

And why is the resurrection a part of the Gospel? The very nature of the Gospel itself involves the resurrection. The Gospel, the saving good news, is that Christ died for our sins, died according to the Scriptures, arose again the third day according to the Scriptures. Christ died for our sins and rose for our justification.

If Christ be now dead, He can save nobody. If Christ be now dead and if the ashes of His decayed body are now scattered in some obscure tomb in Palestine, then the Scriptures are not true; and there is no good news for sinners.

And one must believe the Gospel in order to be saved. Faith in the Bible has two meanings. First, there is acceptance of certain facts as true; second, there is a dependence upon those facts for salvation. One who does not accept as truth that Christ arose from the dead cannot depend upon Him, with saving faith, for salvation.

Believing that Christ rose from the dead is a part of saving faith itself. This is made clear in Romans 10:8,9:

"But what saith it? The word is nigh thee, even in thy mouth, and in thy heart: that is, the word of faith, which we preach; That if thou shalt confess with thy mouth the Lord Jesus, and shalt believe in thine heart that God hath raised him from the dead, thou shalt be saved."

The two simple elements of saving faith here are: first, confessing with the mouth the Lord Jesus; second, believing in the heart that God hath raised Christ from the dead. Actually, the confession with the mouth is simply an expression of faith in the heart, verse 10 says. One who honestly trusts in Christ for salvation is saved. The confession with the mouth is outward evidence of inward faith.

But to confess Christ with the mouth is not an evidence of saving faith, unless the one who so claims Christ honestly believes in his heart that Christ rose from the dead, and that therefore Christ is God come in human form, and now sits at the right hand of the Father, and therefore is able to save us from sin. One cannot have saving faith unless he believes that God raised Jesus Christ from the dead!

Every person who ever exercised saving faith in Christ believed in his heart that God raised Him from the dead, as the Scriptures declare. It may be that many have not understood the implications of the doctrine. It may be that many knew relatively little about the facts of the resurrection. But everyone who ever trusted Christ accepted what God said about raising His Son from the dead. One cannot be saved without believing that Jesus is what He claimed to be, what the Bible declares Him to be—the dying, risen Saviour.

It is interesting to note from the words of Jesus in John 8:21,24 that the deity of Christ must be believed before one can have saving faith. After saying that He was one with the Father, that He was the Light of the world, that He was from above while they were from beneath, Jesus said, "I said therefore unto you, that ye shall die in your sins: for if ye believe not that I am he, ye shall die in your sins" (John 8:24).

One could not believe in the deity of Christ without believing in His resurrection. The resurrection is the proof of His deity. Those who have saving faith must base it on the fact that Christ died and rose again according to the Scriptures.

How wicked, then, the hand of one who would take away the doctrine of the resurrection of Christ! He would destroy the saving Gospel. He would make it impossible for anyone to be saved who agrees with him that Christ did not rise from the dead.

II. RESURRECTION OF CHRIST SINGLE SIGN OF HIS DEITY

Some people believe that Christ's miracles proved His deity. They believe that when Jesus healed the sick, cured lepers, gave sight to the blind, raised the dead, stilled the waters of the Sea of Galilee, that He was thus demonstrating His deity.

But Jesus never claimed that. In fact, He again and again urged people not to tell of some miracle which He wrought. Miracles did not prove the deity of Christ. Moses, Joshua, Elijah, Elisha, Peter, Paul, and others performed miracles by the power of God. None of the miracles of Jesus were intended to prove His deity. He helped the sick because of His compassion on them; He raised Lazarus for the glory of God (John 11:4), not to prove His deity. Miracles prove that one is from God, but they proved that for the apostles as well as for Christ.

The sign of Christ's deity is not simply that He worked miracles but His resurrection from the dead.

Jesus thus quoted in Matthew 12:39,40:

"But he answered and said unto them, An evil and adulterous generation seeketh after a sign; and there shall no sign be given to it, but the

sign of the prophet Jonas: For as Jonas was three days and three nights in the whale's belly; so shall the Son of man be three days and three nights in the heart of the earth."

No sign was to be given concerning His deity except the miraculous sign that after being three days and nights in the earth, the grave, He would come forth from the grave as Jonah came forth from the belly of the great fish.

Jesus' glorification on the Mount of Transfiguration was simply a preview of the glory that He would have after His resurrection. Therefore, the three privileged disciples were commanded, "Tell the vision to no man, until the Son of man be risen again from the dead" (Matt. 17:9).

This truth—that the resurrection of Christ from the dead is the proof of His deity—is given again in Romans 1:3,4. Paul wrote by divine inspiration, "Concerning his Son Jesus Christ our Lord, which was made of the seed of David according to the flesh; And declared to be the Son of God with power, according to the spirit of holiness, by the resurrection from the dead."

Since the resurrection of Christ from the dead is the one miracle that proves His deity, we can understand why Romans 10:9 says, "That if thou shalt. . .believe in thine heart that God hath raised him from the dead, thou shalt be saved." An acceptance of the deity of Christ is essential to saving faith, and the resurrection is the divine proof of His deity.

III. OLD TESTAMENT FORETOLD CHRIST WOULD RISE FROM THE DEAD

When two disciples walking down to Emmaus told the unrecognized Christ who walked beside them how some women claimed that Jesus had been raised from the dead but that they did not believe, Jesus said to them:

"O fools, and slow of heart to believe all that the prophets have spoken: Ought not Christ to have suffered these things, and to enter into his glory? And beginning at Moses and all the prophets, he expounded unto them in all the scriptures the things concerning himself."—Luke 24:25-27.

Jesus meant that the Old Testament prophets foretold His death and resurrection, that the disciples were foolish not to believe the Scriptures and not to expect His resurrection. Then He showed them in all the Scriptures the things concerning Himself.

The clearest Old Testament prophecy about the resurrection of Christ is in Psalm 16:9,10:

"Therefore my heart is glad, and my glory rejoiceth: my flesh also shall rest in hope. For thou wilt not leave my soul in hell; neither wilt thou suffer thine Holy One to see corruption."

This Scripture was used by Peter in Acts 2:26,27, in preaching at Pentecost on the resurrection of Christ. Here we have foretold in the Old Testament the feeling of Christ Himself, rejoicing that, when He should give up the ghost and lay His life down, His flesh would be raised from the grave. The body of Jesus was never to decay, was never to return to dust.

It had to be raised from the dead; then triumphantly the Lord Jesus later ascended to Heaven and that same Saviour, with that same resurrected body, is in Gloryland now waiting for us.

To be good Bible students it is quite clear that the story of Jonah's being swallowed by a great fish was given primarily as a type of the burial and resurrection of Christ. Jesus Himself said,

"There shall no sign be given to it, but the sign of the prophet Jonas: For as Jonas was three days and three nights in the whale's belly; so shall the Son of man be three days and three nights in the heart of the earth."—Matt. 12:39,40.

That Old Testament book of Jonah is meant to teach that Jesus would rise from the dead as Jonah was delivered from the whale or fish.

I doubt if the average modernist and unbeliever even knows that Jesus declared that Jonah's three days and nights in the belly of the whale was a type of His three days in the grave. But the enemy of our souls— Satan—knows it, and that is why he leads unbelievers to attack the Bible account of Jonah.

No doubt the Old Testament ceremony of bringing the firstfruits of the crop to the Lord was intended as a prophecy that the Saviour would be the first to rise from the dead, for I Corinthians 15:20 says, "But now is Christ risen from the dead, and become the firstfruits of them that slept." Then we read in verse 23: "But every man in his own order: Christ the firstfruits; afterward they that are Christ's at his coming."

The Old Testament has many intimations of the future resurrection of Christ which have not been noticed by the average Bible reader.

For example, the second Psalm tells us that when the kings of the earth should set themselves against the Lord and His Christ (anointed), that "He that sitteth in the heavens shall laugh: the Lord shall have them in derision." Why would the Lord laugh when Herod, Pontius Pilate and the leaders of the Jews agree to the crucifixion of Christ? Because God would yet "set my king upon my holy hill of Zion" (vs. 6), says this same Psalm.

Although crucified, Christ is yet to reign over Israel. That necessarily involves the resurrection, though it is not specifically stated.

One of the clearest Old Testament implications of His resurrection is the Jewish priesthood, which was typical of Christ's priesthood. But how could the coming Messiah be both the sacrifice and the priest who offered the sacrifice? Only by rising from the dead after He died!

Melchizedek, mentioned in Genesis 14:18 as "king of Salem" and "priest of the most high God," was particularly a type of the priesthood of Christ. Psalm 110:4 says, "Thou art a priest for ever after the order of Melchizedek," referring to Christ; and Hebrews 5:5,6 tells us that these Scriptures and the type refer to Christ. Hebrews 7:3 says Melchizedek was especially suited to be a type of Christ, since the record of Melchizedek gives no father, no mother, no descendant, no beginning of days nor end of life. These things were omitted from the Old Testament record of Melchizedek so that he would be a fit type of Christ; and Hebrews 7:16 tells us that Christ is such a priest, "who is made, not after the law of a carnal commandment, but after the power of an endless life." Only in having an endless life, not cut short by death, could Christ fulfil the type of Melchizedek, in His priesthood.

Thus the priesthood of the Old Testament, picturing Christ's priesthood, clearly implies His resurrection.

Throughout the Old Testament there is a double picture of Christ.

He is pictured also as the seed of Abraham who is to inherit Palestine, as the seed of David, the branch from the root of Jesse, who is to sit on David's throne.

How can it be true that Messiah, the Saviour, is to be crucified, paying for our sins (as prophesied in Isaiah 53), yet be prophesied to rule over the whole world (as told in Isaiah, chapter 11)? The answer to that is His resurrection from the dead. Jesus died, but He arose again!

This is the divinely inspired interpretation given by Peter in his sermon at Pentecost, recorded in Acts, chapter 2. There Peter says of David:

"Therefore being a prophet, and knowing that God had sworn with an oath to him that of the fruit of his loins, according to the flesh, he would raise up Christ to sit on his throne; He seeing this before spake

of the resurrection of Christ, that his soul was not left in hell, neither his flesh did see corruption."—Vss. 30,31.

Every Old Testament prophecy that Christ should sit on David's throne, that Christ should rule the world, necessarily involves His resurrection. So Peter says, by divine inspiration, that David foretold that God, "according to the flesh," "would raise up Christ to sit on his throne."

Thus the resurrection of Christ is a fundamental doctrine everywhere implied and sometimes plainly declared in the Old Testament.

IV. JESUS OFTEN FORETOLD HIS COMING DEATH AND RESURRECTION

Jesus knew that He was going to die for the sins of the world and often said so. He likewise knew that He would rise from the dead and repeatedly foretold it.

Jesus foretold His resurrection when He referred to Jonah's coming forth from the whale after three days and nights (Matt. 12:39,40).

In Matthew 20:18,19, He told His twelve disciples,

"Behold, we go up to Jerusalem; and the Son of man shall be betrayed unto the chief priests and unto the scribes, and they shall condemn him to death, And shall deliver him to the Gentiles to mock, and to scourge, and to crucify him: and the third day he shall rise again."

Jesus knew the whole program. He, with the Father, had planned it before the world began; but that horrible tragedy of His crucifixion would have a happy ending—"the third day he shall rise again"!

In Matthew 17:9, on the Mount of Transfiguration, "Jesus charged them [the three favored disciples who saw His transfiguration], saying, Tell the vision to no man, until the Son of man be risen again from the dead." The rising from the dead was continually in His mind, as the triumphant finale of the crucifixion.

In Luke 9:22 Jesus straitly charged the disciples not to discuss Him as the Christ of God at the present, "Saying, The Son of man must suffer many things, and be rejected of the elders and chief priests and scribes, and be slain, and be raised the third day."

In John 10:17,18, Jesus said that His crucifixion and resurrection were His own plan:

"Therefore doth my Father love me, because I lay down my life, that I might take it again. No man taketh it from me, but I lay it down of myself. I have power to lay it down, and I have power to take it again.

This commandment have I received of my Father."

Both the crucifixion and resurrection were inevitably connected in the mind and plan of Christ, just as they are connected in the Gospel as preached by Paul and other Bible preachers.

If Christ's resurrection was of so great importance in His own thinking and preaching, it is preeminently important for the thinking of Christians today.

V. BIBLE PREACHERS PROCLAIMED RESURRECTION

On Easter most Bible-believing preachers preach on Christ's resurrection. But how different was the plan of preachers in Bible times! Throughout the book of Acts, we find that almost every time Peter, Paul and others preached, they spoke of the resurrection of Christ. Evidently the resurrection is of far more importance than we realize, and we do well to follow the pattern of Bible preachers.

When Judas Iscariot, the unsaved apostle, hanged himself after betraying the Saviour, the eleven disciples forthwith met. Led by the Spirit, they must elect another apostle at once! Why? They must have twelve in all who had been with Christ from the baptism of John to His resurrection. Acts 1:21,22 says, in the words of Peter,

"Wherefore of these men which have companied with us all the time that the Lord Jesus went in and out among us, Beginning from the baptism of John, unto that same day that he was taken up from us, must one be ordained to be a witness with us of his resurrection."

The primary plan was that these twelve men who had been with Jesus all of His public ministry and who were eyewitnesses of His death and burial, and who had seen Him after His resurrection, talked with Him, handled Him, should continually give a firsthand testimony that Christ had really risen from the dead.

In the second chapter of Acts, verses 24 to 36 are given to Peter's sermon on the resurrection of Christ!

In Acts 3:14,15 Peter, preaching to the multitude gathered in the Temple when the lame man was healed, said, "But ye denied the Holy One and the Just, and desired a murderer to be granted unto you; And killed the Prince of life, whom God hath raised from the dead; whereof we are witnesses."

In the same chapter, in the same sermon, Peter mentions again the resurrection of Christ, saying, "Unto you first God, having raised up his Son Jesus, sent him to bless you, in turning away every one of you from his iniquities" (vs. 26).

The apostles were often arrested. And what was the doctrine they always stressed which aroused the enmity of the leaders? The resurrection!

"And as they spake unto the people, the priests, and the captain of the temple, and the Sadducees, came upon them, Being grieved that they taught the people, and preached through Jesus the resurrection from the dead."—Acts 4:1,2.

When called before the rulers of the Jews, Peter was asked, "By what power, or by what name, have ye done this?" (that is, the healing of the lame man in the Temple). Part of Peter's answer is given in Acts 4:10, "Be it known unto you all, and to all the people of Israel, that by the name of Jesus Christ of Nazareth, whom ye crucified, whom God raised from the dead, even by him doth this man stand here before you whole."

Peter could not preach about Jesus without mentioning His death and resurrection. The resurrection is a part of the Gospel, one of the bases of saving faith.

In Acts 4:31 we find that the apostles and their converts were again filled with the Holy Spirit, and "with great power gave the apostles witness of the resurrection of the Lord Jesus" (vs. 33). The apostles may not have been such good preachers, but they were good witnesses. They had seen the resurrected Saviour and insisted on telling everywhere— in jail and out, before the common people and before the rulers.

May God grant that we too will be faithful witnesses of the resurrected Saviour whom we have met and who has shown His power in our lives.

In Acts 5:29,30 we find that "Peter and the other apostles" faced the Sanhedrin boldly and said, "The God of our fathers raised up Jesus, whom ye slew and hanged on a tree." Naturally they proceeded to say, "Him hath God exalted with his right hand to be a Prince and a Saviour, for to give repentance to Israel, and forgiveness of sins" (vs. 31).

Paul's preaching abounded, likewise, in references to Christ's resurrection. In fact, he based his theology on the fact that Christ, after dying for man's sins, was risen from the dead.

On their first missionary journey, Paul and Barnabas came to Antioch of Pisidia; and there in the synagogue Paul preached a great sermon. Telling how Christ had been crucified, he then declared: "And when they had fulfilled all that was written of him, they took him down from the tree, and laid him in a sepulchre. But God raised him from the dead" (Acts 13:29,30).

Then, to prove the resurrection, Paul quoted Psalm 2 where it is said of Christ, "Thou art my Son; this day have I begotten thee"; and from Psalm 16, verse 10, ". . . neither wilt thou suffer thine Holy One to see corruption." Then in Acts 13:37, in the same service, he says, "But he, whom God raised again, saw no corruption." Then with this background, he preached to them the forgiveness of sins by faith in this resurrected Saviour.

When Paul went to Athens—the center of culture of the world at that time—he preached the resurrection of Christ. Acts 17:18 tells us:

"Then certain philosophers of the Epicureans, and of the Stoicks, encountered him. And some said, What will this babbler say? other some, He seemeth to be a setter forth of strange gods: because he preached unto them Jesus, and the resurrection."

It had already gotten out that Paul was a resurrection preacher! Then when he stood up to preach to them, calling them to worship the unknown God (unknown to their heathen minds, though they had an altar erected to Him), Paul said,

"And the times of this ignorance God winked at; but now commandeth all men every where to repent: Because he hath appointed a day, in the which he will judge the world in righteousness by that man whom he hath ordained; whereof he hath given assurance unto all men, in that he hath raised him from the dead."—Acts 17:30,31.

Paul says that God commands all men everywhere to repent because Christ has been raised from the dead and that authenticates Him as the One who will judge the world. Therefore, men should repent and trust Christ. He is the resurrected Saviour and therefore will be the Judge.

What was the reaction of the Athenians, wise in their own eyes? "And when they heard of the resurrection of the dead, some mocked: and others said, We will hear thee again of this matter" (vs. 32).

Paul's theme was always on the resurrection. After his arrest, when he was brought before Felix, he was allowed to speak for himself. Among other things he said was:

"But this I confess unto thee, that after the way which they call heresy, so worship I the God of my fathers, believing all things which are

written in the law and in the prophets: And have hope toward God, which they themselves also allow, that there shall be a resurrection of the dead, both of the just and unjust."—Acts 24:14,15.

Then again in the same talk before Felix he tells how he had made an issue of the resurrection before the Sanhedrin and says,

"Or else let these same here say, if they have found any evil doing in me, while I stood before the council, Except it be for this one voice, that I cried standing among them, Touching the resurrection of the dead I am called in question by you this day."—Acts 24:20,21.

After two years Festus took the place of Felix as governor, and King Agrippa, with his wife Bernice, came to Caesarea to visit Festus. Festus did not know much about Paul; but as he reported the matter to King Agrippa, he showed that he understood the cardinal teaching of Paul.

The Jews "had certain questions against him of their own superstition, and of one Jesus, which was dead, whom Paul affirmed to be alive" (Acts 25:19). Yes, everywhere dear old Paul went, he affirmed that Jesus was alive!

So it came about that when Paul was called in to speak before King Agrippa, he at once came to the great point: that Jesus, who was crucified for men's sins, had risen from the dead and was able to save all who trusted in Him! Before King Agrippa Paul dramatically said, "Why should it be thought a thing incredible with you, that God should raise the dead?" (Acts 26:8). And then Paul proceeded to tell of his own conversion— how, on the road to Damascus to punish Christians, he was struck down at midday and heard a voice speaking, the voice of this same resurrected Jesus! And how there and then he saw the Saviour.

Remember that after telling of all the eyewitnesses of the Saviour's resurrection, Paul had said, recorded in I Corinthians 15:8, "And last of all he was seen of me also, as of one born out of due time." Paul meant that one day all the remnant of Jews left alive will see the Saviour and that blind spiritual eyes will be opened and they will know and love and serve Him. But Paul was born ahead of time, it seems, converted before the remnant of Jews. He himself saw Jesus. I think it was on the road to Damascus. The glory of that face, that resurrected Jesus struck Paul blind!

I do not wonder that John, on the isle of Patmos, fell at His feet as one dead, when he saw Him (Rev. 1:17). So Paul told King Agrippa of his personal acquaintance with the resurrected Saviour.

In that noble defense before King Agrippa, Paul gives again the substance of his whole Gospel:

"Having therefore obtained help of God, I continue unto this day, witnessing both to small and great, saying none other things than those which the prophets and Moses did say should come: That Christ should suffer, and that he should be the first that should rise from the dead, and should shew light unto the people, and to the Gentiles."—Acts 26:22,23.

Paul preached, proving his points by many Old Testament Scriptures, that Christ was prophesied to suffer on the cross and that He should be the first to rise from the dead.

We can be sure from Paul's statement in I Corinthians 15:3,4 that the resurrection of Christ was part of the saving Gospel he preached and, from the examples given in the book of Acts, that Paul everywhere preached the Gospel.

We can draw no other conclusion than that the resurrection is as vital a part of the Gospel, as preached by New Testament preachers, as the death of Christ itself.

Oh, then let us testify to the fact that Christ is risen from the dead!

VI. RESURRECTION ESSENTIAL BASIS OF OTHER GREAT BIBLE DOCTRINES

We have shown above that Christ's resurrection was the single great proof of His deity and that belief in His resurrection is essential to saving faith, since the resurrection is part of the saving Gospel, as taught in I Corinthians 15:3,4.

But there are certain other great doctrines of the Christian faith based upon the resurrection of Christ. Without His bodily resurrection, these essential facts could not be and these doctrines would be untenable.

First, Christ's resurrection from the dead was essential to our justification. The believer is justified, by which we mean that legally he is counted innocent and just while Christ is counted guilty for our sake.

In Romans, chapter 4, we are clearly taught that "Abraham believed God, and it was counted unto him for righteousness" (vs. 3). And again, "It was imputed to him for righteousness" (vs. 22). Then Romans 4:24,25 says:

"But for us also, to whom it shall be imputed, if we believe on him that raised up Jesus our Lord from the dead; Who was delivered for

our offences, and was raised again for our justification."

Again the theme comes in that the salvation of a sinner would be impossible if Christ had not risen from the dead. And one who believes in Christ must believe that He arose from the dead. God's raising Christ from the dead proved that He was willing to forgive sinners. Christ's rising from the dead proved that He was the Son of God and able to save. And if Christ died to pay for our sins (our offences, verse 25 calls them), He was raised from the dead for our justification.

Having died and risen again, Christ is the perpetual witness that sin has been paid for. He can always present the wounds in His hands and feet, the scar in His side as proof that the demands of the Law have been fully met, that sin has been paid for, that the believing sinner has a right to be classed as just before God, for Christ's sake. The justification of a sinner depends upon Christ's resurrection.

In Romans 5:10, this doctrine is reiterated. "For if, when we were enemies, we were reconciled to God by the death of his Son, much more, being reconciled, we shall be saved by his life." We might say that we were reconciled to God by the death of His Son but we are continually kept by His resurrected life.

Second, a kindred doctrine to our justification by His resurrection is the Bible truth that Christ's high-priestly intercession for us depended upon His resurrection. If Christ were to represent in Heaven before the Father those on earth who have trusted Him for salvation, He must be a living man to represent living men. Christ died as a man, and so Christ must rise as a man to be man's mediator and priest.

This is clearly taught in Hebrews 7:23-25:

"And they truly were many priests, because they were not suffered to continue by reason of death: But this man, because he continueth ever, hath an unchangeable priesthood. Wherefore he is able also to save them to the uttermost that come unto God by him, seeing he ever liveth to make intercession for them."

One trouble with the priests of the Old Testament times, priests of the first covenant, was that "they were not suffered to continue by reason of death." No human priest would be adequate to appear for men before God, if that priest should die and his priesthood end. But not so with Jesus, as verse 24 explains. "But this man, because he continueth ever, hath an unchangeable priesthood."

Thank God for the blessed teaching of verse 25! Christ is able to save us to the uttermost that come to God by Him, "seeing he ever liveth to make intercession for them"!

One of the great essentials of a high priest in the heavenlies is that he be one who "ever liveth." Christ is such a living priest, having risen from the dead.

It is a very shallow and inadequate conception of God's plan of salvation if we think that Christ died once and that henceforth He has nothing to do for the believer. This very day He is at the right hand of the Father, taking the part of every sinner who trusts in Him. That is why the Lord can keep all those He saves. In I John 2:1,2 is this blessed teaching:

"My little children, these things write I unto you, that ye sin not. And if any man sin, we have an advocate with the Father, Jesus Christ the righteous: And he is the propitiation for our sins: and not for our's only, but for the sins of the whole world."

We who have trusted in Christ have an advocate with the Father Jesus Christ the righteous. The living, resurrected Saviour is our mediator, our advocate, our lawyer at the court of Heaven! And this high-priestly intercession of Jesus depended upon His resurrection.

A third great doctrine based upon the resurrection of Christ is that of a coming judgment. In John 5:22 Jesus tells us, "For the Father judgeth no man, but hath committed all judgment unto the Son." The reason given is that God wants "that all men should honour the Son, even as they honour the Father" (vs. 23). Christ is to be the Judge whom all men must face.

Christians must give an account before Christ. "For we must all appear before the judgment seat of Christ" (II Cor. 5:10). But primarily Christ must judge the unsaved world, this world that hates Him, this world that crucified Him, this world that still rejects Him. The Father has committed that judgment into the hands of the Son.

But it required a resurrected Saviour to judge those who crucified Him. So in his sermon at Athens, Paul says by divine inspiration,

"Because he hath appointed a day, in the which he will judge the world in righteousness by that man whom he hath ordained: whereof he hath given assurance unto all men, in that he hath raised him from the dead."—Acts 17:31.

God has given all judgment to the Son. The proof that there will be a great final judgment is that Jesus Christ is risen from the dead! This living Christ, the Christ with a human body (the glorified and perfect One) on the great white throne—before Him shall be gathered all the unregenerate; and the record books shall be opened. Each one will be judged by this risen Christ according to his works! The necessary basis for the coming judgment is the resurrection of Christ.

Another doctrine which depends upon the resurrection of Christ is the return of Christ and His reign on David's throne. God promised David in II Samuel 7:16, "And thine house and thy kingdom shall be established for ever before thee: thy throne shall be established for ever."

Isaiah 11:1 tells how the kingly sprout shall come again from the stump of a tree (now cut down temporarily) of David's dynasty and how "a Branch shall grow out of his roots." That Branch is Christ in His second coming and reign.

In announcing the impending birth of the Saviour, the Angel Gabriel said to Mary,

"He shall be great, and shall be called the Son of the Highest: and the Lord God shall give unto him the throne of his father David: And he shall reign over the house of Jacob for ever; and of his kingdom there shall be no end."—Luke 1:32,33.

Jesus is to have the throne of David and He is to reign bodily thereon. But that requires a resurrected Saviour.

In Acts 2, preaching at Pentecost, Peter quoted Psalm 16 which promised the resurrection of Jesus, and said of David, "Therefore being a prophet, and knowing that God had sworn with an oath to him, that of the fruit of his loins, according to the flesh, he would raise up Christ to sit on his throne" (Acts 2:30). God raised up Jesus according to the flesh, to sit on David's throne.

It is obvious that to believe in the literal coming and reign of Christ one must believe in His bodily resurrection.

Dr. B. H. Carroll, the famous founder of Southwestern Baptist Theological Seminary at Fort Worth and the most prominent theologian Southern Baptists have ever produced, told Dr. W. B. Riley, shortly before Dr. Carroll's death, that he had been greatly impressed with this fact: premillennialists do not turn out to be modernists, while postmillennialists often did. Since Dr. Carroll himself had been widely known as a postmillennialist, his testimony is striking. I use it here, however, wholly to illustrate the fact that those who believe in His literal return and literal reign must believe in His resurrection.

Last, but certainly not least, the blessed hope that Christians have of being called from the grave, of having bodies that never grow old, that are never sick—perfect bodies, glorified bodies—depends wholly on the resurrection of Christ. The Bible repeatedly connects His resurrection with the doctrine of the resurrection of others. In I Corinthians 15:17-23 this solemn and beautiful teaching is given:

"And if Christ be not raised, your faith is vain; ye are yet in your sins. Then they also which are fallen asleep in Christ are perished. If in this life only we have hope in Christ, we are of all men most miserable. But now is Christ risen from the dead, and become the firstfruits of them that slept. For since by man came death, by man came also the resurrection of the dead. For as in Adam all die, even so in Christ shall all be made alive. But every man in his own order: Christ the firstfruits; afterward they that are Christ's at his coming."

If Christ be not raised, our faith is vain and all of us who trusted in Him are still lost!

If Christ be not raised, then all Christians who have fallen asleep are perished, gone forever; and we will never see them again. Small wonder that this passage says that if in this life only we have hope in Christ "we are of all men most miserable"!

But then comes the triumphant statement that Christ is now risen from the dead "and become the firstfruits of them that slept."

We are told here that Christ is the firstfruits, and then afterward they that are Christ's at His coming. When Jesus comes, He will raise the Christian dead and change the Christians who are living. All this is guaranteed by His own resurrection from the dead.

This precious doctrine is taught again in Philippians 3:20,21:

"For our conversation is in heaven; from whence also we look for the Saviour, the Lord Jesus Christ: Who shall change our vile body, that it may be fashioned like unto his glorious body, according to the working whereby he is able even to subdue all things unto himself."

Here we are told that true Christians look happily for the coming of the Saviour, knowing that He "shall change our vile body, that it may be fashioned like unto his glorious body." If Christ, with a resurrected body, came out of Joseph's tomb and lives again, then we will be changed and glorified and receive bodies like unto His glorious body when He comes!

Again, in Romans 8:11, the Holy Spirit tells us that He who raised up Jesus from the dead will also raise up us, in whom the same Spirit dwells. "But if the Spirit of him that raised up Jesus from the dead dwell in you, he that raised up Christ from the dead shall also quicken your mortal bodies by his Spirit that dwelleth in you."

Our resurrection depends on His resurrection. If He is risen, then we, too, who trust in Him and in whom the Spirit makes His home, shall be raised from the dead (if we sleep) and shall be instantly changed and glorified if we are yet alive when Jesus comes.

Any teaching that the body of Jesus decayed and moldered in the dust in a Palestinian grave is not Christianity. Any body of doctrine that omits the personal, literal resurrection of Christ is not Christianity. It is a false religion, a pagan, ungodly religion.

For this reason we must say that the modernist who denies the resurrection of Christ is not a Christian. He has denied the deity of Christ, for Jesus said that His deity would be proved by the one sign of His resurrection. He has denied the integrity of the Bible which everywhere—in the Old and New Testaments—declares or implies the resurrection of Christ. He has turned his back on historic Christianity, the kind preached by the apostles and held by saints and martyrs down through the centuries. Anybody who denies the basic fact of the resurrection of Christ has denied Christianity itself, Christ, the Bible, and the God of the Bible!

Oh, may this doctrine become blessed and real to our hearts! Too many have said the Apostles' Creed, quoting ". . . the third day he rose again from the dead," yet their hearts have not entered into the joyful anticipation and the glorious blessing that is ours because Christ rose from the dead! I suggest, dear reader, that with humble hearts we rejoice and praise God for our living, resurrected Saviour.

His resurrection is part of the blessed Gospel by which we are saved. It is a necessary basis for our justification, for Christ's high-priestly intercession, for the judgment of sinners, for Christ's reign on earth, and for our own resurrection.

VII. BAPTISM GIVEN AS PERPETUAL REMINDER THAT CHRIST WAS RAISED FROM THE DEAD!

Those who turn away from Bible Christianity do so deliberately, willfully. Our Saviour did not leave the great central doctrine of our faith in doubt, nor did He leave it so it could be forgotten by any honest heart.

He gave the Last Supper to commemorate His death and said, "For as often as ye eat this bread, and drink this cup, ye do shew the Lord's death till he come" (as revealed to Paul, I Cor. 11:26).

This oft-repeated ceremony reminds every believing child of God that the death of Christ for our sins is the basis of our salvation.

But remarkably enough, the Lord added another ordinance—baptism—commanded to be observed by every convert, which shows His bodily resurrection. Romans 6:4,5 says:

"Therefore we are buried with him by baptism into death: that like as Christ was raised up from the dead by the glory of the Father, even so we also should walk in newness of life. For if we have been planted together in the likeness of his death, we shall be also in the likeness of his resurrection."

Every person who has been baptized should have remembered that Christ's death and resurrection alike are part of the saving Gospel. The ordinance of scriptural baptism should be carried out faithfully, not as a means of salvation but as a testimony to the death and resurrection of Christ, which is the basis of all of our hope in Him.

Colossians 2:12,13 gives us the same teaching:

"Buried with him in baptism, wherein also ye are risen with him through the faith of the operation of God, who hath raised him from the dead. And you, being dead in your sins and the uncircumcision of your flesh, hath he quickened together with him, having forgiven you all trespasses."

Note that baptism reminds a Christian that Christ rose from the dead. And here we find that baptism typifies not only that the Christian shall be raised from the grave, as Christ was, but that even now the Christian has entered into the resurrection life. The believer is to count himself already alive from the dead. He is to count that, in Christ, he is a new creature, and so is to strive to live as if he had attained to the resurrection.

Of course, all of us are still in this frail, carnal body which is doomed to die; but we can look forward happily with victory in our hearts to the time when our bodies will be raised, as was that of Jesus. And the triumph and happiness in a Christian's life can only come because Christ rose from the dead.

If one comes to you preaching any other doctrine than this doctrine of Christ, II John 10,11 commands us that such an one should not be received into your house, and you should not bid him God speed for he is an enemy of the cross of Christ. The atoning death of Christ for our sins and His resurrection from the grave for our justification are the twin doctrines of the Gospel, the basis of saving faith, the basis of most of the great doctrines of the Bible.

Hold this teaching dear, then, and rejoice that Christ is risen from the dead. Let us have an Easter in our hearts every day in the year, knowing that our Saviour triumphed over death, Hell and the grave and is even now at the right hand of the Father making intercession for us. And one day we will see Him, Jesus our Saviour, the God-man who died and rose from the grave. Then we can put our fingers in the nail prints of His hands and feel the wound in His side, handling Him as did the apostles when He was alive, and rejoice in the physical evidence, as they did, that He arose from the grave.

Oh, resurrected Saviour! Oh, blessed, triumphant hope of the Christian!

> **In the bonds of Death He lay**
>   **Who for our offence was slain;**
> **But the Lord is risen today,**
>   **Christ hath brought us life again.**
> **Wherefore let us all rejoice,**
>   **Singing loud, with cheerful voice,**
>   **Hallelujah!**
>   **—Martin Luther**

He Lives

The triune God conceived a plan,
To pay the debt for ev'ry man
   Regardless of the cost.
He sent His only Son to die,
That we may reign with Him on high
   And thus redeemed the lost.

Christ Jesus struggled up a hill.
It was His Father's sovereign will
   To rend the veil in twain.
The cross, the cross, how large it loomed;
But without blood, the world was doomed,
   And life had been in vain.

How can we now but stand in awe,
In knowing Christ fulfilled the law
   Because our sins He bore.
He rose triumphant over death;
What God required has all been met.
   He lives forevermore!

                —Tom Johnson

CURTIS HUTSON
1934-

ABOUT THE MAN:

In 1961 a mail carrier and pastor of a very small church attended a Sword of the Lord conference, got on fire, gave up his route and set out to build a great soul-winning work for God. Forrest Hills Baptist Church of Decatur, Georgia, grew from 40 people into a membership of 7,900. The last four years of his pastorate there, the Sunday school was recognized as the largest one in Georgia.

After pastoring for 21 years, Dr. Hutson—the great soul winner that he is—became so burdened for the whole nation that he entered full-time evangelism, holding great citywide-areawide-cooperative revivals in some of America's greatest churches. As many as 625 precious souls have trusted Christ in a single service. In one eight-day meeting, 1,502 salvation decisions were recorded.

As an evangelist, he is in great demand.

At the request of Dr. John R. Rice, Dr. Hutson became Associate Editor of THE SWORD OF THE LORD in 1978, serving in that capacity until the death of Dr. Rice before becoming Editor, President of Sword of the Lord Foundation, and Director of Sword of the Lord conferences.

All these ministries are literally changing the lives of thousands of preachers and laymen alike, as well as winning many more thousands to Christ.

Dr. Hutson is the author of many fine books and booklets.

V.

Resurrection of Jesus Christ

CURTIS HUTSON

The Prophecy of His Resurrection
The Proof of His Resurrection
The Purpose of His Resurrection

I come this morning to speak on what I think is the greatest doctrine of the Christian faith: the doctrine of the resurrection of our Lord Jesus Christ.

The resurrection is the foundation for the other great Bible doctrines. For instance, if Jesus Christ was not raised from the dead, as the Bible says, then the Bible is not the verbally inspired, inerrant, infallible Word of God.

Five times before His death, Jesus said, "Destroy this temple, and in three days I will raise it up" (John 2:19). One time He said, "I lay down my life, that I might take it again. No man taketh it from me, but I lay it down of myself. I have power to lay it down, and I have power to take it again" (John 10:17,18). Five times He predicted that He would rise from the dead. If the resurrection is not true, then the Bible is not the inspired Word of God.

If Jesus Christ was not resurrected, we have no Gospel to preach. The definition of the Gospel is found in I Corinthians 15:1-4. Here Paul says,

"Moreover, brethren, I declare unto you the gospel which I preached unto you, which also ye have received, and wherein ye stand; By which also ye are saved, if ye keep in memory what I preached unto you, unless ye have believed in vain. For I delivered unto you first of all that which I also received, how that Christ died for our sins according to the scriptures; And that he was buried, and that he rose again the third day according to the scriptures."

You don't have a Gospel without a resurrection.

It is the foundation stone upon which other doctrines are built. Destroy the resurrection of Jesus and you destroy the grounds of our justification. The Bible states, He "was raised again for our justification" (Rom. 4:25).

Destroy the resurrection of Jesus and you destroy the deity of Christ. Romans 1:4 says He was "declared to be the Son of God with power, according to the spirit of holiness, *by the resurrection from the dead.*"

The resurrection of Jesus distinguishes and makes Christianity superior to all other religions of the world. Someone rightly said, "Christianity begins where other religions end: with the resurrection of Jesus Christ." All other religions of the world can point to a founder; they can point to a founder's grave, but there is no religion other than Christianity that can point to an empty tomb and say, "Our Founder was buried there and on the third day He came out of the tomb."

I suppose no doctrine is hated as much by Satan as the resurrection of Christ. Before Jesus died, Satan had already put it into the minds of men to deny the resurrection. Bible students know that the **Sadducees** did not believe in the resurrection. Someone said, "That is why they were **Sad . . . you . . . see!**"

Not only did the Sadducees deny the resurrection before the death of Jesus, but people in the church at Corinth doubted the resurrection. Paul wrote an entire chapter on the resurrection (I Cor. 15) to try to help them. And in I Corinthians 15:12 he asked, "How say some among you that there is no resurrection of the dead?"

Satan hates this mighty doctrine. The resurrection of Jesus is mentioned forty times in the New Testament. It was the central theme of the disciples' preaching in the book of Acts: "And with great power gave the apostles witness of the resurrection of the Lord Jesus" (4:33). Many people in Jerusalem knew Christ had died, but His disciples knew He had been raised from the dead, and it was the central theme of their preaching. When they were choosing one to take Judas' place, they said, 'We want to choose one to be a witness with us of His resurrection' (Acts 1:22).

Now, as I have time this morning, I want to say three things about the Lord's resurrection. First, I will speak with you briefly about the prophecy of the resurrection. Second, I want to talk about the proof of the resurrection. And if I have time, I would like to talk with you about the purpose of His resurrection. Really this should be three sermons, and it *may* be. I'm not sure.

The Prophecy of the Resurrection

The resurrection was not something that just happened, with no one knowing anything about it or being unable to know about it. Long before Jesus was born, it was prophesied that He would be raised from the dead. Psalm 16:10 says, "For thou wilt not leave my soul in hell; neither wilt thou suffer thine Holy One to see corruption." It was believed in Jesus' day that corruption set in on the fourth day.

You remember the story of Lazarus whom Christ raised from the dead. When Jesus went from Martha and Mary to the cemetery, He said, "Take ye away the stone." They replied, "Lord, by this time he stinketh: for he hath been dead four days" (John 11:39). The body of Jesus did not corrupt. He was raised on the third day, before supposed corruption set in on the fourth day. "For thou wilt not leave my soul in hell; neither wilt thou suffer thine Holy One to see corruption."

Hundreds of years before His birth, His resurrection was prophesied. In Matthew 12:38-40 certain of the scribes and Pharisees came to Jesus and said, "Master, we would see a sign from thee." But He answered, "An evil and adulterous generation seeketh after a sign; and there shall no sign be given to it, but the sign of the prophet Jonas: For as Jonas was three days and three nights in the whale's belly; so shall the Son of man be three days and three nights in the heart of the earth."

"You want a sign that I am the Son of God; I am going to give you one. On the third day I will come out of the grave, then you will know I am the Son of God. That is the only sign I will give you."

If Jesus had not been resurrected, they could have marked Him off as another imposter. Josephus, the early historian, said many people in the days of Christ claimed deity. But this Man who claimed to be Christ said, "I will give you a sign on the third day. I will come out of the grave." And He did!

A skeptic said to a little girl, "I hear you talking about Christ. There were many christs; which Christ do you worship?" The little girl paused a minute and said, "Sir, I worship the One who rose from the dead."

That's the One! There were many christs, but the One we worship is He who came out of the grave after the third day!

In Matthew 16:21 the Bible states, "From that time forth began Jesus to shew unto his disciples, how that he must go unto Jerusalem, and suffer many things of the elders and chief priests and scribes, and be killed, and be raised again the third day." In John 2:19 Jesus said, "Destroy this temple, and in three days I will raise it up." They thought

He was talking about the Temple where they worshiped, but it was the temple of His body. He was prophesying His resurrection, as the later verses in that chapter indicate.

Again and again the Bible said Jesus Christ was going to be raised from the dead. I believe the Bible is the Word of God, if on no other grounds, on the grounds of fulfilled prophecy. No man could know these things ahead of time.

Man cannot predict. He can't even predict the weather. Have you noticed how the weathermen have changed? One said he had to move to another state because the weather didn't agree with him. They don't now say, "It will rain tomorrow." They say, "There is a 20% chance of rain tomorrow . . . a 30% chance of snow or 50% chance that the sun will shine." They don't really know.

You won't find prophecy in any religious books except the Bible, and the reason is simple: if other religious writers had made prophecies, they would have been proven to be in error and discredited many years ago. They knew better than to prophesy.

But God dares to predict the future. And it happens exactly as He says.

Martin Luther said, "Our Lord has written the promise of the resurrection, not in books alone, but in every leaf in springtime."

The Proof of His Resurrection

Second, I want to show the proof of His resurrection. First, I offer the proof of human reasoning. Now, you know what happened. Jesus Christ had a trial, a mock trial. They condemned Him. They scourged Him. They crucified Him. After His death, they took the body down from the cross, placed it in a tomb wherein man had never been laid, and rolled a stone before its mouth.

The religious leaders said, "You remember this Fellow, before He was crucified, said, 'Destroy this temple, and in three days I will raise it up.' If His disciples come and steal Him away and make people believe He was raised from the dead, we'll never get Christianity quieted down. We have to make sure He doesn't come out of that tomb!"

And they did two things to make sure the body of Jesus Christ could not be removed. First, they sealed it with the Roman seal. That is important! For anyone to break the seal of the Roman government meant certain death. The Roman world dared anyone to molest that tomb. They sealed it. You didn't fool with things when the Roman government sealed them. That was a world empire. The whole world stood behind that seal.

But that wasn't enough. They also stationed a guard around the tomb. Roman soldiers stood by day and night to make sure Jesus Christ did not come out of that tomb. The Bible does not indicate how many soldiers guarded the tomb, but four quaternions of soldiers guarded Peter. A quaternion is a squad of four. That means sixteen Roman soldiers guarded Peter. I suppose there were that many or more who guarded the tomb of Christ. Rome dared the entire world to molest the tomb. But after three days and nights the tomb was empty.

Now reason with me. If Jesus Christ came out of that grave, then either *man* took Him out or *God* took Him out. There is no other possibility.

If man took Jesus Christ out of the tomb, it had to be either His friends or His enemies. Do you think His friends—a little band of defenseless disciples—could overpower Roman guards and take the body of Jesus from that tomb? If His friends did take His body, why didn't the Roman government make an effort to find it? It couldn't have disappeared into thin air. They could have found it and said, "They stole His body, but we have found it and want the world to know He did not really come out of that tomb alive, as they said."

The body wasn't to be found. They couldn't produce a corpse. Because there was no corpse to produce! I find it impossible to believe these defenseless disciples overpowered Roman guards and took the body from that tomb. You couldn't believe that.

If it wasn't His friends, then was it His enemies? They were doing everything possible to keep Him *in* the tomb. They *wouldn't* do it. It contradicts human reason.

His friends *couldn't* and His enemies *wouldn't*. That leaves only one alternative: God Almighty raised Jesus Christ from the dead. And that is exactly what the Bible says in Hebrews 13:20, "Now the God of peace, that brought again from the dead our Lord Jesus, that great shepherd of the sheep, through the blood of the everlasting covenant." He is the great Shepherd of the sheep whom God raised from the dead. That is what the Bible says.

Second, I offer to you the proof of the testimony of 500 brethren. Five hundred born-again believers!

We have several attorneys here this morning. And you know very well that sometimes the testimony of two or three witnesses can turn the course of a trial. There have been cases where one witness turned the course of a trial. What would the testimony of 500 witnesses mean?

That is how many witnesses were ready to step forward and say, "Jesus Christ arose from the dead." In I Corinthians 15:6 Paul said, "After that, he was seen of above five hundred brethren at once; of whom the greater part remain unto this present, but some are fallen asleep."

Some modernists say they were having hallucinations. That stretches my imagination. I cannot believe that 500 born-again, blood-washed believers were all having hallucinations at the same time and all seeing the very same thing. That would be a greater miracle than the resurrection of Jesus.

At the time of the writing of I Corinthians, Paul said that most of these people were still alive, still walking around testifying, "I saw Jesus Christ after He was raised from the dead." "I saw Him!" "I saw Him!" Surely the testimony of 500 brethren is sufficient proof for any fair-minded person that Jesus Christ was raised from the dead.

Suppose you are walking down a street in Atlanta, Georgia, with a man who has never seen an American flag. As you pass the post office, he sees the American flag waving in the breeze and asks, "What is that?"

You answer, "That is an American flag."

He inquires, "What does it mean?"

Then you explain, "Many years ago men got together and signed the Declaration of Independence. We became the United States of America, and that is our flag."

You continue walking until you come to a church with a steeple and he asks, "What is that?"

You say, "That is a church."

He inquires, "What does it mean?"

Then you explain, "That means 2,000 years ago a Man named Jesus was crucified, buried, and on the third day He arose from the dead."

Here is the point I am trying to make: there is not an individual in this room who doubts the signing of the Declaration of Independence. There is not a person, I suppose, in America who doubts the signing of that important document. Yet there were more eyewitnesses to the resurrection of Jesus than there were to the signing of the Declaration of Independence—the testimony of 500 brethren!

I offer a third proof of the resurrection of Jesus Christ: the proof of human nature. The first law of life is self-preservation. Normally when you hem up an animal it will fight for its life. When it comes to life or death, most humans will fight for life. But here were men who were willing to give their lives for the resurrection of Jesus Christ.

If friends objected, they would give up those friends. If their job interfered, they would give up the job. If they were threatened with death, they were willing to die. But they were not willing to deny that Jesus Christ was raised from the dead. Everyone has a scale of values. On their scale of values, they placed the resurrection of Jesus Christ above their own lives. Many died because they refused to deny the literal, physical resurrection of Jesus Christ.

The fourth proof is that of common experience. When a loved one dies, hearts are sorrowful. Sometimes it takes a while to get over it.

When I was a little boy growing up, there was a beautiful lady who belonged to the same church we did. She didn't have a boyfriend, and she never married. One day I asked my father, "Daddy, Miss So-and-So is a beautiful woman. Why doesn't she have a husband and children?" Daddy told me this story:

"She was deeply in love and engaged to be married, but the man she loved was killed in an accident. She never got over it. She still has a place in her heart for that man. She still sorrows over him."

I like to get alone when I pray. Sometimes I go to the cemetery. It is a quiet place. One day I noticed a lady sitting at a cemetery lot in a little chair. She went there often and stayed for hours. My wife knew her. She said the lady's son was buried there. That dear woman still sorrows as much as if her son died yesterday.

I am saying it takes a long time to get over sorrow, and some people never get over it. After Jesus Christ was crucified, the disciples were sorrowful. Their hearts were heavy. But after three days and nights, suddenly their sorrow was turned into joy; and you couldn't find a sad disciple in the group!

What brought about the sudden change? The answer is simple: the object of their sorrow was now alive! Their reason to sorrow was gone. Jesus was alive!

> I serve a risen Saviour,
> He's in the world today;
> I know that He is living,
> Whatever men may say . . . .

There is also the proof of changed lives. There are men in this congregation who were once alcoholics. They went everywhere to find a cure, but they searched in vain until they came to Christ. This morning those who once were alcoholics are joyous, happy Christians. A living Christ made the difference!

I can point out women in this congregation who once were dope addicts. This morning they are living without dope. Today they are joyous, happy Christians. A living Christ made the difference!

We have more than a book of rules to follow. We have a Christ to live within us. I'm saying that changed lives are proof of the resurrection of Jesus Christ.

Angels testified to His resurrection. When Mary Magdalene and the other Mary came to the tomb, in Matthew 28:6 the angel said, "He is not here: for he is risen."

Devils in Hell believe in the resurrection. In the 19th chapter of Acts, seven sons of Sceva attempted to cast demons out of a man; and they answered back, "Jesus I know, and Paul I know; but who are ye?" "Jesus I know," present tense. That was after His death, burial and resurrection. They said, "We know Him. We know Jesus. He is alive now!"

It is amazing that demons are more fundamental than some preachers. I could spend the day giving proof of the resurrection.

There is proof of time. Time is a great leveler of human names and events. As time moves across the pages of history, it blots out the lesser names, leaving only the more prominent ones for memory to retain.

Dr. Harry Rimmer was lecturing in a college. Afterwards he gave way for questions.

A young Jew asked, "What did Jesus Christ do that no one else ever did?"

Dr. Rimmer replied, "Sir, you are a Jew. I take it that you know the early history of your people, and you know that Titus and Pilate and the old Roman emperors crucified some 30,000 young Jews."

The young student said, "I agree to that: they crucified some 30,000 young Jews."

Dr. Rimmer continued: "I will name one of those Jews and you name one. I will name Jesus Christ. Now, young man, you name one of the 30,000 whom they crucified."

The young Jew said, "I don't know the name of another one."

He couldn't call the name of one out of 30,000. Why? Because time is a great leveler of human names and events. Why do we remember that name when we can't remember the other 29,999? Because Jesus was the only One who was raised from the dead! He is alive!

Nobody hates a dead man. When a man dies, we forget our hate for him. But the world, for the most part, still hates Jesus Christ.

Two weeks ago, during a morning service in one of the churches here in Atlanta, a woman walked down to the front of the pulpit and began to yell, "Jesus Christ is of the Devil!" She hated Him. But no one hates a dead man. I say, He is alive because they hate Him.

There is also the proof of the five senses. Jesus appeared to His disciples after His resurrection, and in Luke 24:39-43 said:

"Behold my hands and my feet, that it is I myself: handle me, and see; for a spirit hath not flesh and bones, as ye see me have. And when he had thus spoken, he shewed them his hands and his feet. And while they yet believed not for joy, and wondered, he said unto them, Have ye here any meat? And they gave him a piece of a broiled fish, and of an honeycomb. And he took it, and did eat before them."

He said, ". . . handle me"—the sense of feeling. "A spirit hath not flesh and bones, as ye see me have"—the sense of sight. ". . . when he had thus spoken"—the sense of hearing. "And they gave him a piece of broiled fish, and of an honeycomb. And he took it, and did eat before them"— the sense of smell and taste. The proof of the five senses.

I give one more proof: the proof of scientific and archaeological analysis. I read this week about the excavation that took place nearly two hundred years ago in Jerusalem, when General Gordon uncovered the tomb of Christ. Jerusalem has been destroyed by war more than any other city in the world. It has been destroyed so many times that the elevation is twenty feet higher now than it was when Jesus walked its streets two thousand years ago. When General Gordon uncovered the tomb now called Gordon's Tomb, scientists scraped up dirt from the tomb and submitted it to chemical analysis. After a thorough chemical analysis of the dirt, they concluded, "No human body ever decayed in that tomb."

Concerning the body of Jesus, the Bible says in Luke 23:53, ". . . and laid it in a sepulchre that was hewn in stone, wherein never man before was laid."

His body did not decay. He came out on the third day. I am saying the resurrection of Jesus Christ can be proven by any fair-minded person who wants to take time to do so.

It was once tried in court before a jury. Evidence was presented from both sides and the jury gave this verdict: "The resurrection of Jesus Christ is a fact."

I say that Jesus Christ was raised from the dead.

It is said that some years ago there were two brilliant young men in England—one named Lyttleton and the other named West. They got together, and one of them said, "If we could disprove two things we could destroy Christianity—the conversion of the Apostle Paul on the road to Damascus and the resurrection of Jesus."

Lyttleton said, "I'll spend a year investigating the conversion of the Apostle Paul." West said, "I'll spend a year investigating the resurrection of Jesus. Then we will meet again to report our findings."

A year later they met, and Lyttleton said to West, "After a year of investigation, I am convinced that the Bible story of the conversion of the Apostle Paul is true." And not only that, he said, "West, I, too, have been converted."

Then West said to Lyttleton, "I have been investigating the resurrection of Jesus for a year; and Lyttleton, I, too, have discovered that the resurrection of Jesus Christ is a fact. Undeniable. And it may surprise you to know that I have received Him as my Saviour; I'm saved."

The resurrection of Jesus Christ is an undeniable fact. I get amused at these modernistic preachers who try to explain away the resurrection of Christ. One man wrote to a religious editor:

"Dear _____:

"Our preacher said, on Easter, that Jesus just swooned on the cross and that the disciples nursed Him back to health. What do you think?"

He received the following reply:

"Dear _____:

"Beat your preacher with a cat-o'-nine-tails with 39 heavy strokes; nail him to a cross; hang him in the sun for 6 hours; run a spear through his heart; embalm him; put him in an airless tomb for 72 hours and see what happens.

(Signed) "Brother _____."

The resurrection of Jesus is a proven fact.

The Purpose of His Resurrection

Now I have but a few minutes to say something about the purpose of His resurrection. Paul said He was raised for our justification (Rom. 4:25). You must distinguish between justification and regeneration. Regeneration is something that happens to you. Justification is something that happens in the mind of God.

When you are justified, God sees you as if you had never sinned.

He says, "So far as I am concerned, Curtis Hutson has never sinned." Why? Because God SEES me through His Son. And His Son bore my sin, took my guilt and died in my place. The Bible says, ". . . he appeared to put away sin by the sacrifice of himself" (Heb. 9:26). Now God says, "Curtis is not a sinner because Jesus bore the sin." In the mind of God, I'm justified. I am declared guiltless because I am trusting Jesus Christ as my Saviour.

Romans 5:1 states, "Therefore being justified by faith, we have peace with God through our Lord Jesus Christ." That is the purpose of the resurrection.

Another purpose of the resurrection is to declare His deity. When Jesus came out of the grave, it was a declaration to the whole world that He was the Son of God. He was "declared to be the Son of God with power, according to the spirit of holiness, by the resurrection from the dead" (Rom. 1:4).

The resurrection of Jesus assures our own resurrection. The Bible says,

"For if we believe that Jesus died and rose again, even so them also which sleep in Jesus will God bring with him. For this we say unto you by the word of the Lord, that we which are alive and remain unto the coming of the Lord shall not prevent them which are asleep. For the Lord himself shall descend from heaven with a shout, with the voice of the archangel, and with the trump of God: and the dead in Christ shall rise first."—I Thess. 4:14-16.

We are going to be resurrected. Why? Because Jesus was resurrected. He said, ". . . because I live, ye shall live also" (John 14:19). And the Bible states in I Corinthians 15:20, "But now is Christ risen from the dead, and become the firstfruits of them that slept." The firstfruits is an assurance of a main harvest coming later.

When the farmer raised a crop, he gathered the first few ears of corn and brought it to the priest. This was the firstfruits and assurance of a main harvest to follow.

The resurrection of Jesus Christ was a guarantee of a main harvest coming later. He was only the Firstfruits. When Jesus comes again, the body of every saint in the cemetery is going to come out of the grave. His resurrection is an assurance of our own resurrection.

It is also an assurance of reunion. "If we believe that Jesus died and rose again, even so them also which sleep in Jesus will God bring with him" (I Thess. 4:14). He is going to bring our loved ones when He comes, and we are going to be caught up together to meet the Lord in the air (I Thess. 4:16,17).

The resurrection completes the Gospel. If you preach the death of Jesus, you have not preached the Gospel. If you preach His burial, you have not preached the Gospel. You have not preached the Gospel until you preach the death, burial, and resurrection (I Cor. 15: 1-4).

He lives! He lives! He lives! When Jesus came out of the tomb on Easter morning, they had a Gospel to preach. It is the good news of His death, burial, and resurrection.

A man stood looking at a large painting on display in a store window, a painting of Jesus on the cross with the soldiers standing by. A little boy, who attended Sunday school and had learned something about the crucifixion, stood behind the man. After a few moments the boy said, "Mister, Mister, that's Jesus on the cross."

The man didn't say a word but kept staring at the picture.

In a minute the little boy said, "Mister, Mister. Them soldiers there—they killed Him!"

The man still didn't say anything—he just kept looking at the picture.

The boy spoke again, "Mister, Mister. Them disciples there—they buried Him."

Without a word the man walked away. When he was nearly a block down the street, the little boy ran as fast as he could to catch him. Hearing the sound of little feet behind him, the man looked back; and the boy said, "Mister, I forgot to tell you: He came out of the grave on the third day!"

Don't forget to tell them that; it completes the Gospel.

The resurrection of Jesus Christ was an assurance that God was fully satisfied with the payment Jesus made for our sins. Two thousand years ago God took every sin we have ever committed or ever will commit and placed them on Jesus Christ. Isaiah 53:6 states, ". . . the Lord hath laid on him the iniquity of us all." And I Peter 2:24 says, "Who his own self bare our sins in his own body on the tree."

While Jesus Christ was bearing our sins, God punished Him in our place to pay the debt that we as sinners owe. When Jesus Christ cried out from the cross, "It is finished!" it simply meant that full payment for sin had been made.

They took Him down from the cross, placed Him in a borrowed tomb; and three days and nights later God Almighty raised Him from the dead as a declaration of the fact that He was satisfied with the payment Jesus had made for our sins.

I know that God accepted Jesus' payment for my sins because He raised Him from the dead.

Now, dear friend, do you believe that Jesus Christ died for you? Do you believe He fully paid your sin debt? If so, will you trust Him today as your own personal Saviour? You may show your satisfaction with Christ's payment for your sins by simply trusting Him as your Saviour. Tell Him in your own words, "Dear Lord Jesus, I know I am a sinner. I do believe You died for me, and the best I know how I trust You as my Saviour. From this moment on I am depending on You to get me to Heaven. Amen."

If you will pray that simple prayer and write to tell me so, I have some free literature I want to send that will help you as you set out to live the Christian life. All you need do to receive your free literature is fill out the decision form below and mail it to me.

Dr. Curtis Hutson
Sword of the Lord Foundation
P. O. Box 1099
Murfreesboro, Tennessee 37133

Dear Dr. Hutson:

I have read your sermon, "The Resurrection of Jesus Christ." I know I am a sinner and do believe that Jesus Christ died for my sins. I believe, too, that God raised Him from the dead to show His satisfaction with the payment. Today I show my satisfaction with the payment Jesus made for my sins by trusting Him as my Saviour. From this moment on I am fully depending on Him for my salvation and trusting Him to take me to Heaven when I die.

Please send me the free literature that will help me as I set out to live the Christian life.

Name _____

Address_____

City_____State_____Zip_____

How Do I Know?

How do I know that Christ is risen?
  What proof have I to give?
He rescued me from sin's dark prison
  And I began to live.

How do I know He left the tomb
  That Easter long ago?
I met Him at the dawn's fresh bloom
  And life is all aglow.

How do I know He gained for me
  Access to Heaven's door?
Christ's work in me is guarantee
  Of life forevermore.

How do I know that Christ still lives
  Rich blessings to impart?
Abundant grace and peace He gives
  And lives within my heart.

                    —Eugene M. Harrison

R. L. MOYER
1886-1944

ABOUT THE MAN:

Dr. Moyer was an evangelist from 1915-20, then became pastor of the United Brethren Church in Minneapolis. Later Dr. W. B. Riley asked him to become his assistant at First Baptist Church, Minneapolis. When Dr. Riley retired from the pastorate in 1942, Dr. Moyer then became pastor and served in that capacity until his death.

Dr. Moyer was long dean of Northwestern Bible School, and the author of several books.

Dr. H. A. Ironside said:

"Few men have the winsomeness and tenderness combined with sound scriptural teaching that characterizes the ministry of my esteemed friend and fellow laborer, Dr. Robert L. Moyer."

VI.

Supreme Importance of the Resurrection

R. L. MOYER

The resurrection of the dead is the chief truth of the Christian faith. It is a truth that is startling when men first hear it, but it is a truth which lies at the very foundation of the Gospel.

He who takes away the resurrection takes away the Gospel and leaves us no Gospel, or, at best, only a false gospel. He who takes away the resurrection takes away the Bible and leaves us but a mere book. He who takes away the resurrection mantles our future with Egyptian darkness. To take away the resurrection is to leave man with no preeminence above the beast. To have blotted out Paul's hope in the resurrection would have blotted out his hope in Christ. He makes our salvation to rest on the fact of the resurrection. The man, therefore, who does not believe in the resurrection is not a Christian. Other doctrines are important; this is one of the essentials.

And yet, notwithstanding the fact that we have no hope except in the resurrection, there were some in Paul's day who denied it, and so attempted to sap the very foundations of the Christian's hope. And these were men who professed to be Christians! And even today we have the same strange inconsistency—men who pretend to believe the New Testament and yet who deny the resurrection. The Sadducee is still in our midst.

In the section of I Corinthians which we have chosen for exposition, Chapter 15:13-19, Paul shows what the results would be if there be no resurrection of the dead.

No Resurrection, No Saviour

"If there be no resurrection of the dead, then is Christ not risen."—vs. 13.

This is most forcibly put. If men deny the possibility of the resurrection, the resurrection of Christ has not occurred. That means that the

Gospel has come to an end. A dead Christ is, indeed, a disappointing Christ. Everything hinges upon the resurrection of the Lord.

Without the resurrection of Christ away goes our doctrine of the incarnation; for surely, surely God cannot be holden of death. Without the resurrection of Christ, away goes the doctrine of the substitutionary and vicarious sacrifice of Christ, and we are left under the penalty of sins.

The Saviour's resurrection is the proof of sins put away by His sacrifice. Salvation means to believe in the death and resurrection of the Son of God. The Gospel by which we are saved is declared in verses 1 to 4 of this chapter. That Gospel declares that "Christ died." The anointed One of God died, and not as other men—for His own sin—but for our sins. It was not the cross of wood that killed Christ; it was the cross of wills—your will, my will, up against the will of God. Christ died "for our sins."

And He died "according to the scriptures," that is, the Old Testament Scriptures. It was no sudden act of God to remedy an unexpected upset of His plans. That death had been foretold immediately upon the entrance of sin into the world. The Serpent was to bruise the Deliverer's heel. Every sacrifice, from Abel down, represented the death of a Substitute as the hope of the sons of men.

The fact of that death was emphasized by the burial of Christ. He "was buried." The Saviour might have risen from the dead without burial, but proof of His death was strengthened by that burial. He participated in the ordinary lot of men in death. It was only after a considerable interval in the tomb that He was raised from the dead. Athanasius suggested some reasons for the interval of time:

> Not on the same day, lest the real death should be denied; not on the second day, lest His incorruption should not be clearly manifested; not later than the third day, lest the identity of His body should be questioned; His disciples be kept too long in suspense; the witnesses of His death be dispersed and the events forgotten.

The resurrection, also, was "according to the scriptures." That resurrection was foretold in the Old Testament, in Psalms 2 and 16. It was that resurrection which vindicated the claims of the Lord and demonstrated that He was the Son of God. That resurrection was the seal of the Father's approval and acceptance. We repeat: the proof of sins put away by His sacrifice is His resurrection.

No Resurrection, Nothing to Preach

"And if Christ be not risen, then is our preaching vain . . ."—vs. 14.

What we are preaching is just an idle story. There is no reality to it. How can our preaching be anything but utterly "vain," if the central testimony is false? Preaching without the resurrection is "vain," literally "empty." There is nothing in it. Dr. Leon Tucker illustrates this from his own experience:

> Mr. Moody sent me to preach in a tent on North Avenue and Milwaukee. He had several tent meetings under his direction at that time. One night he came into my tent. I was preaching on the text, "When they were come unto a place called Golgotha . . . they crucified him." I said, "Now, friends, I laid Him on the cross tonight—tomorrow night I will tell you what happened afterwards."
>
> The next day I went to a workers' conference, and Mr. Moody saw me. He said, "You are Tucker. You are in tent so and so. Don't go back any more; I don't need your kind of preaching!"
>
> "What have I done? I preached Christ and Him crucified."
>
> "I know you did," he exclaimed, "but you left Him on the cross last night and thought you would tell them the next night what happened afterwards. Don't you know a dead Christ on a cross never saved anybody? How do you know they will come back again? Don't ever preach on that text again without saying, 'God raised Him from the dead.' "

No Resurrection, Faith Is Vain

". . . and your faith is also vain."—vs. 14.

You certainly have a vain, empty faith if you believe in a dead man. His death might demonstrate that He was a true man, but how can the truest man save you from his tomb? The death that proved Him nothing more than a man would prove Him no Saviour. If He were man only, His accusers were right; and He was a blasphemer, worthy of death under the holy law of our holy God. If He died for His own sins, He certainly could not die for ours.

Yes, Paul is right: if Christ be not risen, the Gospel is a fable, and we are reposing our faith in a fallacy. Our faith is as empty as the preaching we heard. There is nothing in it.

If Christ Rose Not, Apostles and Prophets Are Liars

"Yea, and we are found false witnesses of God; because we have testified of God that he raised up Christ: whom he raised not up, if so be that the dead rise not."—vs. 15.

If Christ be not risen from the dead, preaching it is not only useless, it is a falsehood. If Christ be not risen from the dead, the apostles were not merely talkers; they were positive liars.

The question is, At whose instigation was this false testimony borne? Did God send forth the apostles specially accredited by Him to proclaim a lie? If this is sin for man under Moses' law, of what character is our Lord? He is certainly not worthy of our confidence and trust. Here is the solemnity of all false doctrine. It misrepresents God.

Or did the apostles deliberately go of their own volition to proclaim a lie? This would put them into the class of lying prophets of the old dispensation upon whom the judgment of God was fulfilled. False witness in connection with man is bad, but how much worse this misrepresentation against God upon the chiefest of all questions—the salvation of men! The false witness was to be severely dealt with by Moses' law, but consider the character of the apostles. Were they dishonest men? Were they tricksters, serving worldly interests for their own gain? Did they seek to please their audiences? Did they adapt their story to win the world's favor? Did they preach the resurrection in order to obtain greatness and wealth?

We know that this was not true. They gained by their testimony only contempt and hatred, scourging and imprisonments—yes, even martyrdom for each one. We affirm that they declared the resurrection of Christ because they sincerely and wholeheartedly believed it. They had seen the risen Christ. They were not weak-headed enthusiasts preaching an imaginary resurrection. They were not brain-sick men.

We affirm that the witnesses to the resurrection of Christ were honest men, intelligent men. Was Peter a knave? Was Paul a rascal? Was John a deceiver? We have their writings, and to read them is an instant refutation to the charge of dishonesty. We believe that there is not a man in the world today with the master mind of Paul. His testimony to the resurrection is honest and unshakable.

If these apostles were false witnesses, whose testimony is reliable, and what is going to happen to our New Testament? Out go the Pauline epistles; out go the Gospels; out go the writings of John—Gospels, epistles and the Revelation; out goes the Book of the Acts; in fact, out go all of the books. For if Christ be not risen, they are all false and the New Testament is nothing but a lie—a miraculous lie indeed, but only a lie.

The Resurrection Proves Christ, the Bible and Christianity

"For if the dead rise not, then is not Christ raised."—vs. 16.

This is manifestly true. The apostles affirmed, however, that Christ was raised. They testified that He was put to death. Certainly a man of plain common sense ought to know when a man is dead. They testified that they saw the same One alive, after His burial. Certainly a man of plain common sense ought to be able to tell whether another man is alive or not, especially after he had seen that one, heard him, handled him. And they have a right to be emphatic: "Now IS Christ risen from the dead."

How is death known? By the state of the body. How is life known? By the state of the body. How is resurrection known? Only by the body's becoming alive again.

What is death? It is the opposite of life. Life is the result of the union of the spiritual with the physical. Death is the undoing of the bond of union. The dead are those whose parts are severed. Resurrection is the reunion of the sundered spirit (plus soul) and the body. Life at first consists of union; resurrection means reunion.

Elijah brought back into the lifeless body the soul of the son of the widow of Shunem; our Lord brought back into the lifeless body the spirit of the daughter of Jairus. So the prophetic Psalm 16 declares concerning Christ, "For thou wilt not leave my soul in hell; neither wilt thou suffer thine Holy One [His body] to see corruption." The severed body and the soul of our Lord were reunited in resurrection.

The dead do rise; Christ IS risen.

No Resurrection, No One to Trust

"And if Christ be not raised, your faith is vain."—vs. 17.

The word "vain" here is not the same word as translated "vain" in verse 14. "Vain" there means "empty"; "vain" here means an "overthrow," or a frustration. The non-resurrection of Christ would nullify, or frustrate, their faith; for it would prove the failure of His purpose to take them out of their sins. What a wreck of faith is involved in the denial of the resurrection of our Lord! If Christ be not risen, what object has your faith?

No Resurrection, No Forgiveness of Sin

"Ye are yet in your sins."—vs. 17.

If Christ did not come out of the grave, He cannot take men out of their sins. Then we have no justification. We are unforgiven, unrenewed. He has not borne away our sins if He is still in the tomb. If He is still in the tomb, He still lies under our sins—but how can that be? No, if He is still in the tomb, He is there, an imposter, under His own sins; and our sins are still on us. In penalty and power, sin still attaches itself to us.

BUT—we are not in our sins! These Corinthians were not in their sins! "And such *were* some of you: but ye *are* washed, but ye are . . . justified" (I Cor. 6:11). WE ARE NOT IN OUR SINS! That is proof of the resurrection of Christ. Who but a risen, living Christ could save us from our sins?

Mohammed founded a religion and died, was buried and remained in the tomb. Can Mohammed give deliverance from sin? NO! Buddha founded a religion and died and was buried and remained in the tomb. Can Buddha give deliverance from sin? NO! Can Confucius? NO! They all leave us in sin and misery. But where they fail, Christ saves.

"Christ's resurrection is the seal of our justification and the spring of our sanctification," writes Findlay. How true that is! Through the resurrection of our Lord, we have not only deliverance from the penalty of sin, but also deliverance from the power of sin. He was "raised again for our justification," that is, that we might have a perfect legal standing; but more than that, that we might have a vital experience of victory over sin through the power of His resurrection.

Christianity is more than a creed, it is a life. How would you ever explain a Moody, a Spurgeon, a Wesley, a McCheyne, or any saint, apart from the risen Christ?

Have you ever seen an unsaved person die—one conscious of the fact that he was yet in his sins? Several years ago we had a terrible experience in the death of a man whose last moments were spent in agony and horror, and who died shrieking, "The Devil's after me! The Devil's after me! The Devil's got me!" Have you ever seen an unsaved person die?

Have you ever seen a saved person die—one conscious of the fact that he is not in his sins? Just a few weeks since the children gathered round the bedside of a saintly mother and heard her say, "Oh, I see Jesus! He's altogether lovely!" The blood of Jesus Christ has made the way all plain.

> I have heard the voice of Jesus,
> Tell me naught of else beside;
> I have seen the face of Jesus,
> And my soul is satisfied.

Have you ever seen a saved person die? That experience proves the resurrection of Christ, and forgiveness of sins is true because Christ has come up from the dead.

> O joyful day! O glorious hour!
> When Jesus, by almighty power,
> Revived, and left the grave;
> In all His works behold Him great—
> Before, almighty to create,
> Almighty now to save.

If Christ Rose Not, Neither Will Anyone Else!

"Then they also which are fallen asleep in Christ are perished."—vs. 18.

If Christ be not risen, then not only are living "believers" unsaved, but the dead "in Christ" are perished. Indeed, if Christ be not risen, He is like the sailor who plunges into the sea to rescue the man overboard—if the sailor come not back, both are lost. If Christ be not risen, we must go to the grave where sleeps the body of our loved ones, and chisel on the stone: PERISHED.

Does that mean that our dear ones, whom we have laid aside in the hope of a glorious resurrection—that mother of yours, that baby of mine, that precious and loved one to whom we said farewell—are perished like the beast of the field? We fear that it means something even worse than that.

"Perished" does not mean "annihilated." It never does in Scripture. It means that they have gone into the dissolution of death, the body to the grave, and the spirit into the spirit state, but the spirit state of sinners under the wrath of God. "Perished" does not mean "annihilated." It does mean to be before God without a Mediator!

We speak of two classes of the dead: Those who die in Adam, under the penalty of sin and those who die in Christ, forgiven. But if Christ be not risen, all this is wrong; for all have died without help, without pardon. If in life they are yet in their sins, when they die, they die with all their sins upon them. If Christ be not risen from the dead, God and the future still remain; and our loved ones—and we, too—go out to meet them—God and the future—Christless. Then, Heaven is nothing but mocking rhetoric.

What a bleak picture that is! How thankful we ought to be for the clear, satisfactory, conclusive evidence of Christ's resurrection which we possess. What a relief to turn to the confident utterance of Paul, "Now IS Christ risen."

Paul's language here is the language of heart affection. It is impossible that our dear ones are perished. These things are not so. Christ IS risen. So we do not sorrow without hope.

A dear servant of God, a preacher of the Gospel, had one son, and that beloved son died at about the age of thirty. The father mourned, of course, because of the broken cords of love. "I thought that when the years rested heavily upon me, I would have his strong arm to lean upon, and now I am left alone," he wept.

That man of faith preached his own son's funeral sermon and laid his own boy to rest. Those who were with him at the grave said that when he turned away from the burial, the tears were raining down his cheeks; but with uplifted hoary head he gave a veritable shout of triumph: "I am the resurrection and the life!"

If No Resurrection, Then Christians Are Worse Off Than Sinners

"If in this life only we have hope in Christ, we are of all men most miserable."—Vs. 19.

"If in this life only"—nothing beyond the fleeting present—nothing in all the endless future—we are to be pitied, indeed. We have believed a lie; our hope in Christ is fallacious—it must expire in death. "If in this life only"—you have lost your Christ; you have lost your faith; you have lost your dear ones, and nothing precious is left. "Most miserable," indeed! "If in this life only"—then the hope that we shall see Christ, the hope that we shall be with Christ, the hope that we shall be like Christ, is only a dreary blank. If Christ be left to the dishonor of the grave, what relief can He afford you? You are the victim of a vain hope and a supreme folly.

If our hope in Christ does not reach beyond this life, we are pitiable; for we have toiled and suffered in hope of future joy and blessings which are a mere delusion. Many a Christian has surrendered some of the pleasures of the world, and has denied himself certain enjoyments of life, because they conflict with the soul's deepest interest in Christ. The pleasures of the world are not all dead loss. We are not speaking of immorality and debauchery, of the coarse and base things. There are some things of time and hopes of nature that have, at least, some good in them. But the child of God has practiced denial of self in relation to these and has put them far from him in his pursuits. Heaven has been enough for him. "Miserable man"—if Christ be not risen, he has given up earth for Heaven; and there is no Heaven.

We illustrate this by the statement of a brother in Christ in St. Louis who was very fond of music. He said to a Christian worker, "The symphony orchestra is playing tonight. How I would enjoy hearing it!" His friend said, "Well, why don't you go? I'm sure that there would be nothing wrong in that." "Well," replied the man, "I have borne testimony down at the church that Christ is all-sufficient, that He wholly satisfies; and I'm afraid that if someone would see me there, he might think that my satisfaction in Christ is not complete and that I must go to hear the orchestra to supply some lack in Him; therefore, I am going to wait for my music until I get to Heaven." AND THEN—there is no music there! Miserable man, pitiable man. He gave up music here for music there, and he loses both!

Govett says: "The wretchedness of disappointment is felt in proportion to the greatness of the hopes held out." Jesus sets His people against the world's current, both in principles and conduct, and foretells to them trouble as the issue, resting the reasonableness of their obedience to Him on His requital beyond the tomb. But if there be no beyond, His whole system is folly; and the observers of it are cheated dupes.

Secularists get at least the pleasures and profits of time, and may enjoy a good repute. But if there be a resurrection and life beyond the grave, how unhappy are they who live for time alone and despise God's witness of sin and judgment!

Our hope does lie beyond the grave, and that hope is sure.

The late Charles Reade, the well-known writer, wrote his own epitaph; and it is remarkable for his faith in the power of God. The epitaph is as follows:

Here lie,
By the side of his beloved friend,
the mortal remains of
CHARLES READE,
Dramatist, Novelist, and
Journalist
His last words to mankind
are on this stone.

I hope for a resurrection, not from any power in nature, but from the will of the Lord God omnipotent who made nature and me. He created man out of nothing, which nature could not. He can restore man from the dust, which nature cannot. And I hope for holiness and happiness in a future life, not for anything I have said or done in this body, but from the merits and mediation of Jesus Christ. He has promised His intercession for all who seek it, and He will not break His word; that intercession, once granted, and His merit infinite. "Him that cometh to me, I will in no wise cast out." "If any man sin, we have an advocate with the Father, Jesus Christ the righteous: and He is the propitiation for our sins."

T. T. SHIELDS
1873-1955

ABOUT THE MAN:

Dr. Shields was born in Bristol, England, 1873, the son of a Baptist minister.

Converted in his youth.

Received early education in England.

Ordained to the Baptist ministry in 1897.

Held Ontario pastorates in Florence, Delhi, Hamilton and London.

In 1910 was called to Jarvis Street Baptist Church, Toronto.

Elected to the Board of Governors of McMaster University 1920-28.

Received Doctor of Divinity degrees from Temple and McMaster Universities.

Founded THE GOSPEL WITNESS, a weekly magazine, in 1922.

Was author of several books and booklets.

Was president of Baptist Bible Union from 1923-1930.

Founded Toronto Baptist Seminary in 1927.

For many years was president of Union of Regular Baptist Churches of Ontario and Quebec.

In 1948 was elected vice-president of International Council of Christian Churches.

Passed on to be with Christ April 4, 1955.

VII.

Testimony of the Resurrection

(Stenographically Reported)

"And with great power gave the apostles witness of the resurrection of the Lord Jesus: and great grace was upon them all."—Acts 4:33.

If we believe, as most of us here assuredly do, that the Bible is the Word of God and, that being the Word of God, it must be true, we shall have no difficulty in believing in a literal, physical resurrection of our Lord Jesus.

The Acts of the Apostles opens by telling us that Christ "shewed himself alive after his passion by many infallible proofs"; and when the Word of God uses such strong terms as that we must, of course, as in all other cases, take it at its face value and believe that the proofs of the resurrection of our Lord are really "infallible." Throughout the New Testament the resurrection is either proclaimed or assured to be a fact.

We are told in the closing chapters of the Gospels and in Paul's Epistles that Jesus Christ did literally rise from the dead, that He "shewed himself alive," that He appeared unto His disciples again and again.

A certain school of critics in our day has resorted to the expedience of endeavoring to explain away certain things recorded in the Bible instead of openly and directly denying the truthfulness of the record as they formerly did. It is implied that the appearances of our Lord may be explained on psychological grounds, and as being due, in part, to the disciples' imaginations. But how carefully the Holy Spirit has guarded against such attacks upon the reliability of the record at this point! Our Lord did appear to His disciples; they saw Him after His resurrection; and they were able, therefore, to describe the Word of Life as that which they had "seen with [their] eyes."

But to the evidence of the sense of sight there was added also the sense of touch; for when the disciples were frightened and supposed they had seen a spirit, our Lord said, "Handle me, and see; for a spirit hath not flesh and bones, as ye see me have." Surely if the record be true, that puts the fact of the resurrection entirely beyond dispute. Our Lord Jesus said, "I have flesh and bones that answer to the sense of touch. Come and handle Me and see that I am more than a mere spirit."

You remember also His challenge to Thomas. I grant you that Thomas did not do as he was challenged to do. He had said, "Except I shall see in his hands the print of the nails, and put my finger into the print of the nails, and thrust my hand into his side, I will not believe." But how graciously our Lord condescended to his dullness of mind when He said, "Reach hither thy finger, and behold my hands; and reach hither thy hand, and thrust it into my side: and be not faithless, but believing." To his everlasting credit be it remembered that Thomas was never guilty of doing what he had declared to be indispensable to faith, but answered, "My Lord and my God."

As a further proof of the resurrection of His body, our Lord ate a piece of broiled fish and honeycomb before them all; and companied with them in His resurrection body.

After Christ had ascended into the Glory, the apostolic preachers made the truth of His resurrection the burden of their message. We read that the chief priests and scribes were "grieved that they taught the people, and preached through Jesus the resurrection from the dead," and here we are told that "with great power gave the apostles witness of the resurrection of the Lord Jesus." No doubt that was exactly what our Lord meant when He said, "Ye shall receive power, after that the Holy Ghost is come upon you: and ye shall be witnesses unto me." That is to say, they should bear witness to the resurrection of Christ, which was the crown and climax of His career as the Incarnation of redeeming grace; everywhere they should witness to the truth that He who had been crucified was raised again from the dead by the mighty power of God.

Why does the Bible make so much of the resurrection of Christ? Why does the Apostle Paul, by the inspiration of the Holy Ghost, declare that "If Christ be not raised, your faith is vain; ye are yet in your sins"? Because if the literal, physical resurrection of Jesus Christ be not a fact, then we have no Gospel to preach; we have no salvation to enjoy. We do well to follow the apostolic practice and place the emphasis where the apostolic preachers placed it.

I. THE RESURRECTION VERIFIED HIS WORD AS A PROPHET

"God, who at sundry times and in divers manners spake in time past unto the fathers by the prophets, hath in these last days spoken unto us by his Son." Every word that God had spoken previously by the prophets is gathered up, summarized, epitomized, in the testimony of Jesus Christ His Son. And of all the words that came from the lips of our Lord Jesus there is not one that is out of harmony with the Scriptures.

He came to be a Prophet, gathering up in Himself all that God has said. God had sent His servants rising up early and giving to the world line upon line, and precept upon precept, here a little and there a little; then last of all He sent unto us His Son. The Word that was made flesh was, and is, the divine Ultimatum, the last word that God will ever speak to men; for in all the ages that are yet to be, no word will ever come from God that is contrary to the testimony of the divine Prophet, Jesus Christ Himself. He is the Sum of everything, the Alpha and the Omega, the entire Alphabet and Literature of the divine communication to a rebellious world.

Our Lord bore testimony to the prophetic Scriptures as bearing witness to Himself, and *very especially to the prophecies that predicted His own resurrection.*

Take for example the much discussed book of Jonah, and I think we shall do well to go back to the common sense view of Dwight L. Moody. Years ago I was often in his rooms that were his headquarters in Chicago, furnished just as they were in his day. When there I have thought of the simplicity and the sanity of that mighty man of God. He went to the very heart of things when he declared, in effect, that he would judge of any man's orthodoxy by his attitude toward the book of Jonah. The man who can accept that book at its face value, for what it is, a literal, historical, accurate account of a miracle, is likely to be true to all the rest of the Book; but the man who denies that, will be sure to deny the authority of the Scriptures in general.

The book of Jonah has to do with this very subject. Our Lord said, "As Jonas was three days and three nights in the whale's belly; so shall the Son of man be three days and three nights in the heart of the earth"; that while Jonah's experience was historically true, it was prophecy of His own burial and resurrection. By His resurrection, Christ's own testimony to the prophetic Scriptures was verified, and His own authority as a Prophet of God was vindicated.

Furthermore, He *explicitly prophesied His own resurrection.* You remember His saying to the Jews, "Destroy this temple, and in three days I will raise it up." Bear in mind that nobody understood that saying—not even the disciples. And I would again suggest to students of prophecy that you should exercise a reverent caution in dogmatizing in respect to your interpretation of what a particular prophecy may mean; for, remember, that when the disciples actually came to the empty grave, after they had seen that the stone had been rolled away and had seen the linen clothes lying and the napkin folded in a place by itself, even after they were assured that the grave was empty, "as yet they knew not the scripture, that he must rise again from the dead." They knew only that the grave was empty, notwithstanding Jesus Himself had explicitly predicted His own resurrection.

Hence belief in the emptiness of Joseph's tomb does not constitute faith in the resurrection. The Scribes and Pharisees and soldiers all knew that the grave was empty—and they were paid for saying that His disciples had come by night and taken Him away. But not one of them knew the Scripture that He should rise from the dead, the empty grave notwithstanding. The very men who had heard Christ say, "Destroy this temple, and in three days I will raise it up," did not understand what He meant.

But hear this Scripture: "When therefore he was risen from the dead, his disciples remembered that he had said this unto them; and they believed the scriptures [the Old Testament Scriptures] and the word which Jesus had said." His resurrection verified His own specific prediction of His own resurrection and demonstrated that He was a Prophet clothed with divine authority.

The resurrection of the Lord Jesus Christ *verifies the written Word.* It proves it to be what it declares itself to be, the "word of God, which liveth and abideth for ever."

We have a Prophet from the Lord. You remember His teaching? "The rich man also died, and was buried; and in hell he lift up his eyes, being in torments"—and what did he ask for as a final proof to his brethren on earth, the ultimate, authoritative word? He said to Abraham, "I pray thee therefore, father, that thou wouldest send him [Lazarus] to my father's house; for I have five brethren; that he may testify unto them, lest they also come into this place of torment." Abraham answered, "They have Moses and the prophets; let them hear them." To which the rich man—or the once rich man, now poor indeed—replied, "Nay, father Abraham: but if one went unto them from the dead, they will repent."

That is exactly what the Lord has given to us in the person of His Son. He has stamped with His authority the entire Word, even "Moses and the prophets"; and by the resurrection of Christ we are assured that we have a Word from God, that we are not left without God, that we have something upon which our souls can rest for time and for eternity.

II. THE RESURRECTION CERTIFIES HIS WORK AS A PRIEST

The resurrection of Christ not only verifies His word as a Prophet, but certifies His work as a Priest. What is the record of the priesthood of the Old Testament, and of every other priesthood for that matter? "There is a remembrance again made of sins every year." Even the divinely-ordained ritual of the Mosaic economy required the priest every year to enter into the holiest of all with the blood of bulls and of goats. Every time the sacrifice was offered there was a remembrance of sin; and while it pointed to another Sacrifice, at the same time it proclaimed the inadequacy of any and every sacrifice which mere man can offer: "Every priest standeth daily ministering and offering oftentimes the same sacrifices, which can never take away sins."

That is the history of all human religions. It is abundantly evident, therefore, that what was necessary was a Sacrifice adequate to pay the debt of a sinful world, and to cancel all our obligations. Our Lord Jesus said that he had come to do that: "The Son of man came not to be ministered unto, but to minister, and to give his life a ransom for many." He came to play the part of a Redeemer, to pay the price of redemption.

What qualifications had He for that task? Simply this: He said of His life, "No man taketh it from me, but I lay it down of myself. I have power to lay it down, and I have power to take it again. This commandment have I received of my Father." He anticipated the later statement of Scripture that He was made "after the power of an indissoluble life." That is, His life was of such infinite value that He could atone not only for your sins but for mine as well, that He could become the propitiation not for our sins only but "for the sins of the whole world." Thus He said, "I will lay down My life when I am ready: I will be lifted up to die," for He said this signifying by what manner of death He should glorify God.

He selected the particular time, that all that was typified in the Passover might be fulfilled in Himself. He selected the particular place, for He said, "It cannot be that a prophet perish out of Jerusalem." In the manner, at the exact time, and at the particular place which He had ordained from all eternity that He would die, He laid down His life.

But on the third day He took that life again because it "was not possible that he should be holden" of death. His was the very life of God, eternity was in Him; His blood was His life in solution, and it was a sufficient value to atone, had it been necessary, for the sin of a million worlds. "In him was life; and the life was the light of men." He laid down His life, and His resurrection attested the fact that His life was more than human, that it was divine, that He was the "Lamb slain from the foundation of the world."

Thus, my dear friends, the Scripture says He was "slain for our offences"; He died "the just for the unjust that he might bring us to God." But He was raised again "for our justification"; for His resurrection established forever the value of His sacrifice and provided ground for the feet to stand upon. By the resurrection of the Lord Jesus we know that He has satisfied divine justice in our behalf, and He has ascended as our Representative to the right hand of God.

How simple it is! But I wonder how many of us really appreciate His death and resurrection in our behalf? Do you appreciate the fact that when Jesus Christ died on the cross He was your Substitute, your Representative? Was He not your Substitute when He was raised from the dead to become the firstfruits of them that sleep? Did He not equally represent you when He ascended into Heaven, carrying His glorified human body with Him? He did not shed His body; He carried His body with Him.

The incarnation was not a mere parenthesis in His experience; the incarnation is an eternal fact. In Christ a redeemed race is reunited to God. He carried a bit of this material world with Him into the presence of God, redeemed human nature, a pledge and promise of the time when the whole creation which now groaneth and travaileth together in bondage, shall be delivered into the glorious liberty of the children of God.

The resurrection is not only the pledge of the salvation of our souls; it is the pledge of the resurrection of our bodies and of the reunion of all who sleep in Christ.

I say, His resurrection is the certification of the adequacy of His atoning sacrifice and of the effectiveness of His whole priestly ministry. He is ascended into the heavens, is seated on the right hand of God, and He is just as much my Redeemer in Heaven as He was on the cross. That fact is a pledge that some day I shall be there myself. Do you believe that? Hallelujah!

For though here below 'mid sorrow and woe,
My place is in Heaven with Jesus, I know.
And this I shall find that such is His mind,
He'll not be in glory and leave me behind.

III. THE RESURRECTION IS PROOF OF HIS ABSOLUTE SOVEREIGNTY AS KING

He is a Prophet; He is a Priest, but He is also a King. You must look beyond the mere material representation of events. When Pilate wrote the superscription of his accusation to be put over our Lord's head on the cross, he wrote perhaps with bitterness in his heart, perhaps with irony—THIS IS JESUS THE KING OF THE JEWS. When the Jews saw what he had written, they protested and said, "Write not, the King of the Jews; but that he said, I am King of the Jews." Pilate answered, "What I have written I have written." Even as Pilate wrote, an unseen Hand was laid upon him; and he was sovereignly compelled to write what was already written in the counsels of the Eternal.

In the darkest hour the universe has ever seen, Jesus of Nazareth was King! I cannot be content with the acknowledgment that He is going to be King by and by. It is true that in a larger and fuller sense His Kingship shall be manifested, but He is even now *the* King. Yes, He is King now. He is seated on the right hand of the Majesty on high; all authority is His in Heaven and on earth. He is *the* King.

We read that at His death, "having spoiled principalities and powers, he made a shew of them openly, triumphing over them in it." Read the record and see how men tried to shorten His life, how they "led him unto the brow of the hill whereon their city was built, that they might cast him down headlong. But he passing through the midst of them went his way." When the Greeks came saying, "We would see Jesus," they came for no good purpose. He refused to see them. Then it was He said, "I, if I be lifted up from the earth, will draw all men unto me. This he said, signifying what death he should die." In effect He said, "I will not die by the hand of a Grecian assassin; I will die when I am ready to die; I will die in the way I have appointed to die, and for the purpose I came into the world to fulfill. No one shall interfere with My program."

At another time certain of the Pharisees said unto Him, "Depart hence: for Herod will kill thee." To which He majestically and sovereignly replied, "Go ye, and tell that fox, Behold, I cast out devils, and I do cures to day, and to morrow, and the third day I shall be perfected."

Another Herod had tried that long ago, but the angel said soon after to Joseph, "They are dead which sought the young child's life." The Devil said, "Cast thyself down: for it is written, He shall give his angels charge concerning thee." But Christ resisted the temptation to self-destruction.

Sovereignly He went to the grave. He laid down His life at the appointed time, because He was a King, and because there was no power in earth or in Hell that could take His life from Him or in any way interfere with His program.

Thus He went into the grave. I have known some people to be anxious about their burial. Our Lord gave no directions as to how He was to be buried, because that had been arranged before He was born: "He made his grave with the wicked, and with the rich in his death; because he had done no violence, neither was any deceit in his mouth."

Joseph of Arimathaea was a secret disciple: "The same had not consented to the counsel and deed of them" who determined the death of Jesus Christ. He was "a disciple of Jesus, but secretly for fear of the Jews"; but one who did really love the Lord. And when Jesus Christ was dead, he came, out of the love of his heart, not knowing why he came; and Mark says he "went in boldly unto Pilate and craved the body of Jesus." He had a new sepulchre wherein never man had been laid, and he determined to lay Him there.

So the rich man, Joseph of Arimathaea, laid Him in his own grave—and all Hell must have gnashed its teeth stamping roundabout, frustrated again! Sovereignly He chose His own bed in which to rest for those three short days, for He had said, "The scriptures must be fulfilled." And He fulfilled them to the letter!

When the chief priests and Pharisees came to Pilate full of anxiety lest His crucifixion should not wholly remove the menace of His teaching, what an example they provided of the real impotence of those who have power only to kill the body! One feels like saying, "You have had your way. You put thorns on His brow, did you not? You drove nails through His hands, did you not? You fastened Him to a cross. You drove a spear into His side. You killed Him. What more would you do? You have had your way." "Ah," say they, "but we remember that that deceiver said, while he was yet alive, After three days I will rise again."

Is it not strange that His enemies remembered the prophecy more readily than the disciples? They had an inward fear that it might be true. Caiaphas had said, "Ye know nothing at all, nor consider that it is expedient for us, that one man should die for the people, and that the whole nation perish not. And this he spake not of himself; but being high priest that year, he prophesied that Jesus should die for that nation; and not for that nation only, but that also he should gather together in one the children of God that were scattered abroad."

In spite of himself, God the Holy Ghost took the wicked lips of Caiaphas and made him tell the truth—and he prophesied. Now the chief priests and the Pharisees came to Pilate and said, "Command therefore that the sepulchre be made sure until the third day, lest his disciples come by night, and steal him away, and say unto the people, He is risen from the dead: so the last error shall be worse than the first." In effect they said, "Things are bad enough, but if this man's disciples preach a message of resurrection, nothing can withstand them." The Devil knew that from the beginning!

Pilate answered them again with fine irony, "Ye have a watch: go your way, make it as sure as ye can." And can you not see them sealing the tomb and setting a watch? It was as though Pilate had said, "Go on now! You have all the power of the ecclesiastical world on your side! I will give you the authority of Rome. Put Him in the sepulchre, roll the stone upon it, seal it, and gather your soldiers outside. Make it as sure as ye can"! But, as we sang this morning—

> **Up from the grave He arose,**
> **With a mighty triumph o'er His foes:**
> **He arose a victor from the dark domain,**
> **And He lives forever with His saints to reign:**
> **He arose, He arose,**
> **Hallelujah! Christ arose!**

What a glorious triumph over men and the Devil that was! He to whose authoritative word we gladly bow as our supreme Prophet, He who shed His blood for us, and upon whose merit we rely as our one and only High Priest, He is also our sovereign Lord and King. And I rejoice we have such a King.

The Pope is sovereign over the Vatican City. Now at last he is again "recognized in Rome as a temporal prince,"—and he would like to be sovereign over the whole earth. But the day shall come when it shall be proclaimed, "The kingdoms of this world are become the kingdoms of our Lord, and of his Christ: and he shall reign for ever and ever." And when He comes to reign in glory, and the dead are raised to meet Him at His coming, when He shall take to Himself His great power and reign—I do not believe there will be a blade of grass that will not acknowledge the sovereignty of Jesus Christ. His reign will be absolute; there will be no power in the universe comparable to His.

Bring forth the royal diadem,
And crown *Him* Lord of all!

(From *The Gospel Witness*)

VIII.

I Believe It Is the Garden Tomb

WILLIAM W. ORR

We have often sung the song, "There is a green hill far away without a city wall, where the dear Lord was crucified, who died to save us all." There is no doubt that somewhere near the city of Jerusalem is the sacred and hallowed spot where the Lord Jesus Christ, the Lamb of God, gave His life as a ransom for the sins of the world.

And according to the Scripture account, in a place that is called "nigh" to that spot, there must be a rock-hewn tomb answering to the description given in the gospel accounts where the beloved body of the Lord was laid between the time of His death and the time of His resurrection. It is a thoughtful quest on the part of earnest pilgrims to see and know these spots. While it is true that our faith does not depend to any degree upon the identification of these places connected with the life and death of Christ, still it is the earnest desire of many Christians to gaze reverently on these places which are made sacred for all time by the marvelous events which happened there.

The present city of Jerusalem is built largely upon the lines of the city of our Lord's day. A great deal of discussion has centered around the exact locations of the walls, gates and historic places. But most archaeologists seem to concur that the Jerusalem of today sits pretty much upon the foundations of the Jerusalem which our Lord knew. Within the city walls, and a little to the north and west of the city, is the traditional site of the Church of the Holy Sepulchre. This is a very old building erected in 1810 following a disastrous fire which had largely destroyed the building of the Crusaders' time. Five different sects share the supposed holy places within this traditional building. Practically all the spots which could be associated with our Lord's death and resurrection are allegedly grouped there. It seems there is a chapel or an altar to just about everything that happened in those last twenty-four eventful hours.

The front of the building is today braced by an ugly network of steel girders, said to be necessary to prevent the collapse of the structure. At almost any time you will find countless pilgrims from all over the world entering this church to pay earnest, devout worship to the many spots and relics contained therein.

If you were to ask the Moslem guides concerning the credibility of this spot, you will find them all primed with historical allusions. They will tell you how that Queen Helena, mother of Constantine, came to these ruins and, after earnest inquiry, was fully convinced that this was indeed the spot. They will further tell you that the Crusaders in their heyday made extensive search of the various claims of different locations and decided upon this one. They will further point out that both the Greek Catholic Church and the Roman Catholics have dispatched many archaeologists to search diligently surrounding territory, and these have unanimously brought back a verdict of the authenticity of this site.

But the Christian pilgrim finds himself completely dissatisfied with all this. Having been somewhat steeped in the divinely given truths from the gospel account, he turns his face away from tradition and superstition to seek a place upon which his own heart can find satisfaction and, perhaps in addition to this, the spot where the inner voice of the Holy Spirit will add His own approval.

General Gordon Finds What Looks Like Calvary

It is almost a hundred years ago since a British army officer who was called General "Chinese" Gordon was stationed in the Middle East. Being a reverent student of Scripture, he found this dissatisfaction of heart as he moved among the various supposed holy places grouped as the Church of the Holy Sepulchre. Taking his Bible in hand, and asking God to direct him, he searched diligently among the layers of debris outside the present north wall. It was his reward to come upon a tomb that seemed to give great evidence of having been the actual place of our Lord's burial. This was made more real and promising because of its proximity to a rocky knoll which has since been called "Gordon's Calvary." This knoll is a stone cliff, apparently about eighty feet high, which on its face has an uncanny erosion pattern, and in certain light one can easily distinguish the likeness to a decaying human skull, with the sunken eye sockets located beneath a low corroding forehead, and below the eye sockets, the suggestion of a nose bridge and a mouth.

As General Gordon sought for light on these two locations, he became even more convinced that this indeed was the place which the Scriptures would unqualifiedly endorse as the very spots of our Lord's death and burial. In course of time, a number of Christian people, particularly English, became interested in the site; and purchase was made of the area surrounding the tomb. The rocky cliff of Calvary has been for a number of years a Mohammedan cemetery.

Was the City Wall in Jesus' Time Where It Is Now?

The complete identification of this site depends largely on the location of the north wall of the city. Our Lord was crucified without the city, as the Scripture definitely states (Heb. 13:12). If this present north wall is on the same line as the wall in Jesus' time, then this would lead us to believe with all confidence that these sites are genuine.

It is known from history that in the period following our Lord's death, or about the years 66 to 69 A.D., there was an enlargement of the city, and another wall was under construction. This wall was one that opposed the Roman general, Titus, as he sought to conquer the city and the Jews in A.D. 70. This wall, however, would have been the third wall to the north, constructed about thirty-five years following our Lord's death. One need only go north on the Nablus Road about a quarter of a mile, or as far as the American consulate, to find extensive ruins of this third wall which was destroyed by Titus. This would mean that the present north wall is on the site of the one that stood at the time of our Lord's apprehension.

There are two gates in the north wall: the Damascus Gate which is the best looking of all the gates, and Herod's Gate. Beneath the pavement of the present Damascus Gate where people today walk in and out, there is another complete arch, built of Roman architecture of the period when our Lord was living, extending downward some twenty feet or more. This would lead us to think that the present Damascus Gate was built squarely upon a previous gate. This being so, then the present north wall has been built upon the same location as the wall in our Lord's day; and we have established our first point of evidence regarding the exact location of Calvary and the Lord's tomb.

Still Looks Like a Skull

Let us see what other points of biblical description we can find. We note that in Matthew 27:33 the place where Christ is to be crucified is called Golgotha, which is described as a place of a skull. Of course, this might just have been a name for a public execution ground; and yet there is this peculiar erosion effect which is exceedingly striking, to say the least. No one seems to know how old these erosive features are or how they came to be. It seems at first very doubtful that they could have endured in this cliff over a period of two thousand years. Yet the same influences that brought them into being at the first could have been continuing to work.

One thing we do know, and that is that this hill is a continuation of the hill Moriah which extends down to the Temple area within the city. Evidently at some very early time, as a defensive measure perhaps, the hill was cut and a large portion of it removed to another place. The road which lies between the present cliff of Golgotha and the city wall runs to Damascus and is called the Damascus Road. This we know as a road of very great antiquity. The present north wall of the city follows the contour of the hill which lifts it up quite high and, to the person on the Damascus Road, shows the bare face of the portion which has been slashed away. Many have not seen any reason why this strange skull-like cliff face could not have been present in our Lord's day. If so, it is easy to realize how it came to be called Golgotha; because in certain lighting, the resemblance to a skull is striking.

Gordon's Calvary Near Roads and the City

Again, the place where Christ was crucified had to be near a road. Actually the present Calvary is at the convergence of two roads: there is the Damascus Road and the Jericho Road. Both of these were in constant use in our Lord's day. You will remember that the Scripture tells us (Matt. 27:39) that the people who passed by railed on Him, challenging Him to come down from the cross, as if to say that the place of execution was in plain sight of the passers-by.

Even today, while the site is somewhat obscured because of a bus station, one can easily see what goes on at the top of this hill from the present Damascus Road. More than that, if one stands on the city walls over against the hill, it is not unlikely that he could watch the entire proceedings of any event that would occur there. The distance between the face of the cliff and the present city walls would be less than five hundred feet. Thus, the site of Gordon's Calvary seems to answer another description given us by the gospel writers.

As John writes of this event, he mentions that "the place where Jesus was crucified was nigh to the city" (John 19:20). The word "nigh" seems to convey the meaning of real proximity. It is easily less than a quarter of a mile from either the Damascus Gate or Herod's Gate in the north wall.

Garden Tomb Nearby Fits Bible Description

John further tells us (John 19:24) that "the sepulchre was nigh at hand." Here is another point of direction. The rocky tomb which was discovered by General Gordon seems to fulfill in detail the qualifications demanded by the Scripture account. It is even today located in a garden, and the evidence seems to be that it has been a garden for a long time. You will remember that the tomb was owned by a rich man named Joseph of Arimathaea. It is said to be in a garden (John 19:41). Therefore, we would expect it to be a rather extraordinary tomb, such as a rich man would prepare for himself and family.

While there are evidences that in the centuries following the ascent of Christ, efforts were made to obliterate the location of this tomb, still, as it stands today, the uncovered evidence seems beautifully to substantiate the true character of this sepulchre. It is the only one located in this area. It stands alone, but definitely is a family tomb. The interior is about twelve by seventeen feet, and the height is about seven feet. It was dug out by hand. There is one entrance which faces south.

As you step into the tomb, you will notice two main divisions. To your left is an antechamber, or the place of the mourners. This is separated from the right hand portion by two rather large dividers and a step. The right hand portion is the place of the bodies. To the far right is a full-sized resting place which would accommodate an adult body. About halfway up the wall there is a slight ledge, seemingly to indicate the place for another body, after a marble slab had been inserted over the ledge. On the eastern wall a place for another body, but smaller, perhaps of child size.

To the exact right as you come into the tomb, there is a duplicate of the space on the far right with places for two additional bodies when necessary. Both the space for the child's tomb and the space for the additional adult bodies remain unfinished even until this day. This is in agreement with the Scripture which points out that this was a new tomb. As a matter of fact, it was so new that it had not yet been completely finished (John 19:41). The entire tomb was dug out of rather soft limestone and faced the rest of the garden.

One additional feature was a window opening which is to the right of the present door. As you look in through this window, your gaze is immediately centered on the space which is presumed to be our Lord's tomb.

I am well aware that one cannot build a case on intuition. And yet it is the testimony of scores and scores of Bible students that as they have come into the knowledge of this garden tomb and as they themselves have visited the place, their own hearts have been strangely moved by what could be an affirmation of the Holy Spirit regarding the authenticity of this site. Actually, why could not this be? It is the ministry of the Holy Spirit to take of the things of Christ and make them real to us. He has come for the express purpose of exalting the dear Son of God, particularly with reference to His death, burial and resurrection.

While we do not set too great a store by the footprints which our Lord left during His earthly sojourn, the very fact that a reverent heart would seek to know His Lord better by a pilgrimage to a land forever associated with His life and death could easily be divinely affirmed by the Holy Spirit's approval. At the very least, this spot which is kept in quiet reverence today is a most wonderful place for one to sit and meditate upon the great and marvelous events which occurred, if not at this very place, somewhere nearby.

The tomb then seems to fit beautifully into the Scripture account. It is new; it is hewn out; it was a rich man's tomb; its entrance could easily have been closed by a rolling stone. There was only one door, and it was nigh to the place where He was crucified, and it is in a garden. In fact, from the center of the hill Calvary to the entrance of the tomb would not be over five hundred feet.

One might wonder, *How is it possible for two thousand years to pass and still these sacred spots be open and available for visitors to the Holy Land today? Would not the very nature of the passing of time have obliterated them?*

The answer might be contained in God's own loving concern for His children. God does not desire to withhold sources of inspiration. Actually the Christian life is filled with them. Even in the Holy Land the Jordan River still flows, and the Sea of Galilee is as lovely as it ever was. The well of Sychar still contains water, and the Cave of Machpelah holds still the bodies committed to it. It is not an unusual thing that God should allow these inexpressibly holy spots to be a source of continued inspiration and blessing for the reverent pilgrim.

Suffer me a word of personal testimony. I had gone to the tomb with great expectation. Could this really be the place of our Lord's burial?

Were General Gordon and the many other godly examiners correct as they affirmed their conviction of the genuineness of this spot?

It is not always easy to analyze mental processes. As all Bible students, I had formed a thought image of what the area should be like. This had come because of years of teaching and preaching the resurrection story. It was from our study that we had believed a certain interrelation of places and things were necessary. And now we were on the spot itself. Did the tomb fit our own heart picture? Were there any serious objections to the acceptability of this spot? We looked around. We prayed, and we meditated further. And God seemed to confirm with an assurance that has never worn off. "Truly, this is the place," is our profound belief.

Asked to Preach at the Garden Tomb

It was after dinner at the hotel when the telephone rang and I was summoned. The man on the other end was the kind and reverent warden of the tomb. He requested that I give the message at the Easter Sunrise Service. My heart skipped a beat. Surely this would be one of the great privileges of my life, and I answered prayerfully that as God gave me the grace I would do my best.

But what would I say? The occasion almost overwhelmed me to think that I would be standing on the very spot where the most magnificent exhibition of the power of God had taken place. Why, here had been enacted the great consummation of the coming into the world of Jesus Christ. And it was on these stones that God had vindicated for time and eternity the meaning of the life, death and resurrection of His beloved Son. More than that, here sin and death, the bitter enemies of all mankind, had been forever vanquished. And it was on this spot that my own sins had been fully borne and were now remembered no more.

Actually there seemed to be just one message to give. This was no time for sermonizing. I would just speak of what actually happened in this amazing place. That would be thrilling indeed. So at that great Easter morning service I began to tell of the happenings of our Lord's burial and resurrection. Over yonder on that hill to the left the crucifixion had taken place. Joseph of Arimathaea had secured permission from the Roman governor, Pontius Pilate, to take down the body. Here was Nicodemus with the linen clothes and spices. Where should they prepare the body for burial? We will not say "fortunately," for all of this no doubt is God's plan but here is a parcel of ground already owned by one of Jesus' friends, Joseph. Here is the measure of privacy needed. Here the two men God had no doubt ordained for this sacred task could perform their intended ministry. And here is a place of entombment into which no body had ever been laid. So the body is prepared and sorrowfully laid in its place. A stone is rolled in front of the opening, and the dear friends depart to their homes with heavy hearts.

The next day finds Christ's enemies made exceedingly uneasy by the strange happenings of the darkness, the earthquake, the rending of the rocks, and a general atmosphere of "What have we done?" So they went to the Roman governor to request a military guard about the tomb. Pilate, weary of the whole matter, sharply accedes and offers in addition the seal of his government. So the guard is mounted; the stone is sealed; and the tomb is secure, that is, militarily.

The Sabbath passes into night; and as the gray dawn of the first day of the week begins to light the eastern sky, there must have been a sudden flash of heavenly glory. For an angel had come; and, with one look at his lightning-bright countenance, the tough soldiers slumped to the ground in a quivering faint. Then, moving majestically as God's angels must always do, the ponderous stone is effortlessly moved away; and the entrance of the tomb is now accessible to all who were to come to see and to believe. As a crowning gesture of authority, the angel sits upon the stone; and with his permission, the guards again come to life; and still quivering and breathless, they scurry into the city to report the happenings.

Over yonder from the city's still darkened streets come three women. As they walk they talk of the Saviour's death in subdued tones. A packet of spices is in their hands to further anoint the Lord's body. Sorrowfully, uncertainly, apprehensively, they come within sight of the tomb to see in the dim light that the stone has been rolled away.

What was this? Who had done it? It could not be friends of the Lord, for these same friends had placed the body here in order for it to be safe. Therefore, it must be the work of enemies. Now what shall they do? Possibly some greater crime of desecration is being committed! Hastily they hold a conference and decide that one of them, Mary Magdalene, shall hurry back to the city to summon aid. The other two would stay here in the shadows and watch. Mary Magdalene goes quickly.

In the meantime, the light is becoming better; and as the women watch there, they edge closer and closer. No one seems to be on hand, and the door is open. Stealthily they inch up to the entrance and hesitatingly look in. Now what did they see? Why, it was a vision of an angel.

The same one who had frightened the soldiers away and had rolled the stone was seated in the interior. He bids them not to fear and speaks gently, calming their excited hearts and telling them the good news that Christ was risen and urging them to spread abroad this amazing story. They both go back into the city with glad exultancy.

In the meantime, Mary had gone to the home where Peter and John were staying. She tells them of her fears, and they dress hastily and run to the tomb. Breathless, John arrives first and, apparently coming from the right, looks in the window; but what he sees stops him right there. His eyes continue to devour the implications of that scene. Peter arrives a few seconds later and rushes directly in through the door. John now follows; and as their eyes almost strain in their sockets, their hearts beat wildly. They visually examine the scene from one side to the other. Evidently John is first to understand. What he sees is soundly convincing. There are the clothes all right, wrapped around as if they still encased the body. All the convolutions are still there, but they can easily see from the neck opening that there is no body contained therein. John believes there is only one answer to that: the Lord is supernaturally risen!

They must hurry and tell the others! Off they go, running wildly into the city, perhaps through the nearby Damascus Gate.

Shortly after they had gone, Mary Magdalene finally arrives, knowing nothing of what had happened to either of the other groups. Her heart remembers only the clutching fear that someone, and it must have been an enemy, has taken the body. Why did they take it? The only reason that she can see is that they might desecrate it. Her heart was breaking.

As she comes to the entrance, she stoops down and looks; and there to her tear-blurred eyes, she saw what looked like people within. To their inquiry as to why she wept, her sorrow-stupefied heart responded that if they knew where the body had been thrown, would they please tell her.

Weary, she turned again; and going only a few steps away from the door, she cast herself down to weep uncontrollably. Here was deepest anguish added to bitter sorrow. But presently she sensed another person behind her. Her mind suggested this might be the gardener, and he was asking the same question as to why she was weeping. Again she desperately pleaded that if he would only tell her where the body had been cast, she would go and care for it.

But now, joy upon joy, her sorrow was turned into unspeakable happiness; and it was the risen Christ who now spoke her name as none other would speak it. With a wild cry of released joy, she turned to throw herself at His feet and would have clung to Him with desperation; but He tenderly and gently suggested that she too go and tell the glorious news of how the Saviour of mankind lives again.

All of this was my story on the Easter morning. How wonderful, how exceedingly beyond power of words to describe, were these tremendous events. How poor was my tongue to relate them. But this is indeed the message that comes from the inner recesses of that garden tomb. Joybells were ringing loudly in my own heart; and as I watched the eyes of the visitors, I knew that their tears were tears of exquisite happiness as well.

Just before I closed the message with prayer, I turned back to look once more within the tomb's opening. Now the morning sunlight was streaming in, and from where I stood I could see the farthest corner. I looked and I saw and my heart leaped again with joy, for the tomb was still empty, and Jesus Christ lives!

HYMAN APPELMAN
1902-1983

ABOUT THE MAN:

Dr. Appelman was born in Russia and was reared and trained in the Jewish faith. He could speak many languages. The family moved to America in 1914. Dr. Appelman graduated with honors from Northwestern University and from DePaul University where he was one of the highest in the class and was awarded a scholarship. He received his license to practice law from DePaul Law School and was a trial lawyer in Chicago before his conversion—from 1921-25.

At age 28 he was converted. His Jewish family, then living in Chicago, disowned him. His father said to him, *"When your sides come together from hunger and you come crawling to my door, I will throw you a crust of bread as I would any other dog."*

Feeling a definite call to preach, he attended Southwestern Baptist Theological Seminary in Fort Worth from 1930-33.

In 1933 he was elected to be one of the State Evangelists for Texas; he faithfully ministered for eight years in this capacity for the Southern Baptist Convention. Later he launched into larger meetings, both in Texas and outside, and soon was spending some time, year after year, in a foreign country. His meetings were large meetings, with hundreds, sometimes thousands, of conversions in each.

Dr. Appelman made eight or nine trips around the world and several trips to Russia as an evangelist.

His schedule left one breathless. It was hard to find a day in his long ministry of fifty-three years that he was not preaching somewhere. He averaged two weeks at home out of a year. That was the intenseness of a Jew! Of this Jew, at least! His prayer life, hard work and biblical preaching reminded one of the Apostle Paul.

Dr. Appelman was the author of some 40 books.

IX.

Christ Is Risen

HYMAN APPELMAN

"In the end of the sabbath, as it began to dawn toward the first day of the week, came Mary Magdalene and the other Mary to see the sepulchre. And, behold, there was a great earthquake: for the angel of the Lord descended from heaven, and came and rolled back the stone from the door, and sat upon it. His countenance was like lightning, and his raiment white as snow: And for fear of him the keepers did shake, and became as dead men. And the angel answered and said unto the women, Fear not ye: for I know that ye seek Jesus, which was crucified. He is not here: for he is risen, as he said. Come, see the place where the Lord lay. And go quickly, and tell his disciples that he is risen from the dead; and, behold, he goeth before you into Galilee; there shall ye see him: lo, I have told you."—Matt. 28:1-7.

On Christ's resurrection, the authenticity of the Bible stands or falls. The Old Testament predicted it. Christ witnessed to it. The disciples testified concerning it. Paul the apostle preached it.

Christ's resurrection is the infallible proof of his deity. It proved Him to be the Son of God. It proved all His claims regarding Himself. It shows that God accepted Him and His work.

Christ's resurrection is the ground of our standing, the certainty of our state. It gives assurance of eternal life. It shows that believers are justly justified. It gives the saints an accepted Intercessor. It secures the resurrection of those who put their faith in the Lord Jesus Christ.

Center of Church

"The living, risen Christ is the center of the church's creed, the Creator of her character, the inspiration of her conduct. His resurrection is the clearest note in her battle song. It is the sweetest music amid all her sorrows. It speaks of personal salvation. It promises the life that has no end. It declares to bereaved souls that 'them also which sleep in Jesus will God bring with him'; and, therefore, the light of His resurrection falls in radiant beauty upon the graves where rests the dust of the holy dead." Thus spake, again and again, the great Dr. G. Campbell Morgan.

Arthur T. Pierson joins the paean of praise with the following doxology:

> The greatest event that ever happened on this planet thus far is the resurrection. The greatest miracle ever wrought was the resurrection, including all smaller ones. The focal point towards which prophecy points is the resurrection of Jesus Christ. The greatest demonstration that He was the Son of God was the resurrection.
>
> The greatest theme of preaching is the resurrection. The great complement of the redemption on the cross is seen in the resurrection, that event which intervenes between His crucifixion and His coming again. It is a plentiful assurance to all children of God that they shall thus rise from the dead and shall bear the likeness of their glorious Lord. It is a demonstration of the fact that Christ was really deathless, that though He submitted voluntarily to death, it was an impossibility that He should ever be holden of it. It was the preparation for the descent of the Holy Spirit. It is the great assurance to every believer that in Jesus he has the Messiah of the Old Testament, and the Jehovah, the sovereign Lord of all.

Significant Witness

There are many thoughts that flow from these three tremendous words of my text, "He is risen." They are unquestionably, indubitably, the matter of a significant witness. They are a stirring challenge. They are a searching invitation. May we, then, look at these words from the following angle: First, the resurrection; second, the reasons for the resurrection; third, the results of the resurrection.

I. THE RESURRECTION

The resurrection itself supposes, first, that the Lord Jesus Christ was definitely dead when He was taken down from the cross. Malefactors executed in the Roman manner, that is, on the cross, were, in general, a long time dying. To hasten their death, the judge, in the case of the crucifixion of the Lord Jesus Christ and the two thieves with Him, ordered their legs to be broken.

The certainty and reality of our Saviour's death is confirmed by three descriptions of persons.

First, there are the Jews—"The Jews therefore, because it was the preparation, that the bodies should not remain upon the cross on the sabbath day . . . besought Pilate that their legs might be broken, and that they might be taken away" (John 19:31).

Second, there are the soldiers—"Then came the soldiers, and brake the legs of the first, and of the other which was crucified with him. But when they came to Jesus, and saw that he was dead already, they brake not his legs" (John 19:32,33). To make sure work, one of them even went so far as to thrust a spear into the side of the Saviour. "But one of the soldiers with a spear pierced his side, and forthwith came there out blood and water" (John 19:34).

Third, John, the beloved disciple, tells us so in so many words—"And he that saw it bare record, and his record is true: and he knoweth that he saith true, that ye might believe" (John 19:35).

Private Conference

Second, the words, "He is risen," prove not only that the Lord Jesus Christ was dead but that He was also buried. You know without my telling you that this was an act performed by two of His friends, Joseph of Arimathaea, an honorable counselor, and Nicodemus, the ruler of the Jews with whom we had become acquainted much earlier in that wonderful third chapter of the Gospel of John.

One might have thought that this was a most dangerous season to show any love for Christ, especially by two eminent Jews. However, they had never made any open profession of Him. This was the only public opportunity they had to testify their attachment to Jesus. This must lead all of us to believe that both Joseph of Arimathaea and Nicodemus had been often with the Lord Jesus Christ in private conference.

Then the cry, "He is risen," proves not only that the Lord Jesus Christ was dead, not only that He was buried, but also that He lay under the power of death for a season. Unquestionably, this was the fulfillment of prophecy, among others, the words of Hosea 6:2, "After two days will he revive us: in the third day he will raise us up, and we shall live in his sight." Here was the type of the antitype of Matthew 12:40, "For as Jonas was three days and three nights in the whale's belly; so shall the Son of man be three days and three nights in the heart of the earth." Here was the fulfillment of His own word in John 2:19, "Jesus answered and said unto them, Destroy this temple, and in three days I will raise it up." When, therefore, the Lord Jesus Christ was risen from the dead, His disciples remembered that He had said this unto them, "and they remembered his words" (Luke 24:8).

Visible Manifestations

The very slowness and dilatoriness of the disciples in accepting the resurrection of the Lord Jesus Christ are an encouragement to us who also are of trembling faith. If these mighty men of God, having associated with the Lord Jesus Christ in His lifetime, having seen Him perform His mighty miracles, having seen Him voluntarily offer up His life unto death, having had visible manifestations of His resurrected presence, could still doubt, then there is hope for us.

The fact that He is risen is attested by many proofs in the New Testament dispensation. First, we have, in order, the authority of the angels: "And it came to pass, as they were much perplexed thereabout, behold, two men stood by them in shining garments . . . He is not here, but is risen: remember how he spake unto you when he was yet in Galilee" (Luke 24:4,6).

Those to whom the angels spoke could not very well have mistaken the authoritative words of the messengers from Heaven. Surely there was absolutely no chance of misunderstanding so plain a statement. This could never have been invented. It is for our encouragement, for our inspiration, for our counsel, for our comfort, to know that these hesitating disciples were approached by the angels in order that their faith in the Son of God might be assured and insured.

There is, further, the testimony of the disciples themselves:

"And they say unto her, Woman, why weepest thou? She saith unto them, Because they have taken away my Lord, and I know not where they have laid him . . . . Jesus saith unto her, Touch me not; for I am not yet ascended to my Father: but go to my brethren, and say unto them, I ascend unto my Father, and your Father; and to my God, and your God."—John 20:13,17.

The Lord Jesus Christ manifested Himself when, "Afterward he appeared unto the eleven as they sat at meat, and upbraided them with their unbelief and hardness of heart, because they believed not them which had seen him after he was risen" (Mark 16:14).

We are told that He was also seen of about five hundred brethren at once. There is no possibility of misunderstanding the interchange of conversation between the Lord Jesus Christ and Thomas. There is no misunderstanding of the cry of Thomas, "My Lord and my God."

Bitter Truth

We go on from there to the evidence of the Roman soldiers who watched the sepulchre:

"And, behold, there was a great earthquake: for the angel of the Lord descended from heaven, and came and rolled back the stone from the door, and sat upon it. His countenance was like lightning, and his raiment white as snow: and for fear of him the keepers did shake, and became as dead men."—Matt. 28:2-4.

The consternation and dread these warriors experienced surely was not an hallucination, neither an imagination. It forced a bitter truth from their lips. They fled to the city. They showed unto the chief priests all the things that were done. They were bribed with money to deny the fact. This thing was not done in a corner. It was open. It was clear. It was easy to understand and to believe.

To us who are the children of God, one of the greatest attestations of the resurrection of the Lord Jesus Christ is His promise, given to His disciples in chapters 14, 15 and 16 of John: "But when the Comforter is come, whom I will send unto you from the Father, even the Spirit of truth, which proceedeth from the Father, he shall testify of me" (John 15:26); "Nevertheless I tell you the truth; It is expedient for you that I go away: for if I go not away, the Comforter will not come unto you; but if I depart, I will send him unto you" (John 16:7). He renewed this matchless promise after His resurrection, before His ascension: "And, behold, I send the promise of my Father upon you: but tarry ye in the city of Jerusalem, until ye be endued with power from on high" (Luke 24:49).

When the day of Pentecost was fully come, definitely, unmistakably, certainly, in a manner that changed their lives and attitudes from then on until the last day that they lived, the apostles were filled with the promised Holy Ghost:

"And when the day of Pentecost was fully come, they were all with one accord in one place. And suddenly there came a sound from heaven as of a rushing mighty wind, and it filled all the house where they were sitting. And there appeared unto them cloven tongues like as of fire, and it sat upon each of them. And they were all filled with the Holy Ghost, and began to speak with other tongues, as the Spirit gave them utterance."—Acts 2:1-4.

II. THE REASONS FOR THE RESURRECTION

Next, we come to the reasons for the resurrection of the Lord Jesus Christ.

Evident Demonstration

First, the Son of God was raised from the dead, as Paul tells us, that He might be powerfully "declared to be the Son of God with power, according to the spirit of holiness, by the resurrection from the dead" (Rom. 1:4). The Saviour asserted in the days of His flesh again and again that He and God were one. He now proved it, definitely, flatly, by rising again. "No man taketh it from me, but I lay it down of myself. I have power to lay it down, and I have power to take it again. This commandment have I received of my Father" (John 10:18). This glorious, magnificent, miraculous act is an evident demonstration of His divine nature, of the fact that He is God manifest in the flesh. If He had lied in His claims, if he had lied in His testimonies, there would never have been the approval of God upon His life and teaching by His resurrection from the dead.

The Son of God rose that it might be manifested that He had magnified the law, that He had satisfied divine justice. God, sending an angel to roll away the stone from the door of the sepulchre, plainly indicated that Jesus Christ had answered the demands of the law, that He was now at liberty to come forth. Thousands of Jews had died in that fearful Roman fashion, but Jesus Christ was the only One who had been raised from the dead. In the words of a great preacher of today, "The open tomb is a receipt for Calvary."

He was raised from the dead that He might be a Prince and a Saviour.

"Then Peter and the other apostles answered and said, We ought to obey God rather than men. The God of our fathers raised up Jesus, whom ye slew and hanged on a tree. Him hath God exalted with his right hand to be a Prince and a Saviour, for to give repentance to Israel, and forgiveness of sins. And we are his witnesses of these things; and so is also the Holy Ghost, whom God hath given to them that obey him."—Acts 5:29-32.

A Prince, a mighty Prince, a Warrior, a War Lord, the Commander-in-Chief of God's magnificent armies, He spoiled principalities, "And having spoiled principalities and powers, he made a shew of them openly, triumphing over them in it" (Col. 2:15). As a Saviour, He is able—

abundantly able, superabundantly able—to save. "Wherefore he is able to save them to the uttermost that come unto God by him, seeing he ever liveth to make intercession for them" (Heb 7:25).

Alludes to Oblation

"But now is Christ risen from the dead, and become the firstfruits of them that slept" (I Cor. 15:20). The term "firstfruits" is, of course, metaphorical. It alludes to the oblation of the firstfruits in the Levitical law. They were offered both as an acknowledgment that the whole crop was God's and as a pledge and assurance of the Jews' enjoying the whole from God. As certainly as one whole harvest follows the firstfruits, so, surely, shall the saints' resurrection follow the resurrection of Christ, and an effect follows its proper cause.

Christ was the first who rose never to die again; the first who rose by His own power; the first who rose to give others a pledge and assurance of their rising after Him and of their rising like unto Him.

What a wondrous joy it is for us to know that the open tomb of the Son of God guarantees our open tombs! What a blessed peace there comes to us in the confidence of knowing that the resurrected Christ at the right hand of the Father is a presage of the fact that we, too, shall reign and rejoice with Him eternally in the presence of our Father also.

He arose that He might be Judge of the quick and the dead. "And he commanded us to preach unto the people, and to testify that it is he who was ordained of God to be the judge of quick and dead" (Acts 10:42).

Jesus Christ, by virtue of His meritorious passion and glorious resurrection, was constituted Lord of all things.

"For to this end Christ both died, and rose, and revived, that he might be Lord both of the dead and living. But why dost thou judge thy brother? or why dost thou set at nought thy brother? for we shall all stand before the judgment seat of Christ."—Rom. 14:9,10.

He has absolute power to judge all persons. "When the Son of man shall come in his glory, and all the holy angels with him, then shall he sit upon the throne of his glory" (Matt. 25:31). "For we must all appear before the judgment seat of Christ; that every one may receive the things done in his body, according to that he hath done, whether it be good or bad" (II Cor. 5:10).

III. THE RESULTS OF THE RESURRECTION

Our closing thought in this message is the results of the resurrection, the benefits which accrue to us thereby.

Flee to God

First, the Lord Jesus Christ being risen, we are saved from sin through Him. "And she shall bring forth a son, and thou shalt call his name JESUS: for he shall save his people from their sins" (Matt. 1:21). He IS the Saviour of all who put their faith in Him. He IS the Saviour of all who come unto God by Him. The salvation which He purchased with His own precious blood, He holds as a stewardship for all those of us who, cognizant of our need, flee to Him from the wrath of God and the inevitability of the punishment of our sins.

Second, as a result of His resurrection, the Holy Spirit is given to His church, to His people, to the children of God, to the twice-born.

"And I will pray the Father, and he shall give you another Comforter, that he may abide with you for ever: Even the Spirit of truth; whom the world cannot receive, because it seeth him not, neither knoweth him: but ye know him; for he dwelleth with you, and shall be in you."— John 14:16,17.

"What? know ye not that your body is the temple of the Holy Ghost which is in you, which ye have of God, and ye are not your own?" —I Cor. 6:19.

There are all sorts of heresies going the rounds of Christian circles in this day and time. Be it known to you, my beloved friends, that unless you are born of the Spirit of God, you do not become, you cannot become, a child of God. Salvation is an instantaneous and progressive process. First, your sins are forgiven, and the Holy Spirit regenerates your soul.

There is such a thing, however, as the fullness of God's Holy Spirit. There is such a thing as being empowered for service by the infilling of the indwelling Holy Spirit. This is what I mean when I say that by the resurrection of the Lord Jesus Christ, the Holy Spirit is given to His church for the conquests that follow upon the preaching of the Gospel.

In the Presence of Him

Third, our resurrection is absolutely secured. The resurrection of the

Lord Jesus Christ is God's guarantee that we shall not all sleep, but that in like manner as the Lord Jesus Christ rose up from the dead, even so we, also, shall be raised, body and soul, to walk forever in the presence of the Most High. "Blessed be the God and Father of our Lord Jesus Christ, which according to his abundant mercy hath begotten us again unto a lively hope by the resurrection of Jesus Christ from the dead" (I Pet. 1:3).

It is my plea, from the depths of my heart, that this Easter resurrection season may not be so much a time of holiday making, but a time of holy devotion, of holy dedication. May God in His infinite, compassionate grace and mercy give us the wisdom, not so much to show off the finery of our outer apparel, but to show off, in the beauty of holiness, the apparel of the new man which, because of the death, burial, and the resurrection of the Lord Jesus Christ, is created within us by the monition and admonition of God's Holy Spirit.

THE ESSENTIAL DIFFFERENCE

The late Dr. Harry Rimmer, while traveling in Egypt, was negotiating with the then Secretary of State who was a refined and cultured Egyptian. In a conversation regarding their respective faiths, Dr. Rimmer stated that:

"We believe that God has given man three revelations of Himself. First, we believe that He has revealed Himself in the work of creation."

"We, too, believe that," interjected the Egyptian.

"We believe that God revealed Himself in a book, the Bible," continued Dr. Rimmer.

"We, too, believe that God has revealed Himself in a book, the Koran," replied the Egyptian.

"We believe that God has revealed Himself in a Man, and that Man is Jesus Christ," added Dr. Rimmer.

"We also believe that God revealed Himself in a man, and that man is the prophet Mohammed," said the Egyptian.

"We believe that Jesus died to save His followers," said Dr. Rimmer.

"We believe that Mohammed died for his people," replied the Egyptian.

"We believe," continued Dr. Rimmer, "that Jesus is able to substantiate His claims because He rose from the dead."

The Moslem hesitated, then his eyes fell. He had no answer to that statement. Finally he admitted, "We have no information concerning our prophet after death."

Dr. Rimmer was right; he was convinced of the truth of his assertion, because it was founded on the Word of God that has withstood all attacks for over 1,900 years; and there are hundreds of thousands today who would agree with him.

The fact of the resurrection of Jesus Christ is a proven fact of history. The great Apostle Paul states, "For I delivered unto you first of all that which I also received, how that Christ died for our sins according to the scriptures; and that he was buried, and that he rose again the third day according to the scriptures" (I Cor. 15:3,4). Read the whole chapter, and learn more of what Paul taught about the resurrection. This loving Saviour died and rose again that you might have forgiveness of all your sins: past, present, and future. If you will accept Him today, you will be able to say with Paul that you serve a risen, living, omnipotent Saviour. This is beautifully expressed by A. H. Ackley in his inspiring hymn:

> I serve a risen Saviour, He's in the world today,
> I know that He is living, whatever men may say;
> I see His hand of mercy, I hear His voice of cheer,
> And just the time I need Him, He's always near.
>
> In all the world around me, I see His loving care,
> And though my heart grows weary, I never will despair,
> I know that He is leading, through all the stormy blast,
> The day of His appearing will come at last.

D. L. MOODY
1837-1899

ABOUT THE MAN:

D. L. Moody may well have been the greatest evangelist of all time. In a 40-year period, he won a million souls, founded three Christian schools, launched a great Christian publishing business, established a world-renowned Christian conference center, and inspired literally thousands of preachers to win souls and conduct revivals.

A shoe clerk at 17, his ambition was to make $100,000. Converted at 18, he uncovered hidden gospel gold in the hearts of millions for the next half century. He preached to 20,000 a day in Brooklyn and admitted only non-church members by ticket!

He met a young songleader in Indianapolis, said bluntly, "You're the man I've been looking for for eight years. Throw up your job and come with me." Ira D. Sankey did just that; thereafter it was "Moody will preach; Sankey will sing."

He traveled across the American continent and through Great Britain in some of the greatest and most successful evangelistic meetings communities have ever known. His tour of the world with Sankey was considered the greatest evangelistic enterprise of the century.

It was Henry Varley who said, "It remains to be seen what God will do with a man who gives himself up wholly to Him." And Moody endeavored to be, under God, that man; and the world did marvel to see how wonderfully God used him.

Two great monuments stand to the indefatigable work and ministry of this gospel warrior—Moody Bible Institute and the famous Moody Church in Chicago.

Moody went to be with the Lord in 1899.

X.

Jesus Arose: So Shall We Rise

D. L. MOODY

"But now is Christ risen from the dead, and become the firstfruits of them that slept."—I Cor. 15:20.

I think this is one of the grandest chapters in the writings of Paul. It is especially grand to those who have lost friends. No sooner do loved ones pass away than the question arises—Shall we meet them again? Paul answers this question and gives a consolation we can find so clearly stated nowhere else. What a consolation to know, as we lay our friends away, that we shall meet them again in a little while!

As I go into a cemetery I like to think of the time when the dead shall rise from their graves. We read part of this chapter in what we call the "burial service." I think it is an unfortunate expression. Paul never talked of "burial." He said the body was *sown* in corruption, *sown* in weakness, *sown* in dishonor, *sown* a natural body. If I *bury* a bushel of wheat, I never expect to see it again; but if I *sow* it, I expect results. Thank God, our friends are not buried; they are only sown! I like the Saxon name for the cemetery—"God's acre."

The Gospel preached by the apostles rested upon four pillars. The first was the atoning death of Christ; the second, His burial and resurrection; the third, His ascension; the fourth, His coming again. These four doctrines were preached by all the apostles, and by them the Gospel must stand or fall.

In the opening verses of this chapter in Corinthians, we get a clear statement from Paul that the doctrine of the resurrection is a part of the Gospel. He defines the Gospel as meaning that Christ died for our sins, but not that only—He was buried and rose again the third day. Then he summons witnesses to prove the resurrection:

"He was seen of Cephas [Simon Peter], *then of the twelve: After that, he was seen of above five hundred brethren at once; of whom the greater*

part remain unto this present, but some are fallen asleep. After that, he was seen of James; then of all the apostles. And last of all he was seen of me also, as of one born out of due time."—I Cor. 15:5-8.

Now this is pretty clear testimony, strong enough to satisfy a candid inquirer. But the Greeks had no belief in the possibility of the resurrection, and these converts at Corinth had been reared in that unbelief. And so Paul puts the question:

*"Now if Christ be preached that he rose from the dead, how say some among you that there is no resurrection from the dead?"*vs.12.

It was one of the false doctrines that had crept into the church at Corinth, because no orthodox Jew would ever think of questioning it.

To deny the resurrection is to say that we will never see more of the loved ones whose bodies have been committed to the clay. If Christ has not risen, this life is the only one; and we are as the brutes. How cruel it is to have anyone love you if this be true! How horrible that they should let the tendrils of your heart twine around them if, when they are torn away in death, it is to be the end. I would rather *hate* than *love* if I thought there will be no resurrection, because then I would feel no pangs at losing the hated thing.

Oh, the cruelty of unbelief! It takes away our brightest hopes. "If in this life only we have hope in Christ, we are of all men most miserable."

Immortality

Mankind has naturally "yearnings after the infinite." Among the most primitive peoples, philosophers have detected what has been well called "an appetite for the infinite," which belies the teaching that death ends all.

It is one of the points of difference between man and beast. The birds of the air, the beasts of the field, are much the same today as they were in Eden. They eat and sleep and pass their life from sun to sun in unvarying monotony. Their desires are the same, their needs the same.

But the man is always changing. His desires are always enlarging. His mind is always planning ahead. No sooner does he reach one goal than he presses towards the next, and not even death itself can arrest him.

A well-known infidel once said: "The last enemy that shall be destroyed is not death, but the belief of man in his own immortality."

This presentiment of a future life has been beautifully illustrated by the feeling which grows within the bird when winter approaches, impelling it to travel towards the south—"an impulse mysterious and undefined, but irresistible and unerring"—or to "the longing of southern plants, taken to a northern climate and planted in northern soil. They grow there, but they are always failing of their flowers. The poor exiled shrub dreams of a splendid blossom which it has never seen, but which it is dimly conscious that it ought somehow to produce. It feels the flower which it has not strength to make in the half-chilled but still genuine juices of its southern nature. That is the way in which the thought of a future life haunts us all."

Philosophers have many facts to prove this universal reaching forward to the life beyond the grave. It is supposed that many funeral rites and ceremonies, for instance, are due to it. If the body is once more to be occupied by its spirit, it at once suggests itself that is must be protected from harm. Accordingly we find that graves are concealed lest enemies should dig up the remains and dishonor them.

Livingstone tells how a Bechuana chief was buried in his own cattle-pen. Then the cattle were driven about for some hours until all trace of the grave was obliterated. But the body must be protected not alone from ill usage, but, as far as possible, from decay; and the process of embalming is an endeavor in this direction.

Sometimes, indeed, resurrection would be undesirable, and so we find that dead bodies are thrown into the water to drown the spirit. Modern Egyptians turn the body round and round, it is said, to make the spirit giddy and therefore unable to retrace its steps; while certain aboriginal Australians take off the nails of the hands lest the reanimated corpse should scratch its way out of its narrow cell.

When the conception of a second life as a continuation of the present life is held, we find the custom of burying inanimate things, such as weapons and instruments. The dead man will require everything beyond—as he did this side of—death. Not alone inanimate things, but animals are killed in order that their ghost may accompany the ghost of the dead man. The Bedouins slaughter his camel over the grave of their dead comrade; indispensable in this world, it will be the same in the next.

From this, one step leads to the immolation of human beings. Wives follow their husbands; slaves are slain that they may continue to serve their masters. In the words of Tennyson:

"They that in barbarian burials killed the slave and slew the wife
Felt within themselves the sacred passion of the second life."

Doctrine of the Resurrection in the Old Testament

We only catch glimpses of the doctrine of the resurrection now and then in the Old Testament, but the saints of those days evidently believed in it. Nearly two thousand years before Christ, Abraham rehearsed His sacrifice on Mt. Moriah when he obeyed God's call to offer up Isaac. Referring to this Paul writes: ". . . accounting that God was able to raise [Isaac] up, even from the dead: from whence also he received him in a figure." Five hundred years later, we find God saying unto His servant Moses; "I kill, and I make alive."

Isaiah wrote—"He will swallow up death in victory; and the Lord God will wipe away tears from off all faces," and again—"Thy dead men shall live, together with my dead body shall they rise. Awake and sing, ye that dwell in the dust; for thy dew is as the dew of herbs, and the earth shall cast out the dead."

Ezekiel's vivid description of the resurrection of dry bones, setting forth in prophecy the restoration of Israel, is other evidence. When David lost his child, he said he could not call the little one back to him, but that he would go and be with the child. At other times he wrote—"As for me, I will behold thy face in righteousness: I shall be satisfied when I awake with thy likeness"; and—"God will redeem my soul from the power of the grave; for he shall receive me."

The patriarch Job comforted himself with the same glorious hope in the hour of his deep sorrow. He who had asked, "What is my strength that I should hope? and what is mine end that I should prolong my life?" said, "I know that my Redeemer liveth, and that he shall stand at the latter day upon the earth: and though after my skin worms destroy this body, yet in my flesh shall I see God; whom I shall see for myself, and mine eyes shall behold, and not another."

Job must have firmly believed that his body was to be raised to life again, but not on earth, for

"There is hope of a tree, if it be cut down, that it will sprout again, and that the tender branch thereof will not cease. Though the root thereof wax old in the earth, and the [stalk] thereof die in the ground; Yet through the scent of water it will bud, and bring forth boughs like a plant. But man dieth, and wasteth away: yea, man giveth up the ghost, and where is he? As the waters fail from the sea, and the flood decayeth and drieth up: So man lieth down, and riseth not: till the heavens be no more, they shall not awake, nor be raised out of their sleep."—Job 14:7-12.

In Hosea 13, the Lord declares: "I will ransom them from the power of the grave; I will redeem them from death: O death, I will be thy plagues; O grave, I will be thy destruction."

In the last chapter of Daniel we have another glimpse of the same truth: "They that be wise shall shine as the brightness of the firmament; and they that turn many to righteousness as the stars for ever and ever." And his book closes with these words: "Go thou thy way till the end be: for thou shalt rest, and stand in thy lot at the end of the days."

And typically, too, resurrection was set forth in the Old Testament by the firstfruits offered the day after the passover-sabbath as a pledge of the whole harvest. The children of Israel were taught in type of the Messiah who should be "the firstfruits of them that slept." Someone has said that the very first employment of Israel in Canaan was preparing the type of the Saviour's resurrection, and their first religious act was holding up that type of risen Saviour.

In the New Testament

But what was referred to only at long intervals in the Old Testament became in the New Testament a prominent matter of fact and teaching. The word "resurrection" occurs forty-two times in the New Testament. Many times during His ministry did our Lord refer to the resurrection of the dead generally.

The Sadducees once came to Him with a difficult question about the marriage relation hereafter, and Jesus said:

"As touching the resurrection of the dead, have ye not read that which was spoken unto you by God, saying, I am the God of Abraham, and the God of Isaac, and the God of Jacob? God is not the God of the dead, but of the living." —Matt. 22:31,32.

On another occasion Christ said:

"When thou makest a dinner or a supper, call not thy friends, nor thy brethren, neither thy kinsmen, nor thy rich neighbours; lest they also bid thee again, and a recompence be made thee. But when thou makest a feast, call the poor, the maimed, the lame, the blind: And thou shalt be blessed; for they cannot recompense thee: for thou shalt be recompensed at the resurrection of the just." —Luke 14:12-14.

When Lazarus died, Jesus spake the consoling word to his sisters: "Thy brother shall rise again." Martha replied: "I know that he shall rise again in the resurrection at the last day." Jesus then said unto her: "I am the resurrection and the life."

A Splendid Guess

We see, then, that the belief in a future life did not begin with Christ, and nowhere is the claim made that immortality is His gift. We get that from the Creator.

But though the idea existed before Christianity, it was at best only "a splendid guess." The natural man cannot look across the narrowest grave and see what is beyond. Strain his eyes as he will, he cannot pierce the veil of death. It is ever before him, blighting his hopes, checking his plans, thwarting his purposes, a barrier that nothing can break down. Ever since sin entered the world, death has reigned, making the earth one huge graveyard. He has not rested for a moment. In every age and every country, "Dust thou art, and to dust thou shalt return" has been the sentence overhanging mankind. All the generations of men as they pass across the earth do but follow their dead.

Many unexpected things happen to us in this life, but death is not among them. We do not know *how or when* it will come, but come it will, if the Lord tarry.

We have heard of doctors who have performed wonderful cures, but all their skill and knowledge have been unable to undo the work of death. In all these six thousand years since death entered this sin-cursed earth, human means have failed to win back a single trophy from death. Advancing civilization, increased education, progress in commerce and art—none of these things make us superior to the most degraded savages. Death always triumphs in one direction—onward and never backward.

Brought to Light by Christ

What was unknown by the wisest man on earth was revealed by Christ. He did not create immortality, but He "abolished death, brought life and immortality to light through the gospel." "That undiscovered country," spoken of by the poet, "from whose bourne no traveller returns," is *not* an undiscovered country to the believer. Our Lord explored it. He entered the lists against death in His own territory and came off more than conqueror. The sceptre of death is universal still, but it is broken and shall one day crumble into dust. The Christian need no longer speculate about the future; certainty is reached beside the empty tomb of Christ. "Now *is* Christ risen from the dead, and become the firstfruits of them that slept." We can see the trace of His returning footprints.

Triumph

And so we can join in the triumphant strain, "Death is swallowed up in victory." The sting of death is sin, and God has given us the victory through our Lord Jesus Christ. They which have fallen asleep in Christ have *not* perished, but we shall one day see them face to face.

What a Gospel of joy and hope we have, compared to that of unbelief! Dr. Bonar wrote:

> The heathen sorrowed without hope. To them death connected itself with no hope, no brightness, no triumph. It was not *sunset* to them, for that bids us be on the lookout for another sun, as bright as that which set. It was not *autumn* or *winter,* for these speak of returning spring and summer. It was not *seed* cast into rough soil, for that predicts the future tree or flower, more beautiful than the seed. It was pure and simple darkness, all cloud, shadow, desolation. A shattered pillar, a ship gone to pieces, a race lost, a harp lying on the ground with snapped strings and all its music lost, a flower-bud crushed—these were the sad utterances of their hopeless grief.
>
> The thought that death was the gate of life came not in to cheer the parting and brighten the sepulchre. The truth that the grave was the soil and the body the seed sown by God's own hand to call out the latent life; that the race was not lost, but only a little earlier won; that the column was not destroyed but transferred to another building and another city to be "a pillar in the house of God"; that the bud was not crushed, but transplanted for fuller expansion to a kindlier soil and air; that the harp was not broken, but handed to a truer minstrel who will bring out all the rich compass of its hidden music: these were things that had no place in their theology, hardly in their dreams.

An Essential Doctrine

Some people claim that the question of a risen Saviour is not essential. Hear what Paul says:

"If Christ be not risen, then is our preaching vain, and your faith is also vain. Yea, and we are found false witnesses of God; because we have testified of God that he raised up Christ: whom he raised not up, if so be that the dead rise not. For if the dead rise not, then is not Christ

raised: And if Christ be not raised, your faith is vain; ye are yet in your sins."—I Cor. 15:14-17.

I tell you, it is very essential. It is not a mere speculative question that we are dealing with; it is of the greatest practical importance. The resurrection is the keystone of the arch on which our faith is supported.

If Christ has not risen, we must impeach all those witnesses for lying.

If Christ has not risen, we have no proof that the crucifixion of Jesus differed from that of the two thieves who suffered with Him.

If Christ has not risen, it is impossible to believe His atoning death was accepted.

Someone has said that the power of Christ's death to take away sin is always conditioned in the New Testament with the fact of His resurrection.

If Christ has not risen, it is impossible to admire His words and character. He made the resurrection a test-truth of His divinity.

The Jews once asked for a sign, and He answered, "Destroy this temple, and in three days I will raise it up," referring to the temple of His body.

On another occasion, He gave the sign of the prophet Jonah: "As Jonas was three days and three nights in the whale's belly, so shall the Son of man be three days and three nights in the heart of the earth."

Paul says, "Declared to be the Son of God with power by the resurrection from the dead."

"If He had not been divine," says one, "the sins of anyone of us would have been a gravestone too heavy for Him to throw off; the claims of Jehovah's justice would have been bands of death too strong for Him to burst."

What would Christianity be without the resurrection? It would descend to the level of any of the other religious systems of the world. If Christ never rose from the dead, how do His words differ from those of Plato? Other men besides Christ have lived beautiful lives and have left behind them beautiful precepts to guide their followers. We should have to class Christ with these.

"How Are the Dead Raised? and With What Body Do They Come?"

Turning back to the chapter, we find that Paul next deals with the question *how* the dead can be raised and with what body they come.

Thou fool, that which thou sowest is not quickened, except it die:

And that which thou sowest, thou sowest not that body that shall be, but bare grain, it may chance of wheat, or of some other grain:

But God [and all things are possible with God] giveth it a body as it hath pleased him, and to every seed his own body.

All flesh is not the same flesh: but there is one kind of flesh of men, another flesh of beasts, another of fishes, and another of birds.

There are also celestial bodies, and bodies terrestrial: but the glory of the celestial is one, and the glory of the terrestrial is another.

There is one glory of the sun, and another glory of the moon, and another glory of the stars: for one star differeth from another star in glory.

So also is the resurrection of the dead. It is sown in corruption; it is raised in incorruption:

It is sown in dishonour; it is raised in glory: it is sown in weakness; it is raised in power:

It is sown a natural body; it is raised a spiritual body. There is a natural body, and there is a spiritual body.

And so it is written, The first man Adam was made a living soul; the last Adam was made a quickening spirit.

Howbeit that was not first which is spiritual, but that which is natural; and afterward that which is spiritual.

The first man is of the earth, earthy: the second man is the Lord from heaven.

As is the earthy, such are they also that are earthy: and as is the heavenly, such are they also that are heavenly.

And as we have borne the image of the earthy, we shall also bear the image of the heavenly.—I Cor. 15:36-49.

We see the truth of Paul's illustration in the world around us. The analogy of nature does not indeed furnish a *proof* of the resurrection, but it affords illustrations of many things that are just as hard to explain— yet we do not deny the facts.

Take a little black flower seed and sow it; after it has been planted some time, dig it up. If it is whole, you know that it has no life; but if it has begun to decay, you know that life and fruitfulness will follow. There will be a resurrected life, and out of that little black seed will come a beautiful fragrant flower.

Here is a disgusting grub, crawling along the ground. By and by old age overtakes it, and it begins to spin its own shroud, to make its own sepulchre; and it lies as if in death. Look again, and it has shuffled off its shroud; it has burst its sepulchre open, and it comes forth a beautiful butterfly, with different form and habits.

So with our bodies. They die, but God will give us glorified bodies in their stead. This is the law of the new creation as well as of the old: light after darkness; life after death; fruitfulness and glory after corruption and decay.

Thank God, we are to gain by death. We are to have something that death cannot touch. When this earthly body is raised, all the present imperfection will be gone. Jacob will leave his lameness. Paul will have no thorn in the flesh. We shall enter a life that deserves the name of life, happy, glorious, everlasting—the body once more united to the soul, no longer mortal, subject to pain and disease and death, but glorified, incorruptible, "fashioned like unto his glorious body," everything that hinders the spiritual life left behind. We are exiles now, but then we who are saved shall stand before the throne of God, joint heirs with Christ, kings and priests, citizens of that heavenly country.

A bright young girl of fifteen was suddenly cast upon a bed of suffering, completely paralyzed on one side, and nearly blind. She heard the family doctor say to her parents as they stood by the bedside, "She has seen her best days, poor child!"

"No, doctor," she exclaimed, "my best days are yet to come—when I shall see the King in His beauty."

Our Hope

That is our hope. We shall not sink into annihilation. Christ rose from the dead to give us a pledge of our own rising. The resurrection is the great antidote for death. Nothing else can take its place. Riches, genius, worldly pleasures or pursuits—none can bring us consolation in the dying hour.

"All my possessions for a moment of time," cried Queen Elizabeth, when dying.

"I have provided in the course of my life for everything except death, and now alas! I am to die unprepared" were the last words of Cardinal Borgia.

Compare with these the last words of one of the early disciples: "I am weary. I will now go to sleep. Good night!" He had the sure hope of awaking in a brighter land.

At the battle of Inkerman, a soldier was just able to crawl to his tent after he was struck down. When found, he was lying upon his face, his open Bible before him, his hand glued fast to the page by his lifeblood which covered it. When his hand was lifted, the letters of the printed page were clearly traced upon it; and with the ever-living promise in and on his hand, they laid him in a soldier's grave. The words were: "I am the resurrection, and the life: he that believeth in me, though he were dead, yet shall he live."

I want a religion that can comfort even in death, that can unite me with my loved ones. Oh, what gloom and darkness would settle upon this world if it were not for the glorious doctrine of the resurrection! Thank God, the glorious morning will soon break. For a little while God asks us to be on the watch, faithful to Him and waiting for the summons. Soon our Lord will come to receive His own, whether they be living or dead.

A Roman Soldier's Story

A Lenten Meditation

I loved Him not—and yet, I could not hate Him.
  I was A ROMAN . . . He was but a Jew . . .
Yet, there He hung, and agonized for others.
  Was ever love of MAN so pure and true?

Upon the cross between two thieves they hung Him.
  (And now, my stylus falters as I write—
For I must stand and see His awful anguish;
  Must watch the daytime turn to darkest night.)

One thief cried out, "If Thou be Lord, then save us!"
  . . . The other looked at Him with glazing eyes,
And said, "Remember me, Lord, in Thy kingdom.". . .
  Christ said, "Today, thou'lt be in Paradise."

The hours dragged on; yet there He hung suspended
  'Twixt Heaven and earth. Ah, 'twas an awful sight!
I'd seen such sights before—I was a soldier—
  Yet ne'er before did day become as night.

For three long hours the darkness lay around us;
  The rocks were rent and lightning flashed around.
. . . One called, "The veil is rent within the Temple!"
  And saints rose from their graves within the ground.

I dared not look . . . The sky grew darker, darker—
  Until it seemed like midnight all around . . .
And then I cried out, "Stop my ears, O Father!"
  For I had heard His blood drip to the ground.

They said to me, "Go pierce His side, proud Roman."
  But ah . . . my spear hung heavy at my side—
For once more He had cried out to His Father.
  I would that in His place I might have died!

I could not thrust . . . and so they called another.
  The blood and water poured out from His side.
The people smote their breasts and left Golgotha.
  I knew then that it was THE CHRIST who died.

. . . His seamless coat lay folded on the ground there.
  (They said the lot had fallen unto me.) . . .
With reverent, trembling hands I touched its border,
  Then placed it where no human eye could see.

The day grew old. The thieves' legs had been broken;
  And men came now to take our Lord away . . .
More worthy lips than mine shall tell the story
  Of how Christ rose that Resurrection Day.

                    —Mrs. Leo R. Goodwin

H. A. IRONSIDE
1876-1951

ABOUT THE MAN:

Few preachers had more varied ministries than this man. He was a captain in the Salvation Army, an itinerant preacher with the Plymouth Brethren, pastor of the renowned Moody Memorial Church in Chicago, and conducted Bible conferences throughout the world. Sandwiched between those major ministries, Ironside preached the Gospel on street corners, in missions, in taverns, on Indian reservations, etc.

Never formally ordained and with no experience whatever as a pastor, Ironside took over the 4,000-seat Moody Memorial Church in Chicago and often filled it to capacity for 18½ years. A seminary president once said of him, *"He has the most unique ministry of any man living."* Although he had little formal education, his tremendous mental capacity and photographic memory caused him to be called the "Archbishop of Fundamentalism."

Preaching—warm, soul-saving preaching—was his forte. Special speakers in his great church often meant nothing; the crowds came when he was there. He traveled constantly; at his prime, he averaged 40 weeks in the year on the road—always returning to Moody Memorial for Sunday services.

His pen moved, too; he contributed regularly to various religious periodicals and journals in addition to publishing 80 books and pamphlets. His writings included addresses or commentaries on the entire New Testament, all of the prophetic books of the Old Testament, and a great many volumes on specific Bible themes and subjects.

In 1951, Dr. Ironside died in Cambridge, New Zealand, and was buried there at his own request.

XI.

Implications of the Resurrection

H. A. IRONSIDE

Great truths that are stumbling blocks to the natural man are nevertheless the very foundations upon which the confidence of the spiritual man is built, for "faith gives the assurance of that for which we hope, and convinces us of the reality of the unseen." Of course, this is only true when our hopes are based upon the testimony of the Word of God.

That Word is forever settled in Heaven; and, like God who gave it, the Word is unshakable. Men may cavil or quibble regarding its teachings, but "what if some did not believe? shall their unbelief make the faith of God without effect?" It is written in the prophets, "He . . . will not call back his words" (Isa. 31:2). The reverent Christian will therefore accept without question what has been revealed in Scripture, even though it may be beyond his powers of comprehension.

When Festus, the Roman governor of Caesarea, was explaining his perplexity concerning Paul's case to King Agrippa, he expressed his wonder that the accusers of the apostle had nothing definite to bring against him, "but had certain questions against him of their own superstition, and of one Jesus, which was dead, whom Paul affirmed to be alive" (Acts 25:19). This to Festus was such a manifest absurdity that he thought it hardly worth considering. He evidently knew that Jesus had died. It was a matter commonly reported, and he accepted that as the truth, but that any sane man could believe that Jesus was alive again seemed to the cynical Roman utterly absurd and ridiculous. And yet the entire superstructure of Christianity rests on this great fact.

Christ's Resurrection — and Ours

I purpose noting several implications drawn from the truth of Christ's resurrection, as set forth, not in the four gospel accounts, but elsewhere in the Word of God. In the well-known resurrection chapter (I Cor. 15) we are told:

Now if Christ be preached that he rose from the dead, how say some among you that there is no resurrection of the dead?

But if there be no resurrection of the dead, then is Christ not risen:

And if Christ be not risen, then is our preaching vain, and your faith is also vain.

Yea, and we are found false witnesses of God; because we have testified of God that he raised up Christ: whom he raised not up, if so be that the dead rise not.

For if the dead rise not, then is not Christ raised;

And if Christ be not raised, your faith is vain; ye are yet in your sins.

Then they also which are fallen asleep in Christ are perished.

If in this life only we have hope in Christ, we are of all men most miserable.—Vss. 12-19.

In these verses the Holy Spirit develops for us and vigorously defends this great fundamental truth of Christian testimony. Some in Corinth were denying the physical resurrection of mankind generally. To them it seemed impossible that the dead should be brought again to life, but Paul shows that to deny the resurrection of mankind necessarily involves the denial of Christ's resurrection. If He has indeed been raised—and apart from this fact there would be no Gospel to preach—why then should any question the power of God to bring back from the dead the millions who have died through all the millenniums of earthly history?

Surely He who could create a universe out of nought and who brought our physical bodies into existence so marvelously in the first place could resuscitate them even after they had dissolved away into their chemical elements! The miracle of each returning spring bears witness to this. As one looks out upon the apparently lifeless trees of winter, he might well question the possibilitiy that verdant groves would again dot the landscape; but in some strange, mysterious way the trees are enabled to draw from the earth the life-giving sap with all its chemical elements which causes leaves, flowers and fruit soon to appear.

Certainly if one had never seen this miracle performed, he would come to the conclusion the first time that winter spread its blanket over the earth, that all things green and lovely had disappeared forever. But in a very short time he would find that his reasoning was based upon false premises.

Bodily Resurrection

Our faith is based on facts as real as the observed process of nature.

There are those who teach today that our Lord Jesus never came out of the grave in His material body. They admit His continued existence in spirit, but deny His physical resurrection.

But there can be no question as to the testimony of Holy Scripture. There we learn that our blessed Lord arose from the dead in the very body in which He had suffered and died for our sins, though changed in a most wonderful way. Nevertheless, it was a real, material, human body; and we know that it bore in the palms of the hands the print of the nails. There was still the mark where the Roman spear had pierced His side, and one can scarcely question but that these evidences of Christ's love for His church will be seen upon His glorified body throughout all eternity.

We gather from Scripture that no others of the righteous dead will bear similar evidences upon their resurrection bodies of pain and suffering here on earth, for our blessed Lord is going to present the church to Himself as "not having spot, or wrinkle, or any such thing." But as the everlasting testimony to the reality of redemption, He will bear the marks of His passion throughout all the ages to come. When John the Beloved gazed upon the throne in glory, he saw in the midst of it "a Lamb as it had been slain" (Rev. 5:6), or, as Weymouth so tenderly expresses it, "a lamb that looked as though it had once been offered in sacrifice."

> **Thy wounds, Lord Jesus,**
> **Those deep, dark wounds, they tell**
> **The sacrifice that frees us**
> **From sin and death and Hell.**
> **These bind Thee once forever**
> **To all who own Thy grace;**
> **No hand those bonds can sever,**
> **No time those scars efface.**

The redeemed of the Lord will see in those scars the testimony to a love that was stronger than death and which the many waters of judgment could not quench. To Thomas and the other disciples, these were the sure evidences that He who appeared in their midst was actually the same Jesus whom they had known and loved before He went to the cross. He said to them, "Handle me, and see; for a spirit hath not flesh and bones, as ye see me have."

The implication of Christ's bodily resurrection is that if the power of God was put forth in raising Christ from the dead, it is folly to question His ability to raise up the dead bodies of His saints as well as of all men generally. In fact, so definite is the apostle as to this that he insists, "If the dead rise not, then is not Christ raised" (vs. 16).

Proof of Our Redemption

What, then, would be the next implication? Why, "If Christ be not raised, your faith is vain; ye are yet in your sins" (vs. 17). In other words, if our Saviour did not come forth in triumph from Joseph's new tomb, then we have no Gospel to preach to the lost men. A dreaming poet like Arnold may speak of the body of Jesus still sleeping in a Syrian tomb, but that is only the language of unbelief. If it were true, then there would be no redemption for lost sinners, no salvation for guilty men.

All our hopes rest upon the fact that He who was delivered up to death for our offenses was really raised again for our justification. During the time that the body of our Lord lay in the tomb, there was no one on earth who could be sure that redemption was an accomplished fact. If He had not risen, it would have been sure evidence that He was either deceived or a deceiver, for He had definitely predicted His resurrection as well as His sacrificial death.

The fact that He rose from the dead is in itself the proof that His great oblation upon the cross has satisfied the claims of divine righteousness and has met every requirement of infinite holiness. God has raised Him from the dead in token of the satisfaction He has found in His work, and He now sets Him forth a Prince and a Saviour.

A simple illustration may help to make clear what I am trying to say.

Let us imagine the case of a man convicted of a crime and sentenced to spend a certain period of time in prison. In this particular instance, by some arrangement which of course I recognize would not be an ordinary thing, a substitute takes his place, agrees to serve out his sentence. In accordance with this understanding, the substitute is locked up in prison. Now as long as this man remains behind prison bars, the one in whose stead he is suffering can never be absolutely sure that the law may not yet lay hold of him and demand that he serve out at least part of the sentence.

But one day as he goes down the street, he comes face to face with the one who so generously agreed to become his representative before the law and to bear the punishment that his crime deserved. He learns that, having served the sentence, his friend is now free. At once the offender's mind is at rest. He knows the law can have nothing further to say to him. Its claims have all been met; and he, the guilty one against whom the original judgment was rendered, is now once more a free man.

Because Christ's payment of the judgment of sin can be evidenced only by His bodily resurrection, then if Christ be not raised from the dead, there is no possible way of knowing that His redemptive work is an accomplished fact. He said He was to be delivered into the hands of sinful men, that they would crucify Him, and that on the third day He would rise again.

The first two declarations were fulfilled. If the last has not been fulfilled, he stands convicted of false testimony. He was either Himself deluded in thinking that He was the Saviour and could triumph over death, or else He was a deliberate deceiver. It is His resurrection, the fulfillment of His own prediction, which proves that His death was the all-sufficient sacrifice for sin which He proclaimed it to be.

And thus the believing sinner can say, "My sins nailed Him to the cross. He, the sinless One, took my place and there died under the judgment of God, enduring that divine wrath which should righteously have been poured out on me." But having settled the sin question, God has declared His acceptance of the work of His Son by raising Him from the dead and receiving Him into Heaven at His own right hand as the risen glorified Man.

The Essential for Victorious Living

"If Christ be not raised, your faith is vain; ye are yet in your sins." All the millions of saintly souls who have testified to their faith in Christ throughout what we call the Christian centuries were utterly mistaken if Christ did not rise from the dead.

But then the amazing thing to be accounted for is this: What was it that wrought such changes in their lives, that turned them from sin to righteousness, that delivered them from worldliness and selfishness and conformed them to the image of Christ? According to the Word of God, it is as believers are occupied with the risen One that they become like Him. Let those then who deny His resurrection try to explain the transforming power of this faith in Him, who, according to the unbelievers, has no longer any existence.

The apostle's conclusion is that if Christ is no more than a master teacher, if He is only a guide, if His instruction is only meant to serve as a light for our pathway through this world, if the Christ who died has not been raised, we who profess faith in His name, who gladly give up the things of the world for love of Him, are of all men most to be pitied. In that case we are but following a will-o'-the-wisp, a delusion, for the sake of which we are surrendering much that men of the world value. But the experiences of untold millions of Christians prove that the risen Christ is the joy and satisfaction of the hearts of all who thus yield themselves to Him.

Consider the case of Saul of Tarsus. We see him hastening along the Damascus road, bitter hatred filling his heart for Jesus of Nazareth and for all who confess His name. But suddenly the heavens are opened, and light brighter than the sun shines upon the wayward persecutor. A voice from Heaven cries, "Saul, Saul, why persecutest thou me?" And in answer to the hitherto rabid Pharisee's amazed inquiry, "Who art thou, Lord?" the reply comes, "I am Jesus whom thou persecutest."

At once the tremendous change that Jesus called being "born again" takes place. Saul of Tarsus becomes a new creation and soon goes forth as Paul the apostle to preach the faith that once he destroyed. It was his contact with the risen Christ that wrought the miracle, as it has wrought similar miracles in the hearts and lives of untold thousands since.

This message was what the early preachers of the cross proclaimed everywhere they went. They preached "Jesus and the resurrection." Notice, it was not enough to preach Jesus. It was not enough to enlarge upon His excellencies. It was not enough to dwell upon the perfection of His life. It was not enough to occupy people with His sacrificial death. There was something more than this. "This Jesus hath God raised up . . . God hath made that same Jesus, whom ye have crucified, both Lord and Christ" (Acts 2:32,36). This was the message of Pentecost. This was the message which has been blessed and used of God throughout the centuries in the salvation of millions of souls; and this is the message for the preacher today, the only message that will ensure the eternal salvation of all who believe it.

R. A. TORREY
1856-1928

ABOUT THE MAN:

Torrey grew up in a wealthy home, attended Yale University and Divinity School, and studied abroad. During his early student days at Yale, young Torrey became an agnostic and a heavy drinker. But even during the days of his "wild life," he was strangely aware of a conviction that some day he was to preach the Gospel. At the end of his senior year in college, he was saved.

While at Yale Divinity School, he came under the influence of D. L. Moody. Little did Moody know the mighty forces he was setting in motion in stirring young R. A. Torrey to service!

After Moody died, Torrey took on the world-girdling revival campaigns in Australia, New Zealand, England and America.

Like many another giant for God, Torrey shone best, furthest and brightest as a personal soul winner. This one man led 100,000 to Christ in a revival that circled the globe!

Dr. Torrey's education was obtained in the best schools and universities of higher learning. Fearless, quick, imaginative and scholarly, he was a tough opponent to meet in debate. He was recognized as a great scholar, yet his ministry was marked by simplicity.

It was because of his outstanding scholastic ability and evangelistic fervor that Moody handpicked Torrey to become superintendent of his infant Moody Bible Institute. In 1912, Torrey became dean of BIOLA, where he served until 1924, pastoring the Church of the Open Door in Los Angeles from 1915-1924.

Torrey's books have probably reached more people indirectly and helped more people to understand the Bible and to have power to win souls, than the writings of any other man since the Apostle Paul, with the possible exceptions of Spurgeon and Rice. Torrey was a great Bible teacher, but most of all he was filled with the Holy Spirit.

He greatly influenced the life of Dr. John R. Rice.

XII.

Up From the Grave He Arose!

R. A. TORREY

"And if Christ hath not been raised, then is our preaching vain, your faith also is vain. . . . And if Christ hath not been raised, your faith is vain; ye are yet in your sins."—I Cor. 15:14-17, American Standard Version, 1901.

"Now I make known unto you, brethren, the gospel which I preached unto you, which also ye received, wherein also ye stand . . . . For I delivered unto you first of all that which I also received, how that Christ died for our sins according to the scriptures; and that he was buried; and that he hath been raised on the third day according to the scriptures; and that he appeared to Cephas; then to the twelve; then he appeared to about five hundred brethren at once, of whom the greater part remain until now, but some are fallen asleep; then he appeared to James; then to all the apostles; and last of all as to the child untimely born, he appeared to me also."—I Cor. 15:1,3-8, A.S.V.

"Wherefore also he is able to save to the uttermost them that draw near unto God through him, seeing he ever liveth to make intercession for them."—Heb. 7:25, A.S.V.

"Remember Jesus Christ, risen from the dead, of the seed of David, according to my gospel."—II Tim. 2:8, A.S.V.

Our subject is: the wonderful character, the fundamental importance and the demonstrated certainty of the resurrection of Jesus Christ.

Paul preached a Gospel not merely of the crucified Saviour who died and who made a full and perfect atonement for our sins, but still more of a Saviour whose body was raised from the dead and who now lives and is able to save to the uttermost all who come unto God through Him. In our last text, in the last epistle that Paul ever wrote summing up the entire contents of his epistle, he said to Timothy, "Remember

Jesus Christ, risen from the dead . . . according to my gospel."

The subject of the resurrection of Jesus Christ from the dead is one that has many bearings, and I wish to call your attention to them.

I. THE WONDERFUL CHARACTER OF THE RESURRECTION OF JESUS CHRIST

First of all, then, we will look at the wonderful character of the resurrection of Jesus Christ.

A. The first thing to be noted regarding the character of the resurrection of Jesus Christ is that it was a resurrection not merely of His soul and spirit, but a resurrection of His body, the very body that was nailed to the cross and died and was laid in Joseph's tomb.

There are many today who tell you when you ask them if they believe in the resurrection of Jesus Christ, "Oh, certainly I believe in the resurrection of Jesus Christ!" If you question them closely, you soon discover that they do not believe in the resurrection of the body of Jesus Christ at all; but they merely believe that His soul or spirit lived again after His death on the cross.

Doubt about the literal bringing to life again of the body of Jesus that was nailed to the cross and from which the spirit of Jesus departed when He said, "Father, into thy hands I commend my spirit," is very common among people who profess to be Christian and believers in the Bible. Yes, it is quite common among so-called "ministers of the Gospel" and theological professors. But such so-called "ministers of the Gospel" are not the "ministers of the Gospel" that Paul preached nor that which the four gospels present. The four gospels and the epistles of Paul plainly declare the resurrection of the very body of Jesus, the body that was nailed to the cross and laid in Joseph's tomb. The Bible knows nothing of a resurrection of the spirit of Jesus but a resurrection of His body. This is perfectly clear from many passages in the Bible concerning His resurrection.

1. Look, for example, at one of our texts, II Timothy 2:8. Here Paul explicitly declares that Jesus Christ "was raised from the dead" according to his Gospel. Now what was raised? Of course, that which had died or fallen down. Certainly His soul or His spirit did not die. We are told explicitly in I Peter 3:18, that "Christ was put to death *in the flesh*," that is, of course, that His body was put to death; but we are told in the immediately following words that He was "made alive *in the Spirit;* in which [that is, in His Spirit] also he went and preached unto the spirits

in prison." And Peter said in his wonderful sermon about the resurrection of Christ on the day of Pentecost, "Because thou wilt not leave my soul in Hades, neither wilt thou give thy Holy One to see corruption."

A little further on in explaining the meaning of these words quoted from the Old Testament, he says that David, being a prophet and foreseeing the resurrection of the coming Messiah, "spake of the resurrection of the Christ, that neither was he left in Hades nor did *his flesh see corruption*" (Acts 2:27,31, A.S.V.). Here Peter declares that the soul of Jesus went into Hades while His body hung upon the cross and laid in the tomb and that it was "his flesh" that was kept from "corruption" and afterwards raised. Some of our wise modern theologians question the exact verbal accuracy of the Apostle Peter, but it would be a fine thing if the men occupying chairs in our universities and theological seminaries were anywhere as exact and correct as he was.

2. Turn now to another of our texts, I Corinthians 15:3,4, "For I delivered unto you first of all that which also I received, how that Christ died for our sins according to the scriptures; and that he was buried; and that he hath been raised on the third day according to the scriptures." Paul here declares that Jesus Christ "was buried" and "was raised." But what was buried? Nobody has any doubts about that. We all know that it was the body of Jesus that was buried, so it must have been His body that was raised again. Paul himself says in Acts 13:29 that it was that which "they took down from the tree" that was "laid in the tomb." It was certainly His body that was taken down from the cross and that laid in Joseph's tomb, and that was what was raised.

3. This same chapter, I Corinthians 15:12-19, also removes all possibility of doubt on this point on the part of anyone who goes to the Bible to find out what it actually teaches, and not merely to see how he can twist it and distort it to fit his own preconceived philosophical notions or scientific theories. Let me read these verses to you: "Now if Christ be preached that he hath been raised from the dead, how say some among you that there is no resurrection of the dead?"

Mark well that Paul does not say no *immortality of the soul*, but "no resurrection of the dead." Now listen to what follows:

"But if there is no resurrection of the dead, neither hath Christ been raised; and if Christ hath not been raised, then is our preaching vain, your faith also is vain. Yea, and we are found false witnesses of God; because we witnessed of God that he raised up Christ; whom he raised not up, if so be that the dead are not raised. For if the dead are not

raised, neither hath Christ been raised: and if Christ hath not been raised, your faith is vain; ye are yet in your sins. Then they also that are fallen asleep in Christ have perished. If we have only hope in Christ in this life we are of all men most pitiable."

There is no honest mistaking the plain meaning of these words. By "the resurrection of the dead" Paul plainly means the *resurrection of the body;* and in the entire chapter in which these words are found, beyond an honest doubt he is not talking about the "immortality of the soul," but "the resurrection of the body." The whole argument of the chapter turns upon that; and Paul here plainly declares that if the body of Jesus were not raised, then the whole Christian system is a sham and our faith vain and that we Christians are of all men most to be pitied.

These preachers, if they do not believe in the resurrection of the body of Jesus, ought to quit preaching and go to earning an honest living some other way; for any man who does not believe in the resurrection of the body of the Lord Jesus Christ is not earning an honest living when he tries to preach the Gospel. If the body of Jesus was not raised, then Christianity is a lie from start to finish. There is no room in this argument of Paul's (nor is there any room in the four gospel records) for "Pastor" Russell's doctrine that the resurrection of Jesus Christ was not a resurrection of the body that was laid in the tomb, the body that was crucified; but that the body of Jesus Christ which was laid in the sepulchre was carried away and preserved somewhere or else "dissolved into gases."

4. One could easily multiply conclusive scriptural proofs that it was the body of Jesus Christ that was raised, but take only one more illustration, Luke 24:5,6,

"And as they were affrighted and bowed down their faces to the earth, they [that is the angels at the tomb] *said unto them, Why seek ye the living among the dead? He is not here, but is risen: remember how he spake unto you when he was yet in Galilee."*

Here the angels at the tomb from which the body of Jesus had disappeared are reported as saying, "Why seek ye the living among the dead? He is not here, but is risen."

Now what were the women "seeking"? Beyond a question, the body of Jesus, so they could embalm it. The angels told them that what they were seeking (the body of Jesus) was not there but was "risen," and they added in the remainder of the sixth verse and the seventh, "Remember how he spake unto you when he was yet in Galilee, saying that the Son of man must be delivered up into the hands of sinful men, and be crucified, and the third day rise again." Here they told the women in the plainest possible words that what was "crucified" (which, of course, was the body of Jesus) was raised again.

If the actual, literal body of Jesus was not raised, then these angels were liars; and the whole story is a fraud. Do you believe that? Any resurrection that is not a resurrection of the body is no resurrection at all. Every gospel account tells of the resurrection of the body that was nailed to the cross and laid in the tomb. If such a resurrection did not occur, there was no resurrection whatever, and no historical ground for believing in any resurrection at all. Then we are still in our sins, and our preaching is vain.

I have more respect for the intelligence of the infidels who throw the whole story into the wind as a fraud than I have for the intelligence of those who profess to accept the authenticity of the story and then try to put on it a construction that, it is as plain as day, neither Matthew, Mark, Luke, John or Paul ever intended it to bear. Let us at least be honest. The resurrection of Jesus Christ was the resurrection of His body.

B. Second, in regard to the wonderful character of the resurrection of Jesus Christ, while it was the same crucified body that was raised, the body was no longer the same. It was a very different body from what it was when nailed to the cross. It was the old body transformed and glorified. We have not time to go into that in the detail that we should like, but we would like to mention a few points.

1. The resurrection body of Jesus Christ was of such a character that He could appear in a room when the doors were shut and could become invisible to man. This we see in John 20:19,26:

"When therefore it was evening, on that day, the first day of the week, and when the doors were shut where the disciples were, for fear of the Jews, Jesus came and stood in the midst, and saith unto them, Peace be unto you . . . . And after eight days again his disciples were within, and Thomas with them. Jesus cometh, the doors being shut, and stood in the midst, and said, Peace be unto you."

We read in Luke 24:31, "And their eyes were opened, and they knew him; and he vanished out of their sight." The word translated "vanished" literally translated means "became invisible." Our Lord's body after His resurrection was not subject to some of the limitations under which our earthly bodies exist and act.

We should bear in mind in this connection that our resurrection bodies are to be like His. We read in Philippians 3:20,21,

"For our citizenship is in heaven; whence also we wait for a Saviour, the Lord Jesus Christ; who shall fashion anew the body of our humiliation, that it may be conformed to the body of his glory."

2. The resurrection body of Jesus Christ was of such a character that it could be taken up from earth into Heaven in apparent defiance of the law of gravitation. This is clear from Acts 1:9-11,

"And when he had said these things, as they were looking, he was taken up; and a cloud received him out of their sight. And while they were looking stedfastly into heaven as he went, behold, two men stood by them in white apparel; who also said, Ye men of Galilee, why stand ye looking into heaven? this same Jesus, who was received up from you into heaven, shall so come in like manner as ye beheld him going into heaven."

When we get our resurrection bodies, we, too, as we are told in I Thessalonians 4:17, shall be taken up in the same way.

3. The body Jesus now has is a transformed body, "incorruptible" that is, not subject to decay or dissolution or sickness or pain: "glorious," "mighty," "spiritual," "heavenly." This appears from a comparison of Philippians 3:20,21, where we are told that our resurrection body shall be like His resurrection body, with I Corinthians 15:42-50, in which we have the descriptions of our own resurrection bodies.

Certainly the character of the resurrection body that Jesus had was wonderful indeed, wonderful beyond description. Our Lord, before His incarnation, we are told, in Philippians 2:6, "existed [originally] in the *form* of God" that is the outward physical "form of God" and the Father by His resurrection and ascension has again glorified Him with the glory He had with Him before the world began to be (John 17:5).

II. THE FUNDAMENTAL IMPORTANCE OF THE RESURRECTION OF JESUS CHRIST FROM THE DEAD

Now let us look at the fundamental importance of the resurrection of Jesus Christ from the dead.

A. In the first place, the resurrection of Jesus Christ from the dead is mentioned directly at least 104 times in the 260 chapters of the New Testament. It was the most prominent fact in the testimony of the apostles.

It was the central truth that they proclaimed in every sermon recorded in the Acts of the Apostles. Peter on the day of Pentecost, Paul in the synagogue at Antioch of Pisidia and speaking to the philosophers on the Areopagus at Athens based their whole argument and appeal upon the fact to which they bore personal testimony that Jesus had been raised from the dead. This also was the truth Peter declared to the Jewish Sanhedrin when he was brought before it (Acts 8:10), and that Paul drove home when he stood before Felix and before Festus and before Agrippa.

B. In the second place, the one great fact to be remembered about Christ as the very heart of the Gospel was that He rose from the dead. Paul says in one of our texts, "Remember Jesus Christ, risen from the dead . . . according to my gospel" (II Tim. 2:8).

C. In the third place, the Christian faith stands or falls with the resurrection of Jesus Christ from the dead. If He did not rise from the dead, what Christ preached is empty and the Christian faith forceless and useless. Paul says in our first text, I Corinthians 15:14,17, "Then is our preaching vain, your faith also is vain . . . . And if Christ hath not been raised, your faith is vain; ye are yet in your sins." If the body of Jesus Christ that was crucified and laid in the tomb was not raised, Christianity is built on a lie, and all distinctive Christian preaching is baseless, and Christian faith is utter folly.

But if the body of Jesus was raised from the dead, then Christianity rests upon an impregnable foundation of proven fact, and every essential doctrine of Christianity is unmistakably demonstrated truth. And He was raised. His resurrection is the best proven and most indubitable fact of history.

Here we see the utter incredibile folly of those preachers and theological professors who are not only giving up faith in the resurrection of the body of Jesus Christ themselves but are sowing doubt in the minds of others. The Devil well knows that Christianity stands or falls with the truth or falsity of the resurrection of the body of Jesus Christ, and he is exhibiting his cunning and subtilty all over the world by inducing preachers, professors and missionaries to give up faith in, and the preaching of, the resurrection of Jesus Christ. The two points at which the Devil today is aiming his heaviest guns are the beginning and the end of the earthly life of Jesus—His virgin birth and the resurrection of His body from the dead.

However, we can afford to face the Devil at these two points and particularly at the point of the resurrection, for it is the easiest thing in the world to prove the resurrection of Jesus Christ, and the Christian faith rests upon that impregnable fact. Christian faith is not a mere speculation more or less probable, but a certainty demonstrated by indisputable fact.

D. In the fourth place, we see the fundamental importance of the resurrection of Jesus Christ in that the truth of the resurrection of Jesus Christ from the dead is the one truth that has power to save anyone who believes it from the heart.

Listen to what Paul says, Romans 10:9,10:

"If thou shalt confess with thy mouth Jesus as Lord, and shalt believe in thy heart that God raised him from the dead, thou shalt be saved: for with the heart man believeth unto righteousness; and with the mouth confession is made unto salvation."

Is not that plain and unmistakable? and is it not wonderful that there is but one truth that any man needs to believe in order to be saved? That truth is that God raised the body of the Lord Jesus from the dead. Believe that with the heart, that is, with a faith that leads to action in accordance with the truth believed, and you are a saved man. You can be saved in the twinkling of an eye.

But the truth of the resurrection of Jesus Christ inevitably carries with it many other truths. It carries with it many essential doctrines of Christianity. Believe in the resurrection of Jesus Christ and you are logically compelled to believe every essential truth of the Christian faith.

III. THE DEMONSTRATED CERTAINTY OF THE RESURRECTION OF JESUS CHRIST

Now just a few words about the demonstrated certainty of the resurrection of Jesus Christ. I shall not go at length into the argument for the historical certainty of the four gospel narratives of the resurrection of Jesus Christ from the dead. Many others have shown that the evidence of the resurrection of Christ is so clear and convincing and overwhelming that no candid man or woman, no man or woman who sincerely desires to know the truth and who is genuinely willing to obey it, could sit down and thoroughly consider the evidence for the resurrection of Jesus Christ and come to any other conclusion than that Jesus Christ actually rose from the dead as is recorded in the four Gospels.

Those who deny the resurrection often call themselves "scholarly," but in reality they are either utterly unscholarly on this question (and that is usually the case) or else they are utterly insincere and determined not to believe. We see by indubitable evidence, discovered by careful study of the four Gospels and the comparison of them one with the other that they could not have been a fiction or a fabrication, that they must be a competent and exact record by four independent witnesses of facts just as they occurred, and therefore, that the body of Jesus Christ must have been raised from the dead just as is recorded in the four Gospels.

We see furthermore that there is abundant circumstantial evidence that conclusively proves the resurrection of Jesus Christ from the dead, that there are certain facts that are admitted to be facts even by scholarly rationalists, that demand the resurrection of the body of Christ to account for them.

In addition to all this, the opening verses of the chapter from which I have taken most of my text, I Corinthians 15, prove the certainty of the resurrection of Jesus Christ. Just let me read these verses:

"For I delivered unto you first of all that which also I received, how that Christ died for our sins according to the scriptures; and that he was buried; and that he hath been raised on the third day according to the scriptures; and that he appeared to Cephas; then to the twelve; then he appeared to about five hundred brethren at once, of whom the greater part remain until now, but some are fallen asleep; then he appeared to James; then to all the apostles; and last of all, as to the child untimely born he appeared to me also."—Vss. 3-8.

Now the first epistle to the Corinthians is one of the epistles of which the Pauline authorship has never been denied, even by the rationalistic critics who are so fond of pulling the Bible to pieces and saying that its various books were written by other men than those whose names they have borne from the earliest times. It is admitted by all that Paul wrote this book. Its testimony, therefore, has very great weight.

In the 5th verse Paul tells us that Jesus was seen after His resurrection by Cephas (Peter). This appearance is recorded in Luke 24:34. Peter's own testimony to the resurrection of Jesus we find in the Gospel of Mark, and Peter's direct testimony to the resurrection of Christ is also found in his epistle (I Pet. 1:3). As Paul was intimately acquainted with Peter, meeting him on various occasions, his testimony here given that the risen Lord was seen by Cephas (Peter) is unimpeachable.

After His appearance to Cephas (Peter), the Lord Jesus appeared to the entire apostolic company together. Sometime after this appearance to the twelve, the risen Christ "appeared to above five hundred brethren at once," that is to say, He was seen visibly by them. That ought to settle the question that He actually rose from the dead and was bodily visible to men after His crucifixion. The greater part of those five hundred men were living when Peter spoke and could therefore be appealed to.

Here we see the great importance of the admission of all scholarly rationalists that Paul wrote this epistle. Of course, Paul could not make a statement like this, that nearly five hundred were still living who saw Jesus after His resurrection, unless it were substantially correct. We speak of "scholarly rationalists" in order to distinguish them from the obstinate unintelligent skeptics who simply say, "I don't believe," and make no pretense of ever having investigated the evidence. The whole foundation for doubt with this class of skeptics is their ignorance, and ignorance on a subject so vital as this is unpardonable. It is admitted that Paul wrote this epistle, and Paul clearly asserts that there were nearly five hundred living in his day who had seen Jesus after His resurrection. Either then Jesus had risen or else Paul was a most prolific liar.

Of course, it is impossible to believe that Paul deliberately lied about this matter. Paul laid down his life for his testimony to the truth of the resurrection of Jesus Christ; and men do not give up every earthly ambition and prospect, endure thirty-five years of hardships and untiring toil, and finally die for a lie. Moreover, if this were a lie, it was a lie that could easily have been proven at that time. So it is simply impossible for it to be a lie. If then anything can be proven by testimony, it is proven that Jesus Christ rose from the dead.

David Strauss, the ablest infidel and denier of the resurrection of Jesus Christ that Judaism ever produced, suggests that this appearance of Jesus to the five hundred must have been due to visions. Does any honest-minded, normal-minded student think for a moment that five hundred men may have the same vision at the same time? Suppose a lawyer in court today, when only a dozen persons had testified to having seen the same thing should argue that they had not really seen what they testified to, but had seen a vision. He would be laughed out of court. And these ingenious deniers of the actual resurrection of Jesus should be laughed out of court. If there is an historic fact absolutely proven, it is that Jesus was raised from the dead. It is one of the most amazing things in literature how God through all these centuries has guarded, at every point, the evidence of this supreme fact of history.

The resurrection of Jesus Christ from the dead is a scientifically demonstrated certainty. That certainty is of stupendous importance.

(Sermon taken from *The Uplifted Christ*, by R. A. Torrey. Copyright 1965 by Zondervan Publishing House. Used by permission.)

Easter Morning . . .

As dawn crept o'er the garden fair,
   Around the vault where Jesus lay,
The heavy-hearted women came,
   Their last sad solemn dues to pay
To Him who through the gladness years
   Their hearts and souls so strangely stirred,
Who haled their hurts, who stilled their fears,
   Who spake the True and Living Word.

A glance within the opened tomb,
   The message of the angel given,
On joyous eager feet they run
   To tell the news: The Lord is risen;
The promise made has been fulfilled;
   Within the tomb He may not stay;
But bursting from the bonds of death
   Comes forth this first glad Easter Day.

With joyful hearts repeat the news
   To men bowed down with grief and pain:
O'er sin and death the victory's won;
   The Lord returns with us to reign.
Triumphant o'er the powers of Hell,
   The gates of life He opens wide.
Rejoice! Rejoice! Exalt His Name!
   The risen Lord be glorified!

               —E. R. Bingham

CHARLES H. SPURGEON
1835-1892

ABOUT THE MAN:

Many times it has been said that this was the greatest preacher this side of the Apostle Paul. He began preaching at the age of 16. At 25 he built London's famous Metropolitan Tabernacle, seating around 5,000. It was never large enough. Even when traveling he preached to 10,000 eager listeners a week. Crowds thronged to hear him as they came to hear John the Baptist by the River Jordan. The fire of God was on him as on the Prophet Elijah facing assembled Israel at Mount Carmel.

Royalty sat in his Tabernacle, as did washerwomen. Mr. Gladstone had him to dinner; and cabbies refused his fare, considering it an honor to drive for this "Prince of Preachers." To a housewife kneading bread, he would say, "Have you ever tried the Bread of Life?" Many a carpenter was asked, "Have you ever tried to build a house on sand?"

He preached in all the principal cities of England, Scotland and Ireland. And although invited to the United States on several occasions, he was never able to visit this country.

HOW GREAT WAS HIS HEART: for preachers, so the Pastors' College was founded; for orphans, so the orphans' houses came to be; for people around the world, so his literature poured forth in an almost unmeasurable volume. He was a national voice; so every national issue affecting morals, religion or the poor had his interpretation, his counsel.

Oh, but his passion for souls! You can see it in every sermon.

Spurgeon published thousands of poems, tracts, sermons and songs.

HIS MESSAGE TO LOST SINNERS WILL LIVE AS LONG AS THE GOSPEL IS PREACHED.

XIII.

The Tomb of Jesus

CHARLES H. SPURGEON

"Come, see the place where the Lord lay."—Matt. 28:6.

**His cross, His manger, and His crown,
Are big with glories yet unknown.**

All His weary pilgrimage—from Bethlehem's manger to Calvary's cross—is, in our eyes, paved with glory. Each spot upon which He trod is, to our souls, consecrated at once, simply because there the foot of earth's Saviour and our own Redeemer once was placed.

When He comes to Calvary, the interest thickens. Then our best thoughts are centered on Him in the agonies of crucifixion; nor does our deep affection permit us to leave Him, even when, the struggle being over, He yields up the ghost.

When His body is taken down from the tree, still lovely in our eyes, we fondly linger around the motionless clay. By faith we discern Joseph of Arimathaea and the timid Nicodemus, assisted by those holy women, drawing out the nails and taking down the mangled body; we behold them wrapping Him in clean, white linen, hastily girding Him round with belts of spices; then putting Him in His tomb and departing for the Sabbath rest.

On this occasion we shall go where Mary went on the morning of the first day of the week, when, waking from her couch before the dawn, she aroused herself to be early at the sepulchre of Jesus. We will try, if it be possible, by the help of God's Spirit, to go as she did, not in the body, but in soul; we will stand at that tomb, examine it, and we trust we shall hear some truth-speaking voice coming from its hollow bosom which will comfort and instruct us, so that we may say of the grave of Jesus when we go away, "It was none other than the gate of Heaven"—a sacred place, deeply solemn, and sanctified by the slain body of our precious Saviour.

I. AN INVITATION GIVEN

I shall commence my remarks this morning by inviting all Christians to come with me to the tomb of Jesus. "Come, see the place where the Lord lay." We will labor to render the place attractive. We will gently take your hand to guide you to it. And may it please our Master to make our hearts burn within us while we talk by the way.

Away, ye profane, ye soul whose life is laughter, folly and mirth! Away, ye sordid and carnal minds who have no taste for the spiritual, no delight in the celestial. We ask not your company; we speak to God's beloved, to the heirs of Heaven, to the sanctified, the redeemed, the pure in heart; and we say to them, "Come, see the place where the Lord lay." Surely ye need no argument to move your feet in the direction of the holy sepulchre; but still we will use the utmost power to draw your spirit thither. Come, then, for 'tis the shrine of greatness, 'tis the restingplace of the Man, the Restorer of our race, the Conqueror of death and Hell.

Men will travel hundreds of miles to behold the place where a poet first breathed the air of earth; they will journey to the ancient tombs of mighty heroes or the graves of men renowned by fame, but whither shall the Christian go to find the grave of one so famous as was Jesus? Ask me the greatest man who ever lived—I tell you the Man Christ Jesus was "anointed with the oil of gladness above his fellows." If ye seek a chamber honored as the resting place of genius, turn in hither; if ye would worship at the grave of holiness, come ye here; if ye would see the hallowed spot where the choicest bones that e'er were fashioned lay for awhile, come with me, Christian, to that quiet garden, hard by the walls of Jerusalem.

Come with me, moreover, because it is the tomb of your best Friend. The Jews said of Mary, "She goeth unto his grave to weep there." Ye have lost your friends, some of you; ye have planted flowers upon their tombs; ye go and sit at eventide upon the green sward, bedewing the grass with your tears, for there your mother lies and there your father or your wife.

Oh! in pensive sorrow come with me to this dark garden of our Saviour's burial; come to the grave of your best Friend—your Brother, yea, one who "sticketh closer than a brother." Come thou to the grave of thy dearest relative, O Christian, for Jesus is thy Husband, "Thy Maker is thy husband, the Lord of Hosts is his name." Doth not affection draw you? Do not the sweet lips of love woo you? Is not the place sanctified where one so well-beloved slept, although but for a moment? Surely ye need no eloquence; if it were needed, I have none. I have but the power, in simple but earnest accents, to repeat the words, "Come, see the place where the Lord lay." On this Easter morning pay a visit to His grave, for it is the grave of your best Friend.

Yea, more, I will further urge you to this pious pilgrimage. *Come, for angels bid you.* Angels said, "Come, see the place where the Lord lay." The Syriac version reads, "Come, see the place where *our* Lord lay." Yes, angels put themselves with those poor women and used one common pronoun—*our.* Jesus is the Lord of angels as well as of men. Ye feeble women—ye have called Him Lord; ye have washed His feet; ye have provided for His wants; ye have hung upon His lips to catch His honeyed sentences; ye have sat entranced beneath His mighty eloquence; ye call Him Master and Lord, and ye do well. "But," said the seraph, "He is my Lord, too." Bowing his head, he sweetly said, "Come, see the place where *our* Lord lay."

Dost fear then, Christian, to step into that tomb? Dost dread to enter there, when the angel pointeth with his finger and saith, "Come, we will go together, angels and men, and see the royal bed-chamber"? Ye know that angels did go into His tomb, for they sat one at His head and the other at His foot in holy meditation.

I picture to myself those bright cherubs sitting there talking to one another. One of them said, "It was there His feet lay"; and the other replied, "and there His hands, and there His head"; and in celestial language did they talk concerning the deep things of God. Then they stooped and kissed the rocky floor, made sacred to the angels themselves, not because there they were redeemed, but because there their Master and Monarch, whose high behests they were obeying, did for awhile become the slave of death and the captive of destruction.

Come, Christian, then, for angels are the porters to unbar the door. Come, for a cherub is thy messenger to usher thee into the deathplace of death himself. Nay, start not from the entrance; let not the darkness affright thee; the vault is not damp with the vapors of death, nor doth the air contain aught of contagion. Come, for *it is a pure and healthy place.* Fear not to enter that tomb. I will admit that catacombs are not the places where we, who are full of joy, would love to go. There is something gloomy and noisome about a vault. There are noxious smells of corruption; ofttimes pestilence is born where a dead body hath lain. But fear it not, Christian, for Christ was not left in Hell—in Hades— (the realm of death), neither did His body see corruption.

Come, there is no scent, yea, rather a perfume. Step in here; and if thou didst ever breathe the gales of Ceylon or winds from the groves of Araby, thou shalt find them far excelled by that sweet, holy fragrance left by the blessed body of Jesus, that alabaster vase which once held divinity and was rendered sweet and precious thereby. Think not thou shalt find aught obnoxious to thy senses. Corruption Jesus never saw; no worms ever devoured His flesh; no rottenness ever entered into His bones; He saw no corruption. Three days He slumbered, but not long enough to putrefy. He soon arose, perfect as when He entered, uninjured as when His limbs were composed for their slumber.

Come then, Christian, summon up thy thoughts, gather all thy powers; here is a sweet invitation; let me press it again. Let me lead thee by the hand of meditation, my brother; let me take thee by the arm of thy fancy, and let me again say to thee, "Come, see the place where the Lord lay."

There is yet one reason more why I would have thee visit this royal sepulchre—*because it is a quiet spot.* Oh! I have longed for rest, for I have heard this world's rumors in my ears so long that I have begged for

A lodge in some vast wilderness,
Some boundless contiguity of shade,

where I might hide myself forever. I am sick of this tiring and trying life; my frame is weary; my soul is mad to repose herself awhile. I would I could lay myself down a little by the edge of some pebbly brook, with no companion save the fair flowers or the nodding willows. I would I could recline in stillness, where the air brings balm to the tormented brain, where there is no murmur save the hum of the summer bee, no whisper save that of the zephyrs, and no song except the caroling of the lark. I wish I could be at ease for a moment. I have become a man of the world; my brain is racked; my soul is tired.

Oh! wouldst thou be quiet, Christian? Merchant, wouldst thou rest from thy toils? wouldst thou be calm for once? Then come hither. It is in a pleasant garden, far from the hum of Jerusalem; the noise and din of business will not reach thee there: "Come, see the place where the Lord lay." It is a sweet resting spot, a withdrawing room for thy soul, where thou mayest brush from thy garments the dust of earth and muse for awhile in peace.

II. ATTENTION REQUESTED

Thus I have pressed the invitation; now we will enter the tomb. Let us examine it with deep attention, noticing every circumstance connected with it.

And, first, mark that it is a *costly tomb*. It is no common grave; it is not an excavation dug out by the spade for a pauper, in which to hide the last remains of his miserable and overwearied bones. It is a princely tomb; it was made of marble, cut in the side of a hill. Stand here, believer, and ask why Jesus had such a costly sepulchre. He had no elegant garments; He wore a coat without seam, woven from the top throughout, without an atom of embroidery. He owned no sumptuous palace, for He had not where to lay His head. His sandals were not rich with gold or studded with brilliants. He was poor. Why, then, does He lie in a noble grave?

We answer, for this reason: Christ was unhonored till He had finished His sufferings; Christ's body suffered contumely, shame, spitting, buffeting and reproach, until He had completed His great work. He was trampled under foot. He was "despised and rejected of men; a man of sorrows, and acquainted with grief." But the moment He had finished His undertaking, God said, "No more shall the body be disgraced. If it is to sleep, let it slumber in an honorable grave. If it is to rest, let nobles bury it. Let Joseph, the councillor, and Nicodemus, the man of Sanhedrin, be present at the funeral. Let the body be embalmed with precious spices. Let it have honor; it has had enough of contumely, shame, reproach and buffeting; let it now be treated with respect."

Christian, dost thou discern the meaning? Jesus, after He had finished His work, slept in a costly grave; for now His Father loved and honored Him, since His work was done.

But, though it is a costly grave, *it is a borrowed one.* I see over the top of it,

SACRED TO THE MEMORY OF THE FAMILY
OF JOSEPH OF ARIMATHEA;

yet Jesus slept there. Yes, He was buried in another's sepulchre. He who had no house of His own, and rested in the habitation of other men who had no table, but lived upon the hospitality of His disciples; who borrowed boats in which to preach, and had not anything in the wide world, was obliged to have a tomb from charity.

Oh! should not the poor take courage? They dread to be buried at the expense of their neighbors; but if their poverty be unavoidable, wherefore should they blush, since Jesus Christ Himself was interred in another's grave?

I wish I might have had Joseph's grave to let Jesus be buried in it. Good Joseph thought he had cut it out for himself and that he should lay his bones there. He had it excavated as a family vault, and lo, the Son of David makes it one of the tombs of the kings!

But he did not lose it by lending it to the Lord; rather, he had it back with precious interest. He only lent it three days; then Christ resigned it. He had not injured, but perfumed and sanctified it, and made it far more holy, so that it would be an honor in the future to be buried there.

It was a borrowed tomb; and why? I take it, not to dishonor Christ, but in order to show that as His sins were borrowed sins, so His burial was in a borrowed grave. Christ had no transgressions of His own; He took ours upon His head. He never committed a wrong, but He took all my sin and all yours, if ye are believers. Concerning all His people, it is true He bore their griefs and carried their sorrows in His own body on the tree; therefore, as they were others' sins, so He rested in another's grave; as they were sins imputed, so that grave was only imputedly His. It was not His sepulchre; it was the tomb of Joseph.

Let us not weary in this pious investigation, but with fixed attention observe everything connected with this holy spot. The grave, we observe, *was cut in a rock.* Why was this? The Rock of Ages was buried in a rock; a Rock within a rock. But why? Most persons suggest that it was so ordained that it might be clear that there was no covert way by which the disciples or others could enter and steal the body away. Very possibly it was the reason; but O! my soul, canst thou find a spiritual reason?

Christ's sepulchre was cut in a rock. It was not cut in mould that might be worn away by the water, or might crumble and fall into decay. The sepulchre stands, I believe, entire to this day; if it does not naturally, it does spiritually. The same sepulchre which took the sins of Paul, shall take my iniquities into His bosom; for if I ever lose my guilt, it must roll off my shoulders into the sepulchre. It was cut in a rock, so that if a sinner were saved a thousand years ago, I, too, can be delivered; for it is a rocky sepulchre where sin was buried—it was a rocky sepulchre of marble where my crimes were laid forever—buried never to have a resurrection.

You will mark, moreover, that tomb was *one wherein no other man had ever lain.* Christopher Ness says that when Christ was born, He lay in a virgin's womb; and when He died, He was placed in a virgin tomb. He slept where never man had slept before. The reason was that none might say that another person rose, for there never had been any other body there, thus a mistake of persons was impossible. Nor could it be said that some old prophet was interred in the place, and that Christ rose because He had touched his bones. You remember where Elisha was buried; and as they were burying a man, behold he touched the prophets bones and arose. Christ touched no prophets' bones, for none had ever slept there; it was a new chamber where the Monarch of the earth did take His rest for three days and three nights.

We have learned a little, then, with attention; but let us stoop down once more before we leave the grave and notice something else. We see the grave, but do you *notice the graveclothes,* all wrapped and laid in their places, the napkin being folded up by itself? Wherefore are the graveclothes wrapped up? The Jews said robbers had abstracted the body; but if so, surely they would have stolen the clothes; they would never have thought of wrapping them up and laying them down so carefully; they would be too much in haste to think of it.

Why was it then? To manifest to us that Christ did not come out in a hurried manner. He slept till the last moment; then He awoke. He came not in haste. They shall not come out in haste, neither by flight, but at the appointed moment shall His people come to Him. So at the precise hour, the decreed instant, Jesus Christ leisurely awoke, took off His cerements, left them all behind Him and came forth in His pure and naked innocence, perhaps to show us that as clothes were the off-spring of sin—when sin was atoned for by Christ, He left all raiment behind Him; for garments are the badges of guilt—if we had not been guilty we should never have needed them.

Then the napkin, mark you, was laid by itself. The graveclothes were left behind for every departed Christian to wear. The bed of death is well sheeted with the garments of Jesus, but the napkin was laid by itself; because when the Christian dies, he does not need that; it is used by the mourners, and the mourners only. We shall all wear graveclothes, but we shall not need the napkin. When our friends die, the napkin is laid aside for us to use; but do our ascended brethren and sisters use it? No; the Lord God hath wiped away all tears from their eyes.

We stand and view the corpses of the dear departed; we moisten their faces with our tears, letting whole showers of grief fall on their heads; but do *they* weep? Oh, no. Could they speak to us from the upper spheres they would say, "Weep not for me, for I am glorified. Sorrow not for me; I have left a bad world behind me and have entered into a far better." They have no napkin—they weep not. Strange it is that those who endure death weep not, but those who see them die are weepers. When the child is born, it weeps while others smile (say the Arabs); and when it dies, it smiles while others weep. It is so with the Christian. O blessed thing! The napkin is laid by itself, because Christians will never want to use it when they die.

III. EMOTION EXCITED

We have thus surveyed the grave with deep attention and, I hope, with some profit to ourselves. But that is not all. I love a religion which consists, in a great measure, of emotion. Now, if I had power, like a master, I would touch the strings of your hearts and fetch a glorious tune of solemn music from them, for this is a deeply solemn place into which I have conducted you.

First, I would bid you stand with *emotions of deep sorrow* and see the place where the Lord lay. Oh come, my beloved brother, thy Jesus once lay there. He was a murdered Man, my soul, and thou the murderer.

> **Ah, you my sins, my cruel sins,**
> **His chief tormenters were,**
>
> **Each of my crimes became a nail,**
> **And unbelief the spear.**
>
> **Alas! and did my Saviour bleed?**
> **And did my Sov'reign die?**

I slew Him—this right hand struck the dagger to His heart. My deeds slew Christ. Alas! I slew my best Beloved. I killed Him who loved me with an everlasting love. Ye eyes, why do you refuse to weep when ye see Jesus' body mangled and torn? Oh! give vent to your sorrow, Christians, for ye have good reason to do so.

I believe in what Hart says, that there was a time in his experience when he could so sympathize with Christ, that he felt more grief at the death of Christ than he did joy.

It seemed so sad a thing that Christ should have to die, and to me it often appears too great a price for Jesus Christ to purchase worms with His own blood. Methinks I love Him so much, that if I had seen Him about to suffer, I should have been as bad as Peter, and have said, "That be far from thee, Lord"; but then He would have said to me, "Get thee behnd me, Satan"; for He does not approve of that love which would stop Him from dying. "The cup which my Father hath given me, shall I not drink it?"

But I think, had I seen Him going up to His cross, I could fain have pressed Him back and said, "O Jesus, Thou shalt not die! I cannot have it. Wilt Thou purchase my life with a price so dear?" It seems too costly for Him who is the Prince of Life and Glory to let His fair limbs be tortured in agony, that the hands which carried mercies should be pierced with accursed nails, that the temples that were always clothed with love should have cruel thorns driven through them. It appears too much.

Oh! weep, Christian, and let your sorrow rise. Is not the price all but too great, that your Beloved should for you resign *Himself?* Oh! I should think, if a person were saved from death by another, he would always feel deep grief if his deliverer lost his life in the attempt.

I had a friend who, standing by the side of a piece of frozen water, saw a young lad in it, and sprang upon the ice in order to save him. After clutching the boy, he held him in his hand and cried out, "Here he is! Here he is! I have saved him." But, just as they caught hold of the boy, he sank himself; and his body was not found for some time afterwards, when he was quite dead.

Oh! it is so with Jesus. My soul was drowning. From Heaven's high portals He saw me sinking in the depths of Hell; He plunged in:

He sank beneath His heavy woes,
To raise me to a crown;
There's ne'er a gift His hand bestows,
But cost His heart a groan.

Ah, we may indeed regret our sin, since it slew Jesus.

Now, Christian, change thy note a moment. "Come, see the place where the Lord lay," *with joy and gladness.* He does not lie there now. Weep, when ye see the tomb of Christ, but rejoice because it is empty. Thy sin slew Him, but His divinity raised Him up. Thy guilt hath murdered Him, but His righteousness hath restored Him. Oh! He hath burst the bonds of death; He hath ungirt the cerements of the tomb and hath come out more than conqueror, crushing death beneath His feet. Rejoice, O Christian, for He is not there—He is risen.

"Come, see the place where the Lord lay."

One more thought, and then I will speak a little concerning the doctrines we may learn from this grave. "Come, see the place where the Lord lay," *with solemn awe,* for you and I will have to lie there, too.

Hark! from the tomb of doleful sound,
Mine ears, attend the cry,

Ye living men, come view the ground
Where ye must shortly lie.

Princes, this clay must be your bed,
In spite of all your powers.
The tall, the wise, the reverend head,
Must lie as low as ours.

It is a fact we do not often think of, that we shall all be dead in a little while. I know that I am made of dust and not of iron; my bones are not brass, nor my sinews steel. In a little while my body must crumble back to its native elements. But do you ever try to picture to yourself the moment of your dissolution?

My friends, there are some of you who seldom realize how old you are, how near you are to death. One way of remembering our age is to see how much remains. Think how old eighty is, and then see how few years there are before you will get there. We should remember our frailty.

Sometimes I have tried to think of the time of my departure. I do not know whether I shall die a violent death or not, but I would to God that I might die suddenly, for sudden death is sudden glory. I would I might have such a blessed exit as Dr. Beaumont and die in my pulpit, laying down my body with my charge and ceasing at once to work and live. But it is not mine to choose.

Suppose I lie lingering for weeks, in the midst of pains and griefs and agonies; when that moment comes, that moment which is too solemn for my lips to speak of, when the spirit leaves the clay—let the physician put it off for weeks, or years, as we say he does, though he does not—when that moment comes, O ye lips, be dumb and profane not its solemnity. When death comes, how is the strong man bowed down! How doth the mighty man fall! They may say they will not die, but there is no hope for them; they must yield, the arrow has gone home.

I knew a man who was a wicked wretch, and I remember seeing him pace the floor of his bedroom, saying, *O God, I will not die! I will not die!* When I begged him to lie on his bed, for he was dying, he said he could not die while he could walk; and he would walk till he did die. Ah! he expired in the utmost torments always shrieking, *O God, I will not die!* Oh! that moment, that last moment. See how clammy is the sweat upon the brow, how dry the tongue, how parched the lips. The man shuts his eyes and slumbers, then opens them again; and if he be a Christian, I can fancy that he will say:

> Hark! they whisper: angels say,
> Sister spirit, come away.
> What is this absorbs me quite —
> Steals my senses — shuts my sight —
> Drowns my spirit — draws my breath?
> Tell me, my soul, can this be death?

We know not when he is dying. One gentle sigh, and the spirit breaks away. We can scarcely say, "He is gone," before the ransomed spirit takes its mansion near the throne.

Come to Christ's tomb, then, for the silent vault must soon be your habitation. Come to Christ's grave, for ye must slumber there. And even you, ye sinners, for one moment I will ask you to come also, because ye must die as well as the rest of us. Your sins cannot keep you from the jaws of death. I say, sinner, I want thee to look at Christ's sepulchre, too; for when thou diest, it may have done thee great good to think of it.

You have heard of Queen Elizabeth crying out that she would give an empire for a single hour. Or have you heard the despairing cry of the gentleman on board the *Arctic*, when it was going down, who shouted to the boat, "Come back! I will give you 30,000 pounds if you will come and take me in." Ah! poor man, it were but little if he had thirty thousand worlds, if he could thereby prolong his life: "Skin for skin, yea, all that a man hath, will he give for his life."

Some of you who can laugh this morning, who came to spend a merry hour in this hall, will be dying, and then ye will pray and crave for life and shriek for another Sunday. Oh! how the Sundays ye have wasted will walk like ghosts before you! Oh! how they will shake their snaky hair in your eyes! How will ye be made to sorrow and weep, because ye wasted precious hours, which, when they are gone, are gone too far to be recalled. May God save you from the pangs of remorse.

IV. INSTRUCTION IMPARTED

And now, Christian brethren, "Come, see the place where the Lord lay," to learn a doctrine or two. What did you see when you visited "the place where the Lord lay"? "He is not here: for he is risen." The first thing you perceive, if you stand by His empty tomb, *is His divinity*. The dead in Christ shall rise first at the resurrection; but He who rose first, their Leader, rose in a different fashion. They rise by imparted power. He rose by His own. He could not slumber in the grave because He was God. Death had no more dominion over Him. There is no better proof of Christ's divinity than that startling resurrection of His when He arose from the grave by the glory of the Father. O Christian, thy Jesus is God; His broad shoulders that hold thee up are indeed divine; and here thou hast the best proof of it—because He rose from the grave.

A second doctrine here taught well may charm thee, if the Holy Spirit apply it with power. Behold, His empty tomb, O true believer, is a sign of *thine acquittal* and thy full discharge. If Jesus had not paid the debt, He ne'er had risen from the grave. He would have lain there till this moment if He had not cancelled the entire debt by satisfying eternal vengeance. O beloved, is not that an overwhelming thought?

> **It is finished, it is finished,**
> **Hear the rising Saviour cry.**

The heavenly turnkey came; a bright angel stepped from Heaven and rolled away the stone, but he would not have done so if Christ had not done all. He would have kept Him there. He would have said, "Nay, nay! Thou art the sinner now; Thou hast the sins of all Thine elect upon Thy shoulder, and I will not let Thee go free till Thou hast paid the uttermost farthing." In His going free I see my own discharge,

> **"My Jesus' blood's my full discharge."**

As a justified man, I have not a sin now against me in God's book. If I were to turn over God's eternal book, I should see every debt of mine receipted and cancelled.

> **Here's pardon for transgressions past,**
> **It matters not how black their cast,**
> **And O my soul, with wonder view,**
> **For sins to come, here's pardon too.**
> **Fully discharged by Christ I am,**
> **From Christ's tremendous curse and blame.**

One more doctrine we learn, and with that we will conclude—*the doctrine of the resurrection.* Jesus rose; and as the Lord our Saviour rose, so all His followers must rise. Die I must—this body must be a carnival for worms; it must be eaten by those tiny cannibals; peradventure it shall be scattered from one portion of the earth to another; the constituent particles of this my frame will enter into plants, from plants pass into animals, and thus be carried into far distant realms. But, at the blast of the archangel's trumpet, every separate atom of my body shall find its fellow; like the bones lying in the valley of vision, though separated from one another, the moment God shall speak, the bone will creep to its bone; then the flesh shall come upon it; the four winds of heaven shall blow, and the breath shall return.

So let me die, let beasts devour me, let fire turn this body into gas and vapor, all its particles shall yet again be restored. This very selfsame, actual body shall start up from its grave, glorified and made like Christ's body, yet still the same body; for God hath said it. Christ's same body rose; so shall mine.

O my soul, dost thou now dread to die? Thou wilt lose thy partner body a little while, but thou wilt be married again in Heaven. Soul and body shall again be united before the throne of God.

The grave—what is it? It is the bath in which the Christian puts the clothes of his body to have them washed and cleansed. Death—what is it? It is the waiting room where we robe ourselves for immortality, the place where the body, like Esther, bathes itself in spices that it may be fit for the embrace of its Lord. Death is the gate of life; I will not fear to die, then, but will say,

> **Shudder not to pass the stream;**
> **Venture all thy care on Him;**
> **Him whose dying love and power**
> **Stilled it tossing, hushed its roar,**
> **Safe in the expanded wave;**
> **Gentle as a summer's eve.**
> **Not one object of His care**
> **Ever suffered shipwreck there.**

Come, view the place then, with all hallowed meditation, where the Lord lay. Spend this afternoon, my beloved brethren, in meditating upon it; and very often go to Christ's grave, both to weep and to rejoice. Ye timid ones, do not be afraid to approach, for 'tis no vain thing to remember that timidity buried Christ. Faith would not have given Him a funeral at all; faith would have kept Him above ground, and would never have let Him be buried; for it would have said that it would be useless to bury Christ if He were to rise. Fear buried Him. Nicodemus, the night disciple, and Joseph of Arimathaea, secretly, for fear of the Jews, went and buried Him. Therefore, ye timid ones, ye may go, too.

Ready-to-halt, poor Fearing, and thou, Mrs. Despondency, and Much-afraid, go often there; let it be your favorite haunt. There build a tabernacle, there abide. And often say to your heart, when you are in distress and sorrow, "Come, see the place where the Lord lay."

(From the book, SPURGEON'S SERMONS, Vol. I., published by Zondervan Publishing House.)

The Lord Is Risen

THE LORD IS RISEN, the resurrection morning
  Has dawned, and from my troubled heart has fled
The fear of death, and now in place of mourning
  Joy, sweetest joy and peace are mine instead.

THE LORD IS RISEN, the reign of sin has ended,
  He holds the key of death, and from its sway
My soul is freed, for now in Him ascended
  Life, everlasting life is mine today.

THE LORD IS RISEN, He Satan's power has broken,
  And from the foe, my ransomed soul is free;
THE LORD IS RISEN, and by this wondrous token
  I too shall rise His glorious face to see.

                              —Marion E. C. Netherton

B. H. CARROLL
1843-1914

ABOUT THE MAN:

B. H. Carroll was a giant of a preacher. That was true *physically*—he was 6' 4" tall and his beard flowed almost to his waist, giving him the semblance of an old prophet. And he was a giant *intellectually*.

He was born in Carrollton, Mississippi, one of twelve children. At age 18 he graduated from Waco University, taught some school, and engaged in numbers of great debates. He was 28 years pastor of the First Baptist Church, Waco, Texas, then became Dean of Bible at Baylor University, helped found and later became president of Southwestern Baptist Seminary in Fort Worth (1908 until his death in 1914).

He not only was a voracious reader, but he wrote! Doubtless, his most important contribution was his *Interpretation of the English Bible*—commentaries and messages that have become a Christian classic.

Whether as pastor, educator or writer, B. H. Carroll was a giant for God. With his erudite mind and evangelistic heart, for half a century he served the Lord well. At a memorial service for him, Dr. George Truett said,

"The man was a giant of the Faith, a great preacher and a man who influenced men in a positive way toward faith in Christ. The pulpit was his throne, and he occupied it like a king."

XIV.

Infallible Proof of the Resurrection of Christ

A Careful Examination of Claims, Theories and Scriptures

B. H. CARROLL

"And the angel answered and said unto the women, Fear not ye: for I know that ye seek Jesus, which was crucified. He is not here: for he is risen, as he said. Come, see the place where the Lord lay."—Matt. 28:5,6.

"To whom also he shewed himself alive after his passion by many infallible proofs, being seen of them forty days, and speaking of the things pertaining to the kingdom of God."—Acts 1:3.

We want to show that all New Testament claim on inspiration rests upon the proof of a simple historical fact, namely, that Jesus of Nazareth, claiming to be the Messiah of the Old Testament, did arise from the dead.

It is, therefore, quite needless to multiply or to complicate issues. All controversies between Christians upon the one hand and the opposers of Christianity, of whatever name, throughout the universe, on the other hand, may be narrowed to one decisive battlefield. The whole case compacts itself as a single kernel into one nutshell of historical fact. If Jesus of Nazareth rose from the dead at the date previously assigned by Himself, and as a proof of His claim, then He is no imposter nor a deluded enthusiast. God would not raise from the dead one who made such a blasphemous claim, one who was an imposter. So that if He did rise from the dead, He is divine. If He be divine, just one word from Him authenticated the inspiration of both Testaments. The Testaments being inspired by the fact become the supreme standard of human conduct and creed and thought by which the world will be judged and eternal destiny fixed.

Jesus Proposes the Test SIX Times

Let us, therefore, glance rapidly at the proof that He Himself, while living, did propose this test and that the challenge was accepted and that the demonstration did come in the way claimed. I read six distinct statements of this proposed issue at different periods in His life here upon the earth, the first early in His ministry, the last at the close of His ministry. This proves that it was no afterthought but that from the beginning He recognized this to be the crucial point upon which all of His claims depended.

(1) Early in His ministry He came suddenly to His Temple, in fulfillment of prophecy; and when by virtue of the authority claimed He scourged from that Temple the robbers and thieves who held it, they demanded a sign of His authority. I read it from chapter 2 of John, commencing at the 18th verse:

"Then answered the Jews and said unto him, What sign shewest thou unto us, seeing that thou doest these things? Jesus answered and said unto them, Destroy this temple, and in three days I will raise it up. Then said the Jews [not understanding], *Forty and six years was this temple in building, and wilt thou rear it up in three days? But he spake of the temple of his body. When therefore he was risen from the dead, his disciples remembered that he had said this unto them; and they believed the scripture, and the word which Jesus had said."*—Vss. 18-22.

It is admitted that when here He first set forth His test, they misapprehended his language.

(2) I read the next instance in order of time, and from chapter 12 of Matthew (He is now in Galilee and not in Jerusalem).

"Then certain of the scribes and of the Pharisees answered, saying, Master, we would see a sign from thee. But he answered and said unto them, An evil and adulterous generation seeketh after a sign; and there shall no sign be given to it, but the sign of the prophet Jonas: For as Jonas was three days and three nights in the whale's belly; so shall the Son of man be three days and three nights in the heart of the earth."—Vss. 38-40.

This time they did not misunderstand Him, as will be clearly shown later.

(3) I cite the next instance from the sixteenth chapter of Matthew:

"From that time forth began Jesus to shew unto his disciples, how that he must go unto Jerusalem, and suffer many things of the elders and chief priests and scribes, and be killed, and be raised again the third day."—Vs. 21.

Mark's record and Luke's record accord exactly with this record by Matthew. This time the test was not proposed to His enemies but to His friends, to His disciples; but through His disciples the knowledge of it rapidly reached His enemies.

(4) In the order of history I read the next instance from chapter 17 of Matthew:

"And while they abode in Galilee, Jesus said unto them, The Son of man shall be betrayed into the hands of men: And they shall kill him, and the third day he shall be raised again. And they were exceeding sorry."—Vss. 22,23.

(5) I read the next presentation of the test in the order of the history, and this time from the 10th chapter of John. He had just told them that He was the Good Shepherd and would lay down His life for the sheep, adding the significant statement:

"No man taketh it from me, but I lay it down of myself. I have power to lay it down, and I have power to take it again. This commandment have I received of my Father. There was a division therefore again among the Jews for these sayings."—Vss. 18,19.

(6) I cite the next instance. This time Matthew, Mark and Luke all record it. I read from chapter 20 of Matthew, commencing at the seventeenth verse:

"And Jesus going up to Jerusalem took the twelve disciples apart in the way, and said unto them, Behold, we go up to Jerusalem; and the Son of man shall be betrayed unto the chief priests and unto the scribes, and they shall condemn him to death, And shall deliver him to the Gentiles to mock, and to scourge, and to crucify him: and the third day he shall rise again."—Vss. 17-19.

The Testimony of the Two Ordinances and the Promise of the Holy Spirit

Three other things occurred in His lifetime bearing upon the same signification.

The first is the institution of the ordinance of baptism, which has no signification apart from the resurrection of the dead, it being a picture of a burial and an emergence from the grave. That this institution was appointed before He died, that it was appointed for perpetual obligation, showed the clearest apprehension in His mind of the nature of the test and the worth of this monumental evidence.

The second is the institution of the Lord's Supper, whose only hope is in the resurrection of the dead. In the very act of commemorating His death, He assures them that He will drink this wine anew with them in His Father's kingdom and that while this ordinance is to be a perpetual obligation and points significantly backward, it also points still more significantly to the future, in that it was to be observed until He came again. For 1900 years these two monuments have stood in the eyes of the world.

The third thing was that when they were saddened over the clear announcement of His departure from them by death, He gave them an assurance based upon His resurrection that He would not leave them always; that when He rose from the dead and reached His Father's house, He would send the Holy Spirit, whose coming would confer upon them power to do all He had commanded them to do.

Thus the institution of baptism and the supper as perpetual ordinances and the promise of the Holy Spirit, all conditioned on His resurrection, take their place with the test six times preannounced. That a mere man, and particularly that an imposter, would make such conditions of faith in himself is inconceivable.

How the Test Was Considered by His Enemies

After these citations it is necessary to show you how this proposed test, that is, the proof of one historical fact, was considered by His enemies. I now read from chapter 27 of Matthew. He is hanging on the cross. He has been delivered up, and they are putting Him to death, and while He is dying they say this:

"And they that passed by reviled him, wagging their heads, And saying, Thou that destroyest the temple, and buildest it in three days, save thyself."—Vss. 39,40.

I submit a much more conclusive statement. He is now dead. Those who have had charge of His execution have officially certified that He is dead. His body has been taken down from the cross, pronounced dead by the official executioner, received as dead by His friends, both hands and feet pierced and a spear driven into His heart; cold and dead, and He had been put in the grave and an immense stone rolled to the mouth of that sepulchre. I read from chapter 27 of Matthew:

"Now the next day, that followed the day of the preparation, the chief

priests and Pharisees came together unto Pilate, Saying, Sir, we remember that that deceiver said, while he was yet alive, After three days I will rise again. Command therefore that the sepulchre be made sure until the third day, lest his disciples come by night, and steal him away, and say unto the people, He is risen from the dead: so the last error shall be worse than the first. Pilate said unto them, Ye have a watch: go your way, make it as sure as ye can. So they went, and made the sepulchre sure, sealing the stone, and setting a watch."—Vss. 62-66.

The Body—Not Soul—to Be Resurrected

Now I submit to you, have I not proved from this Book that while He was alive He Himself rested all of His claims upon the proof of one historical fact, and that He gave this as the sign, and that the challenge was accepted by His enemies? They understood its significance. They did not understand the resurrection of the dead, as some moderns claim, to mean regeneration. They did not understand it to mean the deliverance of the soul from the body at the dissolution of the body. They understood it to apply to the body and not to the soul. They brought no word to Pilate as to the whereabouts of His disembodied soul. They sought not to seal up the gate that hides the invisible world. They sealed a grave. They established a guard to see that the body should not be wrested from the grave. They understood His test to be that His body, put to death upon the cross, would rise from the dead upon the third day; and any man who talks about the resurrection meaning any other thing does violence to the literal, primary and commonly accepted signification of the word, and advertises himself as incompetent to deal with a critical question.

No Doubt About His Actual Death

Now, let us see where we stand. First, according to these records, there was a Jew named Jesus of Nazareth who claimed to be the Messiah of the Old Testament; second, that the scribes and Pharisees disputed His claim, demanding a sign; third, that He, while living, repeatedly to His friends and repeatedly to His enemies and in answer to the demand that one who made such claim should have some adequate credentials, must furnish some proof of such high claim, gave as His credentials, as the authentication of His mission, as the divine establishment of His divinity, that after they put Him to death on the third day He would rise again.

The record shows that they did take Him and try Him and condemn Him and crucify Him, and that the authentication of His death was everything that evidence could supply.

You cannot meet this question by saying that He only seemed to be dead, and His alleged resurrection merely as resuscitation of suspended life. A Roman centurion, charged with the execution of the prisoner, who goes back to the one in authority and reports that this prisoner has been executed and is dead, would make no mistake upon a point of that kind. You could not consistently affirm that anyone now sleeping in our cemetery is dead and then deny the sufficiency of the evidence that the Man Jesus of Nazareth died and was buried. So thus far we are clear.

No Doubt About Empty Tomb

I cite next the Scripture in connection with the text. The third day is just about to dawn, the critical hour, the precise time. The lesson reads:

"In the end of the sabbath, as it began to dawn toward the first day of the week, came Mary Magdalene and the other Mary to see the sepulchre. And, behold, there was a great earthquake: for the angel of the Lord descended from heaven, and came and rolled back the stone from the door, and sat upon it. His countenance was like lightning, and his raiment white as snow: And for fear of him the keepers did shake, and became as dead men. And the angel answered and said unto the women, Fear not ye: for I know that ye seek Jesus, which was crucified. He is not here: for he is risen, as he said."

So then we have come to this fact, that at the time designated by the test, the tomb is empty, the body is gone. So far there has been perfect agreement upon every fact stated: there was a Man named Jesus of Nazareth; He claimed to be the Messiah of the Old Testament; He was challenged to give a sign that would authenticate His high claim; He did fix the sign and specified the time of the test; He did die; He was buried, and at the appointed time, though a guard stood there to prevent imposture, the body is gone.

What, then, became of the body of Jesus of Nazareth? If He did not rise, either the Jews got the body or the disciples got it. The Jews were in this dilemma: If they took that body away, why didn't they exhibit it as dead and identify it as the very body that had been crucified, and disprove all claim of the resurrection.

In our thinking thus far we are at the grave of Jesus—the empty grave of Jesus. We are at the disappearance of the dead body that had been put in the grave, and with the question pending: What became of that body?

I have never heard of but two theories concerning the disposition of the dead body of our Lord Jesus Christ. Both of the theories are possible. Both of them make allegations legitimately belonging to the domain of testimony; that is, they are matters upon which testimony may be received and susceptible of sufficient proof.

Did the Disciples Take Jesus' Body?

The first theory is set forth in the following language: "Some of the watch came into the city, and shewed unto the chief priests all the things that were done," that is, they told the chief priests that an earthquake came, and that there was a dazzling appearance of an angel from Heaven, and that they fell down like dead men, and that when they arose from the prostration by the power of the heavenly messenger the grave was empty. Those were the facts they recited to the chief priests. Then the record adds:

"And when they [the chief priests] *were assembled with the elders, and had taken counsel, they gave large money unto the soldiers, saying, Say ye, His disciples came by night, and stole him away while we slept. And if this come to the governor's ears, we will persuade him, and secure you. So they took the money and did as they were taught: and this saying is commonly reported among the Jews until this day."*

This first theory, therefore, was that the body of our Lord Jesus Christ was stolen by night by His disciples and stolen for the purpose of making a claim that He was raised.

This was a possible solution of the question, and it was an allegation that could be sustained by adequate testimony. We know that there have been such things as robbers of graves. We know of many historical instances where dead bodies have been taken from the grave for some purpose: medical students, for example, who carry them to the dissecting table, or robbers, whose object is to obtain a large ransom from the afflicted relatives. So then, if the evidence is sufficient, there is nothing in the theory itself to make it objectionable.

The witnesses are sufficient in number. That guard constituted enough witnesses to prove any fact, so far as numbers go. The only thing is that what they testify must be subjected to the rules of evidence such as are commonly recognized among men. Let us look, then, at their statement.

They first gave a different account. In the second place, they accepted a bribe of a large sum of money to put this theory in circulation. In the third place, what they finally allege was absolutely impossible, so far as their knowledge could go, to wit, that the disciples stole that body while they were asleep. If they were asleep, they could not testify as to any disposition of the body. They could not prove that anyone removed that body. Moreover, on the face of it, their last story is exceedingly improbable, namely, that when a special guard had been detailed for the express purpose of preventing the very thing which they now allege did take place and when the very time had been given when they must be most particular in their vigils, it is unreasonable to suppose that a guard so appointed would have relaxed their vigilance.

It becomes more improbable from the death penalty assigned to a Roman sentinel who went to sleep upon the post of duty. It is still more improbable from the fact that no adequate motive can be suggested or conceived of why the disciples should want this dead body. It would be of no use to them. So that as far as this theory goes—and it is one of the only two that have ever been advanced—we may at once reject it.

To say that the disciples took away the dead body forces a question of unavoidable logic: What did they want with it dead? What could they do with it dead? What purpose would it answer for them? They felt that the battle was lost. They were cowed to death. They supposed that they were orphaned. What courage could come into their hearts by stealing that body, then lying with reference to it, and then destroying it so that it never could be found? A man's gullibility must be huge to believe that these cowed disciples stole that body and reported that He was risen from the dead. So the important question is now fairly stated.

The Second Theory: Christ Arose

Now, what is the other theory? The other theory is that Jesus Himself rose from the dead. The particular point upon which human testimony is to be brought is not to show the processes by which He overcame death and brought back life to Himself. No witness is introduced who alleges that he actually saw Him rise from the dead. The only thing upon which they are to bear testimony is that they did see Him alive after He was dead.

Here we are met by a pertinent and important inquiry: Is the thing concerning which evidences is to be introduced a legitimate matter for evidence? I take it for granted that there are no other things upon which human testimony is accepted more readily than upon these two points: First, that a man is dead, and second, that a man is alive.

We accept evidence upon both of those points and act upon that evidence on innumerable occasions. It is oftentimes necessary to prove death. It is oftentimes necessary to prove life. In either case, it is easy to be understood what amount of testimony is sufficient to prove that death has taken place or to prove that a man is alive.

The evidence of His death is abundant, official, and has never been denied. Therefore, let us look at the evidence that Jesus showed Himself alive after His death to His apostles and others. There are extant four independent histories of Jesus of Nazareth, written while multitudes who also knew Him personally were yet alive. There are extant also twenty-three other books, written by contemporaries, and written while thousands were yet alive who personally knew Jesus Christ. I refer to the 27 books of the New Testament. The most notable event in all of these records is that Jesus of Nazareth rose from the dead. To this fact, according to these records, hundreds and thousands of eyewitnesses bear testimony and counted it the chief business of their subsequent life to repeat that evidence.

The Evidence of Multiple Appearances

In other words, henceforth their life mission was to be witnesses of the resurrection. Fifteen distinct appearances of our Lord Jesus Christ, at least, are given in the New Testament, perhaps more, including the several appearances to Paul, to Stephen and to John on the Island of Patmos. But there are ten distinct appearances mentioned in those four histories.

These appearances, many of them, are connected with the most minute details of identification of the body. Sometimes He appeared to just one, as to Mary Magdalene, to Peter, to James. Sometimes He appeared to two, then again to three, then again to seven, then to ten, then to eleven and finally to five hundred at one time.

These appearances covered a period of forty days. Some of them were in the morning, some of them at brightest midday, some of them at night; some in the house, some out in the road, some in the suburbs and some in the city of Jerusalem; some by the sea and some on the mountains of Galilee.

Speaking collectively of these witnesses, they saw Him often. They ate with Him just as they had done before His death. They heard Him often in both brief and long-sustained conversation. They witnessed closely every familiar mannerism of speech and tone and gesture. They handled Him critically, touching the prints of the well-known wounds received at His crucifixion, and feeling of His flesh and of His bones, to assure themselves that a material substance was before them.

Intimate Friends Could Not Be Mistaken

And this, too, by those who knew Him most intimately in His lifetime, those who could least easily be mistaken as to the identity of His person—including one of His own who was skeptical as to His resurrection, well-nigh incorrigible—and their tremendous interests at stake, required upon their part the most patient and exhaustive examination, and demanded abundant and infallible proof, not only to the bodily senses of sight, of hearing and touch, and to the keener mental tests of memory, intuition and reason, but to that more subtle and more satisfactory proof—spiritual recognition. They must not only know positively, unmistakably and absolutely that this was the very body which had died and was buried and was now alive, but also that it was reanimated by the same spirit which warmed it before death, so that in every respect, and beyond all possibility of doubt, this was the same person, the same Jesus who had been their Teacher, and also that He possessed and made over to them power to do things that would make that resurrection a declaration that He was the Son of God with power.

In all the cases of the establishment of identity known to history there has never been one where the proof has been so abundant, so critical and so comprehensive, covering all departments of investigation, nor where the testimony was so unequivocal and so consistent. If these witnesses could not establish the proof that Jesus was alive, then no evidence could possibly prove any man to be alive.

So you have before you the two theories and the evidence upon which those two theories rest: the first that the disciples stole the dead body, and next, that Jesus showed Himself alive to His people after His death, not only by proofs but many proofs, not only by many proofs but by many infallible proofs.

Rules of Evidence Applied Proving
Christ's Resurrection

I submit the following fundamental rules which govern matters of evidence: First, In trials of fact by oral testimony the proper inquiry is, not whether it is possible that the testimony may be false, but whether there is sufficient probability that it is true. Second, A proposition of fact is proved when its truth is established by competent and satisfactory evidence. Third, In the absence of circumstances which generate suspicion, every witness is to be presumed credible until the contrary is shown, the burden of impeaching his credibility lying on the objector. Fourth, The credit due to the testimony of witnesses depends upon, first, their honesty; second, their ability; third, their number and the consistency of their testimony; fourth, the conformity of their testimony with experience; and fifth, the coincidence of their testimony with collateral circumstances.

Now if we apply these four rules of evidence to what is said concerning the stealing of His body, that statement goes to the wall. If we apply them to the evidence that Jesus showed Himself alive after death to His people, no sane man can question that the requirements of every one of them is met in every particular.

The honesty of these witnesses cannot be impeached. Their ability of competency depends upon their being acquainted previously with the person of Jesus Christ, their having good sense enough to recognize One whom they had previously known, their opportunities for seeing the One who is identified by their testimony.

There can be no question of the competency of these witnesses. There is nothing in their testimony that bears on its face suspicion. What, let me ask you, can create a suspicion against this evidence? It is consistent. What one says is consistent with what another says.

Now let us look at these people who gave this evidence and see if in all the collateral circumstances what they say is affirmed. For these men to state that Jesus was alive meant that they must take upon themselves the lifetime obligation of the publication of the fact of His resurrection; that to do this they must go counter to the world, its pleasures, its habits, its business; that they must entail upon themselves the most grievous burdens in life and the greatest hazards of death.

They joyfully assume all these responsibilities. When they speak of Jesus as risen, they impress every man that hears it with their sincerity. They testify to it before kings, and the kings tremble as they listen. They testify to it when chained to the martyr's stake; and while the flames are burning their bodies and with shouts and hosannas of triumph, they declare in their own dying agonies that Jesus is risen.

No amount of intimidation was ever able to shake their testimony. It was tried by imprisonment, tried by stripes, tried by poverty, tried by fire, tried by casting them to the ravenous, wild beasts in the Roman amphitheater, and in every way possible to human effort; many experiments of the most excruciating kind were resorted to shake the testimony of these men and these women.

I submit that if any man with an unbiased mind will read the Acts of the Apostles and see how that narrative glows, he will feel the power of these men giving this evidence.

The Testimony of Pentecost

But we come now to another question in connection with it. Our Lord had told them in the last interview He had with them there should come a confirmation that neither Heaven nor Hell could doubt. He said, "I go to my Father, and if I go I will send upon you the Holy Spirit."

The history recites that ten days from that time a most remarkable transaction occurred openly in the city of Jerusalem. There were certain things visible in connection with it. Tongues as of fire seemed to rest upon their heads. There was the further remarkable phenomenon that these fishers of Galilee were able, under His power bestowed upon them, to speak in the languages of all of the nations of the earth, as if they had been born and reared in those tongues. It was evident that a power characterized them utterly foreign to their previous experience; and when they were called upon to explain, what was their explanation? Let me read it to you.

"Ye men of Israel, hear these words; Jesus of Nazareth, a man approved of God among you by miracles and wonders and signs, which God did by him in the midst of you, as ye yourselves also know: Him, being delivered by the determinate counsel and foreknowledge of God, ye have taken, and by wicked hands have crucified and slain: Whom God hath raised up, having loosed the pains of death: because it was not possible that he should be holden of it . . . he hath shed forth this, which ye now see and hear."—Acts 2:22-24,33.

They gave no other account of their power. They could heal the sick. They could raise the dead. They could perform other wonders impossible to men not Spirit-endued. They distinctly disclaimed that the power rested in themselves, and affirmed that it came to them from the risen and ascended and glorified Lord Jesus Christ.

The Importance of the Resurrection to the Apostles

The next question to be determined is, What significance did they attach to this doctrine of the resurrection? How important was it in their sight? How much in their judgment was involved in that issue?

I read first from chapter 17 of the Acts of the Apostles. Paul is standing on Mars' Hill, and he says:

"The times of this ignorance God winked at [or overlooked] *but now commandeth all men every where to repent; Because he hath appointed a day, in the which he will judge the world in righteousness by that man whom he hath ordained; whereof he hath given assurance unto all men, in that he hath raised him from the dead."*—Vss. 30,31.

Is there to be a judgment, and must all men stand before that divine bar and answer for the deeds which are done in the body? The only proof that there will be a judgment is the resurrection of the dead.

Is there a Heaven? There is but one proof of it, that Jesus when alive said to His people, "I go to prepare a place for you. And if I go and prepare a place for you, I will come again, and receive you unto myself; that where I am, there ye may be also . . . . In my Father's house are many mansions" (John 14:2,3). Or let us read from the 15th chapter of the first letter to Corinthians, where this doctrine of the resurrection of the dead is specifically discussed.

"Now if Christ be preached that he rose from the dead, how say some among you that there is no resurrection of the dead? But if there be no resurrection of the dead, then is Christ not risen: And if Christ be not risen, then is our preaching vain, and your faith is also vain. Yea, and we are found false witnesses of God; because we have testified of God that he raised up Christ: whom he raised not up, if so be that the dead rise not. For if the dead rise not, then is not Christ raised: And if Christ be not raised, your faith is vain; ye are yet in your sins. Then they also which are fallen asleep in Christ are perished. If in this life only we have hope in Christ, we are of all men most miserable."—Vss. 12-19.

Trust in All Bible Doctrine Depends
Upon Resurrection

Whenever before in issues made by man has there been such a readiness to stake everything upon one single fact; such an openness to concede that preaching is vain; faith is vain; forgiveness of sin is a falsehood; your fathers and mothers who died, perished; there is no judgment; there is no Heaven; there is no Hell; there is no hope, if there is no resurrection of the dead?

It is a matter of unspeakable sadness to me, particularly in the case of young people, to hear them speak lightly of the doctrine of the resurrection of the dead. And there are some who imagine that they can be skeptical upon this point and remain Christians. Is there anything left of Christianity with this surrendered? If its preaching be vain, if its faith be vain, if there be no such thing as the forgiveness of sin, if there be no such thing as the judgment, if there be no such place as Hell, if all who have professed it are now utterly annihilated in their graves, what infinitesimal shred of Christianity is left?

When you say that you are only skeptical concerning the resurrection of the dead, you mean or ought to mean that you are skeptical about the whole matter, in its height and width and length and breadth, in its center, in its solidarity and in it circumstances. You do not believe any of it. There is nothing to profess if you deny this doctrine.

TOM MALONE
1915-

ABOUT THE MAN:

Tom Malone was converted and called to preach at the same moment! At an old-fashioned bench, the preacher took his tear-stained Bible and showed Tom Malone how to be saved. He accepted Christ then and there. Arising from his knees in the Isbell Methodist Church near Russellville, Alabama, he shook the circuit pastor's hand; and this bashful nineteen-year-old farm boy announced: "I know the Lord wants me to be a preacher."

Backward, bashful and broke, yet Tom borrowed five dollars, took what he could in a cardboard suitcase and left for Cleveland, Tennessee. Immediately upon arrival at Bob Jones College, Malone heard a truth that totally dominated his life and labors for the Lord ever after—soul winning!

That day he won his first soul! The green-as-grass Tom, a new convert himself, knew nothing of soul-winning approaches or techniques. He simply asked the sinner, "Are you a Christian?" No. In a few minutes that young man became Malone's first convert.

Since that day, countless have been his experiences in personal evangelism.

Mark it down: Malone began soul winning his first week in Bible college. And he has never lost *the thirst* for it, *the thrill* in it, nor *the task* of it since. Pastoring churches, administrating schools, preaching across the nation have not deterred Tom Malone from this mainline ministry.

It is doubtful if young Malone ever dreamed of becoming the man he is today. He is now Doctor Tom Malone, is renowned in fundamental circles for his wise leadership and great preaching, is pastor of the large Emmanuel Baptist Church of Pontiac, Michigan, Founder and President of Midwestern Baptist Schools, and is eagerly sought as speaker in large Bible conferences from coast to coast.

Dr. John R. Rice often said that Dr. Tom Malone may be the greatest gospel preacher in all the world today!

XV.

The Biggest "IF"

TOM MALONE

(Preached in the Emmanuel Baptist Church, Easter Sunday, March 29, 1970, and mechanically recorded for use in *The Baptist Vision*.)

READ: I Corinthians 15:1-28

"But if there be no resurrection of the dead, then is Christ not risen."—I Cor. 15:13.

Now there is an occasion for this particular verse in I Corinthians 15. Some of these people at Corinth had said to Paul, "There is no such thing as the resurrection of the dead." Verse 12 makes it clear that there were some who denied the resurrection—"How say some among you that there is no resurrection of the dead?"

Paul says, "I want to show you what would be true if there were no resurrection from the dead."

Not only were there people at Corinth who did not believe in the resurrection of the dead, but it has always been true that there were people who did not believe in the resurrection.

Bible students believe the oldest book in the Bible is not Genesis, nor Exodus—none of the books of the Pentateuch, but the book of Job. In 14:14 Job posed the question way back centuries ago: "If a man die, shall he live again?"

Even then men were debating, "If a man die, will he ever come out of the grave? If a man die, will he live again? Is there any such thing as the resurrection of the dead?" It is the oldest question ever pondered by the human mind, the oldest question ever debated by human beings. If a man die, will he live again?

You find that there were people in the Bible who didn't believe in the resurrection. Some people were constant thorns in the side of Jesus, constant enemies of our Lord while He was on this earth. There were the Sadducees who said that there was nothing miraculous; everything could be rationalized, explained; nothing was supernatural. The Sadducees did not believe in the resurrection of a body from the grave. Nor did they believe in angels. Luke 20:27 says, "Then came to him certain of the Sadducees, which deny that there is any resurrection."

So there have always been people who did not believe that a body could ever be raised from the dead.

In Luke 8 is an instance of a little twelve-year-old girl who had died—an only child of wealthy parents. Jesus took the parents and, with Peter, James and John, went in a room, secluding themselves from all other followers. With these He said, "Weep not; she is not dead, but sleepeth. And they laughed him to scorn, knowing that she was dead" (Luke 8:52,53).

People began to laugh and ask, "What can You do about death?" Here is the Son of God; here is the resurrection; here is the Author of all life—people laughed at Him and said, "There is no such thing as one who was dead coming back to life." Always there have been enemies of the resurrection of our Lord.

In Acts 17:18 read what they said to Paul when he went to Athens to preach: "What will this babbler say?" Why did they say that? Here is why. They said, "He seemeth to be a setter forth of strange gods: because he preached unto them Jesus, and the resurrection."

When Paul preached Jesus and the resurrection, they thought this man a babbler. "What strange things he has to say! He is talking about a strange God when he talks about the power of God to raise people from the dead."

In another instance, Paul was preaching mostly to Pharisees, religious people, when he said, "Why should it be thought a thing incredible with you, that God should raise the dead?" (Acts 26:8).

So there have always been enemies to the resurrection of the human body and to the resurrection of Jesus Christ from the dead.

When He was crucified, two well-to-do men, both of whom had been saved, came and begged the body of Jesus. He was not placed out in the potter's field. Because of a fulfillment of Bible prophecy that He be numbered with the rich in His death, Nicodemus and Joseph of Arimathaea came and got permission to bury the body of Jesus in a tomb.

When the body was surrendered to the kind hands of those who loved Him, the enemy said, "Sir, we remember that that deceiver said, while he was yet alive, After three days I will rise again" (Matt. 27:63). Talking about Jesus, they said, "Now this deceiver said He will rise again. We don't believe in nor want any resurrection. So these Roman soldiers will stand at the door of that tomb and see that He never comes forth."

People have not only doubted but have hated the glorious, wonderful truth of the resurrection of our Lord. So Paul, even at Corinth, said, "But if there be no resurrection . . . ."

Now in this passage that I read, Paul said, 'But *if* there is no resurrection then seven other facts hold to be true'—the greatest *"if"* in human language.

Let me mention to you how some people try to explain away the resurrection. There is, first of all, what theologians call the *swoon theory*.

Some say, "They took Him down from the cross before He died and placed Him in a tomb. He didn't have to rise from the dead because He never died. He was merely in a coma."

Now anyone who is honest and intelligent, whether he believes all the Bible or not, would know that this could not be true. For six hours He was nailed to the cross. A spear opened up His body until blood and water gathered in a crimson pool beneath the cross. The Roman soldier came and saw that Jesus was dead, so he did not execute the Roman law to break the legs. The *swoon theory*, they say!

Then there is a theory called the *hallucination theory*. They said, "All these who say they saw Him after He rose from the dead were having nightmares, hallucinations, a series of visions."

Now, let me ask you something. The Bible says that He was seen by as few as one and by as many as five hundred. Could five hundred people have the same nightmare at the same time and tell the same story of it? "After that, he was seen of above five hundred brethren at once . . ." (I Cor. 15:6). Paul said, "Five hundred brethren saw Him at once, and most of them are still alive and still witnesses that Jesus came forth from the grave."

Then there is the *kidnap theory:* "Now you put these Roman soldiers here because these Christians will probably try to kidnap Him. They are going to steal His body and then say that He rose from the grave."

No, that did not happen. An earthquake came; two angels came; Roman soldiers fell to the ground as though they were dead; Jesus walked out of the grave with the keys of death and Hell at His side and said, "I am alive for evermore." It is an attested fact of human history that Jesus Christ arose from the dead.

It is said that the British Archaeological Society made a chemical analysis of the dirt found in the Garden Tomb when it was excavated a little over a hundred years ago, and their analysis was that no human body had ever decayed in that tomb. The dirt showed no evidence that one bone or bit of flesh had ever decayed there. Jesus lay in the tomb in the cold grip of death; but, thank God, on the morning of the resurrection, He walked forth with His feet upon the neck of death and said, "I am alive for evermore."

"But if there be no resurrection of the dead, then is Christ not risen."—I Cor. 15:13.

I. IF THERE BE NO RESURRECTION, THE RESUR- RECTION OF JESUS CHRIST WOULD BE A FALLACY

In the first place, if there be no resurrection of the dead, then it stands to reason that Jesus did not arise. If there is no such thing as the resurrection of the human body out of the grave, then the resurrection—the personal, bodily, literal, physical resurrection—of Jesus would be nothing but a fallacy.

You say, "Brother Malone, is it important to consider this?"

Think what the resurrection means. First, it proves His redemption to be of God. Three days before this, while dying upon the cross, Jesus cried out, "It is finished."

He claimed that on the cross the sins of the world were to be laid upon Him. The Bible tells us that God laid upon Him the iniquity of us all (Isa. 53:6). Three days before this, robed in blood and crowned with thorns, He claims to die for the sin of the world.

If there had been no resurrection, the redemptive work of Jesus would have been set at naught and proven to be a fallacy, for the Bible says, "Who was delivered for our offences, and was raised again for our justification" (Rom. 4:25).

In Matthew 16 He told His disciples how ". . . he must go unto Jerusalem, and suffer many things of the elders and chief priests and scribes, and be killed, and be raised again the third day" (Matt. 16:21).

If Jesus didn't arise on the third day, I am not going to believe that He died for my sins. The two go together. His resurrection is God's "amen" to His death on the cross.

While Jesus was alive, He said, "For as Jonas was three days and three nights in the whale's belly; so shall the Son of man be three days and three nights in the heart of the earth" (Matt. 12:40). Jesus is saying, "Three days and three nights I will be in the earth, then I will come forth."

If Jesus Christ didn't come forth, He is the world's greatest imposter. If Jesus didn't arise on the third day, He is the world's biggest liar. He deceived more people than any other personality that ever walked across the face of this earth. If there be no resurrection, the resurrection of Christ would be a fallacy. His redemption work could not have been proven to be of God. All of the Christian's system of truth tumbles if the resurrection goes down.

I thought of a picture that I saw some years ago of a great arch made of stone. In the Bible lands you see them by the hundreds. Many date back to the time of Jesus and before. There was the Arch of Triumph. Gates and many doors were made in the shape of an arch. One stone in an arch, the most important stone, is called the arch stone. It is a V-shaped stone and fits right in the middle of the bottom of the arch. The weight of all stones rests upon that arch stone.

It is said that if you want to tear down that arch, you don't have to dig at the foundation or put pressure on the top but just remove that arch stone, the one in the center which holds the weight; and the arch will come down.

So it is with all the truth of Christianity. If by some subtle power of the Devil the resurrection of Christ could be disproved, the whole system of Christianity would come tumbling to the ground. All the Bible would become a legendary myth.

Again and again the resurrection of Jesus is taught in the Bible. It was even prophesied and demonstrated in the Old Testament. There were three resurrections of people in Old Testament times; so if there be no resurrection, we have no Bible. If there be no resurrection, then Christ is not raised from the dead. If Jesus did not rise from the dead, then all His words become meaningless and fraudulent.

In John 2:19 Jesus said, "Destroy this temple, and in three days I will raise it up." He said to Mary and Martha whose brother lay yonder in the cold grave in death, "I am the resurrection, and the life: he that believeth in me, though he were dead, yet shall he live: And whosoever liveth and believeth in me shall never die" (John 11:25,26).

If there is no resurrection of the dead, then you cannot believe what Jesus said. All of His words become meaningless and fraudulent. If there is no resurrection of the dead and Christ didn't arise, then the keeping power of Jesus would be a figment of deluded imagination. If Jesus did not arise from the dead then you could not have assurance that God would keep you until He comes again to receive you unto Himself.

The verse I have been talking about is Romans 4:25, "Who was delivered for our offences, and was raised again for our justification."

Yonder at the throne He keeps us by His power. He was raised not only that we might be saved, but that we might be kept. The Mediator at the throne, the Lawyer at God's right hand, is a risen Jesus, raised for our justification. So if Christ did not arise from the dead, then the keeping power of Jesus would be a statement of deluded imagination.

So, we have a risen Saviour.

"But if there be no resurrection of the dead, then is Christ not risen."—I Cor. 15:13.

II. IF THERE BE NO RESURRECTION, ALL BIBLE PREACHING WOULD BE MEANINGLESS

Paul said, "If there be no resurrection of the dead, then all Bible preaching would be meaningless and in vain." He said, "If there is no such thing as a resurrection of the human body, all preaching is vain."

Just think of all the preaching this world has heard! Noah preached the Bible 120 years. Moses lived 120 years, and forty years of that he preached the truth of God every day. Elijah was a preacher. Elisha was a preacher. The book of Ezekiel is almost entirely sermons by this great preacher, Ezekiel. Isaiah preached 62 long years the truth of God.

Jeremiah wept as he preached through a long and fruitful ministry. Jonah was a preacher. John Wesley preached to as many as twenty-five thousand people in the open fields. Dwight L. Moody probably preached to more people than any man in the last hundred years.

Fifty years I have devoted my life, my mind, my heart, my eyes, my body, to one thing—the preaching of the Gospel.

One of the dearest men I ever knew was Dr. Bob Jones, Sr., who for over sixty years preached the death, burial and resurrection of Jesus.

Here comes Paul in the Bible who says, "If there be no resurrection of the dead, all your preaching is in vain." Jesus' last words were, "Go ye into all the world, and preach the gospel to every creature" (Mark 16:15).

If there is no resurrection, all that preaching, in all the world, in all these ages, has been in vain. We read in I Corinthians 1:18, "For the preaching of the cross is to them that perish foolishness; but unto us which are saved it is the power of God."

"Preach the word; be instant in season, out of season; reprove, rebuke, exhort with all longsuffering and doctrine."—II Tim. 4:2.

"But if there be no resurrection of the dead, then is Christ not risen."—I Cor. 15:13.

III. IF THERE BE NO RESURRECTION, FAITH BECOMES AN EMPTY DREAM

The Word of God says that if there is no resurrection of the dead, then your faith is in vain. If there is no resurrection, then there is nothing to believe in. "Vain," in this instance, means absolutely meaningless. If there is no resurrection of the dead, faith becomes an empty dream.

Stop and think. The Bible says that we have to have faith to be saved: "For by grace are ye saved through faith; and that not of yourselves: it is the gift of God: Not of works, let any man should boast" (Eph. 2:8,9).

Paul says, "If there is no resurrection from the dead, your faith is vain." You have to have faith to pray. Every Christian could stand and say, "One time at least in my life God answered my prayer." Jesus said on the matter of prayer, "According to your faith be it unto you" (Matt. 9:29).

You have to have faith to please God, "But without faith it is impossible to please him" (Heb. 11:6).

You have to have faith to be kept and to commit your soul to God. Paul said, "For I know whom I have believed, and am persuaded that he is able to keep that which I have committed unto him against that day" (II Tim. 1:12).

It takes faith to be saved, to get answers to prayer, to please God, to be kept as a Christian. Paul says, "If there is no resurrection of the dead, your faith is all in vain."

I think of a dear old lady who used to claim Hebrews 13:5, "I will never leave thee, nor forsake thee." One day a Greek scholar came along and said to this dear lady who had made this promise a dear thing in her life, "You know, in studying Hebrews 13:5, we Greek scholars find that there are five negatives in it and that it could read like this, 'I will never, never, never, never, never leave thee, nor forsake thee.' "

The elderly lady said, "My faith is so strong in God that the Lord only one time had to say, 'I will never leave you' for me to believe Him the rest of my days."

Thank God, our faith is not in vain! It is in Jesus who lives. It is in Jesus who conquered death and who arose from the grave.

"But if there be no resurrection of the dead, then is Christ not risen."—I Cor. 15:13.

IV. IF THERE BE NO RESURRECTION, ALL CHRISTIANS ARE FALSE WITNESSES

Paul said, "If there be no resurrection of the dead, all Christians are false witnesses." Just think of the Christians involved.

First, Paul himself is involved. He said, "And last of all he was seen of me also, as of one born out of due time" (I Cor. 15:8). He declared, "I saw Him alive. He spoke to me on the Damascus Road. A risen Saviour in Heaven said, 'I am Jesus whom thou persecutest.' " Paul said, "I saw Him. I saw Him!"

Now Paul was used of God to write fourteen books of the New Testament. If he didn't see Jesus, then Paul was a false witness and more than half of your New Testament is immediately gone.

John on the Isle of Patmos heard Jesus say, "I am he that liveth, and was dead; and, behold, I am alive for evermore, Amen; and have the keys of hell and of death" (Rev. 1:18).

Peter said that Jesus lived: "Blessed be the God and Father of our Lord Jesus Christ, which according to his abundant mercy hath begotten us again unto a lively hope by the resurrection of Jesus Christ from the dead" (I Pet. 1:3).

Stephen, a deacon, being stoned to death and "being full of the Holy Ghost, looked up stedfastly into heaven, and saw the glory of God, and Jesus standing on the right hand of God, And said, Behold, I see the heavens opened, and the Son of man standing on the right hand of God" (Acts 7:55,56). Stephen said that He was alive.

Paul said, "If there be no resurrection of the dead, we are all false witnesses."

Paul said, "I saw Him."

John said, "I saw Him."

Peter said, "I saw Him."

Stephen said, "I saw Him."

And the Bible says, "If there is no resurrection . . . all these are false witnesses."

It includes all Christians. If there is no resurrection of the dead, then all of us are false witnesses in the sight of man.

A famous conductor, Reichel, was preparing for a great choir to sing the "Messiah." At the last practice, a lady soprano with a most beautiful voice was singing the solo, "I know that my Redeemer liveth." Her intonation was wonderful; her voice was as clear as a bell; it was a talent that came from God.

It is said that after she finished singing, many were almost breathless. But the famous conductor said at the last practice to this talented lady, "Do you really believe what you are singing?"

The great singer said, "Why, Sir, with all my heart I believe that my Redeemer liveth."

Reichel, the great conductor, admonished, "Then, Lady, sing it so as to make me believe it, and sing it so as to make the whole world believe that Jesus lives. Now, take it again."

She again began to sing but this time with a living Redeemer filling her body. She sang with her eyes upon the Lord, with her soul absorbed with His presence. She sang until the tears flowed.

In the midst of it the great conductor cried out, "I believe it! I believe it! I believe it! I believe Jesus lives."

I believe with all my heart and soul I have a Redeemer, not only from Calvary but an Advocate at the throne. As the years come and go and we take those frequent trips to the Silent City of the Dead, by the hope given to us at the resurrection of Jesus Christ, because He lives, we, too, shall live forever.

Thank God for the resurrection and a living Saviour!

"But if there be no resurrection of the dead, then is Christ not risen."—I Cor. 15:13.

V. IF THERE BE NO RESURRECTION, WE ARE YET IN OUR SINS

Says I Corinthians 15:17, "And if Christ be not raised, your faith is vain; ye are yet in your sins."

Someone may say to me, "Preacher, if He died on the cross but didn't rise from the grave, do you think we would still be in our sins?" That is not what I *think* and not something I conjectured; God says so in the Bible. If He did not rise from the dead, God says you are yet in your sins.

You say, "Why is that true?"

If you will read in the Bible what it takes to be saved, then you will know why it is true. It says that you can't be saved without believing in the resurrection of Jesus Christ from the dead.

Look at Romans 10:9,10—a passage so often quoted, but how many really understand it:

"That if thou shalt confess with thy mouth the Lord Jesus, and shalt believe in thine heart that God hath raised him from the dead, thou shalt be saved. For with the heart man believeth unto righteousness; and with the mouth confession is made unto salvation."

In order to be saved, you have to "confess with thy mouth the Lord Jesus, and . . . believe in thine heart that God hath raised him from the dead." You can't be saved without believing in the resurrection of Jesus Christ.

You say, "Well, I thought one only had to believe that Jesus died for our sins."

The Bible says that if Jesus did not arise from the grave, you are yet in your sins. So if you do not believe in the resurrected Christ, the Bible says there is no way to be saved.

I have often pointed out a misinterpreted passage. Romans 5:10 says that "we shall be saved by his life." Many have said, "Yes, all one has to do is imitate Jesus. Look at His life; see how He lived a spotless life, never sinned or spoke an evil word or thought an evil thought or committed an evil act. If one can live like Jesus and follow Him as an example, he can be saved."

That is not true. It is not even talking about from the age of thirty until He died upon the cross three years later. It is not talking about that perfect, exemplary life that He lived before men. It is not talking about His life yonder side of the cross when the Bible says that we shall be "saved by his life." Romans 5:10 is talking about His life this side the cross. It is talking about His life at the throne. It is talking about His mediatorial work. It is talking about His advocacy for us as He mediates our cause at the right hand of God. We shall be saved by His life, that is, kept saved, justified, declared righteous by our Lord Jesus.

No doubt that is what He meant in John 14:19 when He said, "Because I live, ye shall live also." When did He say that? John 13 closes with Jesus making the announcement to His disciples, "I am going to die and leave you. Separation is going to come." Simon Peter and all these others loved Him (with the exception of Judas Iscariot). Simon spoke up, saying, "I would rather die with You than to be left behind."

Then Jesus begins to comfort them. "Let not your heart be troubled: ye believe in God, believe also in me. In my Father's house are many mansions: if it were not so, I would have told you. I go to prepare a place for you" (John 14:1,2).

He says to those men who were saddened at His death, "Because I live, ye shall live also."

So the Bible says that if there be no resurrection, you are yet in your sins. Hebrews 7:25 teaches it: "Wherefore he is able also to save them to the uttermost that come unto God by him, seeing he ever liveth to make intercession for them."

So if there be no resurrection, you are yet in your sins.

"But if there be no resurrection of the dead, then is Christ not risen."—I Cor. 15:13.

VI. IF THERE BE NO RESURRECTION, OUR LOVED ONES ARE PERISHED

Look at I Corinthians 15:18, "Then they also which are fallen asleep in Christ are perished."

If there is no resurrection, forget about your loved ones who preceded you to Glory. Forget about precious gray-haired Dad who loved the Lord, read the Bible, prayed and won you to Christ. If there is no resurrection, you will never see him again.

Forget about the sweet little child who one day was plucked from your home. God took that little flower out of your life. If there is no resurrection, you will never see her again. "Then they also which are fallen asleep in Christ are perished."

How wonderful is the teaching of the Bible! Many times when Paul was writing his letters, he said,"I would not have you to be ignorant." In the matter of money, Paul said, you don't need to be ignorant. "I will tell you how you can use your money." In the matter of meats, Paul would not have you to be ignorant. In the matter of marriage, Paul would not have you to be ignorant.

When it comes to talking about people who have died in the Lord, I Thessalonians 4:13-17 says:

"But I would not have you to be ignorant, brethren, concerning them

which are asleep, that ye sorrow not, even as others which have no hope. For if we believe [as it is in the King James Version, but in the Greek New Testament, 'for since we believe'] *that Jesus died and rose again, even so them also which sleep in Jesus will God bring with him. For this we say unto you by the word of the Lord, that we which are alive and remain unto the coming of the Lord shall not prevent them which are asleep. For the Lord himself shall descend from heaven with a shout, with the voice of the archangel, and with the trump of God: and the dead in Christ shall rise first: Then we which are alive and remain shall be caught up together with them in the clouds, to meet the Lord in the air: and so shall we ever be with the Lord."*

Paul said, "If there be no resurrection of the dead . . . they also which are fallen asleep in Christ are perished" (I Cor. 15:13,18). Paul said that if there is no resurrection, then our loved ones are perished.

As I have mentioned many times, my brother and I spent most of our boyhood on my grandfather's farm. Uncle Fred, my mother's brother, had, I think, actually an even dozen children. Two boys were about the age of my brother and I. My brother and the other two were big fellows, real men.

Where I was raised, the "pastime" was fighting. A fellow would fight half a day, then sit down and talk about it a while, then get up and fight some more. I didn't enjoy that with such big guys, so I would get me a ringside seat and watch. When I thought I was going to get involved, I would flee to safety. That kept me alive for many years!

The four of us were together constantly. We worked in the fields many hours together; we played together, went swimming together. We did most things together.

One of those boys, with no education, moved down to Louisiana and somehow became quite a wealthy man. When he was forty-seven years old, he took sick and died. They called me long distance to come to Lafayette, Louisiana, to preach his funeral. My brother and I got in my plane, and we flew down to Lafayette, and I preached my cousin's funeral. He was the same age I was. It was a sad day.

I never will forget my dear country aunt whose boy was lying in that casket. My dear Aunt Ella came and bent over the casket that held one of her children. With tears running down her face, she said, "Goodbye, Son—but I'll see you in the morning."

That is the hope of a Christian—"Goodbye, but I will see you in the morning."

A mother of two grown children said when I preached the funeral of one of her daughters, "It is goodbye, but not forever. Goodbye, but not forever."

Thank God, because Jesus arose our loved ones have not perished. I thank God for the sweet and wonderful hope of a reunion in Glory with all those who have preceded us in death and those who died with faith in Christ.

"But if there be no resurrection of the dead, then is Christ not risen."—I Cor. 15:13.

VII. IF THERE BE NO RESURRECTION, "WE ARE OF ALL MEN MOST MISERABLE"

We find in I Corinthians 15:19, "If in this life only we have hope in Christ, we are of all men most miserable." Why did Paul say that?

I have heard many people say, "If there were not any God or Christianity, I would still be glad that I had lived a Christian life."

That may be true; but the Bible says that if in this life only we have hope, we are of all men most miserable. Why did Paul say this?

I think for one reason. He is thinking about all of his suffering for the cause of Christ—the shipwreck, the beatings, the storms, the imprisonment, the suffering, the ridicule—all of this. Paul is thinking, *If there is no resurrection, no life hereafter, no place somewhere where everything is right, I am the most miserable man in the world to take all I have taken and all I have suffered.*

Paul said, "If there be no resurrection, we are of all men most miserable!"

Luke 9:23 says, "And he said to them all, If any man will come after me, let him deny himself, and take up his cross daily, and follow me." The cross bearing is something that every real Christian has to do. If there is no life beyond the grave, what a ridiculous thing to bear a cross through this journey of life! So Paul is saying, "If there is no resurrection, we are of all men most miserable."

Then he adds to this passage by saying, ". . . but now is Christ risen." Thank God for that!

I am like the dear old lady who said, when there was talk about God's being dead, "My God is alive. Sorry about yours!"

That is the way I feel about it. Mine is alive! You say, "How do you know?" I talked to Him today. Like the bells that tinkled upon the bottom of the robe of the high priest beyond the veil, I have talked to Him and heard the bells of Heaven ring. I know the Lord is alive. I have hope in Christ. I do not ask for pity from the world. I feel fortunate that, out of the millions on earth, He sought me, found me, saved me. For thirty-five wonderful years, He has kept me every step of the way.

It was Dr. George Truett, I believe, who some years ago told about a couple in Fort Worth, Texas. They had a twelve-year-old boy who died. The mother had been afflicted with a heart ailment, and everyone was concerned about her.

When the pastor came and people gathered in the home, that wonderful woman said, "I appreciate your prayers and interest, but don't worry about me. I know I have a bad heart, and many people think that this may kill me. My heart is broken, but pray for my husband. I am saved. I know the Lord. My boy was a Christian. I led him to Christ at my knee. But my husband is lost. I have hope; my boy has hope, but my husband has none. Pray for him. I am going to meet my boy again in Glory. Pray for my husband; he has no hope."

I thank God for hope in Christ.

"But if there be no resurrection of the dead, then is Christ not risen."—I Cor. 15:13.

SAM MORRIS
1900-

ABOUT THE MAN:

Sam Morris was for many, many years best known as "J. Barleycorn's No. 1 Enemy." He was proclaimed by the liquor industry as "the most valuable man to have entered the service of the drys in several generations." For years he successfully fought liquor on the strongest stations in America and Mexico on his "Voice of Temperance" radio broadcast.

"HOWDY, NEIGHBOR!" Morris' listeners packed out great halls to hear his friendly greeting. One well-known writer described the mighty response that followed it: "I have been watching crowds closely all my life, but I never saw anything like this before. I have seen admiration, respect and veneration in the faces of people as they listened to Bryan or Billy Sunday. These people, packed tightly together in great auditoriums, had all that—but much more. It was massed, concerted, personal friendship and love . . . ."

Dr. Morris was not only a great temperance speaker; he was also a successful pastor in Weatherford and Stamford, Texas, before being offered time for his temperance talks on the world's most powerful radio station XERA, located across the border in old Mexico.

Dr. Morris also conducted great revival campaigns in some of America's largest churches.

No one can estimate the influence Morris had on the lives of individuals.

His 16 publications were very popular, among them: *Blessed Assurance, Mother's Bible, Voice of Temperance Scrapbooks, The Booze Buster,* and *Rats in the Brewery Vats.*

He taught Bible in Hardin-Simmons University; got his M.A. degree from Brown University in Providence, Rhode Island.

XVI.

"He Is Risen"

SAM MORRIS

This is Easter week. It reminds us of the resurrection of Christ. The Bible says that very early on the morning of the first day of the week, following the crucifixion of Christ, certain women came to the tomb bringing with them spices for the purpose of anointing His body. When they arrived, they found the stone rolled away and were told by angels, "He is not here: for he is risen, as he said."

I want to speak on that text this morning—"He is not here: for he is risen, as he said." It suggests three things: an empty tomb, a risen Lord, and a fulfilled prophecy."

"He is not here: for he is risen, as he said."

The Empty Tomb

Christ's tomb was empty. That was contrary to the precaution of His enemies. They did not want that to happen. They tried to make sure it would not happen. They had sealed the tomb with the Roman seal of authority which would mean death to anyone who broke that seal. They had likewise placed armed guards before it to keep vigil.

But Roman seals and armed soldiers are no match for the power of God, and so on the third day the tomb was opened and emptied of His body.

It was contrary to the precaution of His enemies.

It was likewise contrary to the expectation of His friends. They did not expect Him to rise from the dead. They were all down in the dumps, sad, mournful, and had "taken out." They had given up. They thought the show was over.

These women had in their hands certain spices with which to anoint His body. When they ran and told His disciples that He had risen from the dead, those disciples did not believe them. Two of them ran to the tomb to look and verify for themselves the story. And Thomas, when told that Christ had risen, said: "Oh, no! You have seen a ghost, you've had a vision, you are fooled. I won't take your word for it; I won't believe it unless I can see Him for myself and stick my finger in the nail prints of His hand."

Boy, wasn't he skeptical!

But not more so than the rest of them. They did not, any of them, believe it at first. Christ's tomb was empty, contrary to the expectation of His friends.

It was empty, contrary to all other tombs of history.

The pyramids of Egypt are famous because in them were found the mummified bodies of ancient Egyptian potentates. Westminster Abbey in London is famous because in it are the bodies of Browning, Tennyson and other English notables. Arlington Cemetery in Washington is famous for it is the honored resting place of famous Americans. Mount Vernon is famous because there is the body of Washington.

That is the difference between the tomb of Christ and other famous tombs. They are famous and draw visitors from afar because of what they contain. The tomb of Christ is famous because of what it DOES NOT CONTAIN. They are famous because they are full; it is famous because it is empty. If it were not empty, you would never have heard of Christ.

The Risen Lord

Now if Christ's tomb was empty, what became of the body? That is the question. Either the body had been removed, or He had risen from the dead. One or the other of those two things had to be true. There is no other alternative.

But there were only one of two groups that could have removed His body, and those were His friends or His foes. Well, for His friends to remove the body was out of the question. The tomb was sealed and the guard marched in front of it to prevent that very thing from happening. So even if His friends had wanted to take away the body, they could not. On the other hand, His foes WOULD NOT have taken the body away. That is the very thing they did not want to happen. That is why they sealed the tomb and placed the guard there to protect it.

His friends could not rob the tomb of His body, and His foes would not.

Then the other alternative stands.

He arose from the grave.

That's what the angel said.

That's what Mary said.

That's what Simon Peter said.

That's what Matthew wrote.

That's what Mark wrote.

That's what Luke wrote.

That's what John wrote.

That's what Paul wrote and preached.

That's what Christian people have written and said for two thousand years. If it were not the truth, then preachers and the New Testament and Christian churches are a farce and the Christian faith is the biggest hoax the world ever witnessed. There is no getting around that.

I never saw Plato nor Alexander the Great nor Caesar nor Napoleon nor John Bunyan nor Charles Haddon Spurgeon nor George Washington. I never saw nor talked with anyone who ever did see them. But there is not the shadow of doubt in my mind that such men did once live. I believe they did because we have records left by them and their friends who say they did, and those who made those records were honest, trustworthy people.

And, ladies and gentlemen, the records are too plain, unvarnished and undeniable, about the resurrection of Christ. Men who wrote the New Testament about His life and deeds and death and resurrection preached those things in their lifetime, and for that testimony they were put in jail; they were beaten and abused and ridiculed and hounded and killed.

Men do not suffer and die for myths. Men do not suffer and die voluntarily for Santa Claus stories. Men do not go to jail and bleed and suffer and lay down their lives for funny books and things they do not believe.

These men were on the spot. Nobody could fool them. They lived when it happened. They were there and knew all about it. It could not be a "put-up job" on them. And they were transformed by this great fact and spent their lives telling it. They laid down their lives to defend it. They wrote the New Testament record that we might know its certainty. The resurrection of Christ is as well established as any fact of history could be established by the records of men.

The Fulfilled Prophecy

Now notice the third thing in this text—the fulfilled prophecy. "He is not here: for he is risen, **as he said**."

Things had a habit of happening "as he said."

A father came asking Him to heal an afflicted child, and Jesus told the father to go his way, the child would be made whole. It happened "as he said."

He told His disciples they would find a colt tied in a certain place. It happened "as he said."

He instructed Peter to go catch a fish and in the mouth of the fish he would find a piece of money with which to pay taxes. It happened "as he said."

He told them they would meet a man carrying a pitcher in whose home they would eat the passover. It happened "as he said."

He told them that they were going up to Jerusalem and that He would be betrayed into the hands of sinners and be crucified and buried but that on the third day He would rise from the dead. It happened "as he said."

His enemies remembered that prediction and took precautions to prevent it. His disciples forgot the prediction and were astonished when it happened "as he said."

But it took place just the same, "as he said."

The Pledge of Our Resurrection

His resurrection is the pledge of our resurrection. If He could keep the prediction of His own resurrection, then we may rest assured that He is able and will keep His promise that we shall rise. If He could throw off the robes of death and rise, then surely He can raise our dead bodies.

Listen to His promise:

"This is the Father's will which hath sent me, that of all which he hath given me I should lose nothing, but should raise it up again at the last day. And this is the will of him that sent me, that every one which seeth the Son, and believeth on him, may have everlasting life: and I will raise him up at the last day." —John 6:39,40.

That is His promise. He will make it good. "We shall not all sleep, but we shall all be changed."

"Christ the firstfruits; and afterward they that are Christ's at His coming." "The dead in Christ shall rise first." Because He lives, we shall live also. This is the Christian's hope of the resurrection.

The Condition to This Hope

But do not be fooled. Do not get misled. This hope is not universal.

It is not held out to everybody, everywhere, all the time. It is limited to believers. It is for "they that are Christ's." It is only to "the dead in Christ." Jesus said it was for "every one which seeth the Son and believeth on him." So if you want this hope and wish to claim this promise, then you must accept Christ and believe on Him.

That is why we have that wonderful promise in the book of Romans 10:9,10:

"If thou shalt confess with thy mouth the Lord Jesus, and shalt believe in thine heart that God hath raised him from the dead, thou shalt be saved. For with the heart man believeth unto righteousness; and with the mouth confession is made unto salvation."

Last week I was called home for the death of Mrs. Morris' mother. She was nearly 82 years of age. She has lived a faithful, godly, Christian life before her children and her neighbors all of these years. When I reached her bedside just before she passed away, she was conscious and recognized me; and I talked with her. I said: "Mother, how are you feeling?" She replied: "Well, I am still alive." I said: "You certainly are, and that's something to be thankful for. But it would still be all right if you were not because we know where you are going when you die, don't we?" She feebly tried to clap her frail hands and began to shout, as I had seen her do so many times in Sunday school and church, and she said: "It certainly would. Praise the Lord! Praise His holy name! Praise Him! Praise Him! Praise His holy name!"

That, my friends, is the way my wife's mother said farewell to this world last week. We laid her body away by the side of her husband's in the little graveyard in Detroit, Texas. But some day when Jesus returns, we shall greet her again.

My Risen Lord

I never walk the sandy shore
   But that I think of Galilee,
And how the One who stilled the waves
   Can calm the storms of life for me.

I never gaze upon a crowd
   Without a sense of brotherhood,
A thankful gladness that He had
   Compassion on the multitude.

I never seek my garden's peace
   And loveliness and ecstasy
Without a poignant thought of Him
   Who suffered in Gethsemane.

I never see a lonely hill
   But that I think of Calvary—
Three crosses dark against the sky,
   On one the Lord who died for me!

I never weep beside a grave
   In hopeless anguish for my dead;
I see by blessed, risen Lord,
   And so my heart is comforted!

               —Martha Snell Nicholson.

LOUIS T. TALBOT
1889-1976

ABOUT THE MAN:

Born in Sydney, Australia, Louis, as he grew up, assisted his father in the brewing business, becoming a distributor of alcoholic beverages.

But with the help of his mother's prayers, he, now in his manhood and still unsaved, became restless, dissatisfied, disillusioned as to the business he was in. He dreamed of America and a new life. His brother Jim, in Moody Bible Institute, was to be a preacher: "Why couldn't there be two preachers in the family?" So "Louie" followed Jim to Moody, now cut loose from the liquor evil and ready for a fresh adventure.

He was far along in his studies at Moody when, under the preaching of John Harper of London, he was genuinely converted.

After Moody Institute, this young Australian went from pastorate to pastorate in the United States and Canada until he received a call to the great Church of the Open Door in Los Angeles, the very church the mighty R. A. Torrey had founded. Dr. Talbot was also president of the Bible Institute of Los Angeles (BIOLA).

He met and married Audrey Hogue while pastoring a Congregational church in Paris, Texas.

The story of Dr. Louis Talbot's activities in Los Angeles make a fiction tame. He found a church of 1,200 discouraged members; he left it with 3,500 and the future bright. He came to a debt of over a million dollars; he left the church free from debt and thousands of dollars raised on new promotional enterprises. He extended the missionary program to where literally hundreds of American missionaries and native workers circle the globe, supported by this great church. He came to 300 students in the Bible Institute; he left it with more than a thousand. His ministry over the air was phenomenal.

Few men in this generation achieved success as Dr. Talbot did. He had tremendous faith and was absolutely loyal to the Bible, and he loved the Lord with all his heart.

XVII.

Christ Lives!

LOUIS T. TALBOT

"Because I live, ye shall live also." —John 14:19.

The greatest single event in human history, displaying at once the most tremendous force and exerting the most powerful influence upon the entire world, was not a mighty military victory. It was not an amazing achievement of the arts. It was not an ingenious invention of man. It was not a stupendous scientific discovery—not even the development of the atom bomb of our day. Honest research into history results in but one conclusion: the world-shaking and world-shaping occurrence of all time was the resurrection from the dead of our Lord Jesus Christ in the land of Palestine, nearly two thousand years ago.

Since that time, no phase of life upon the earth in any age has been unaffected by the fact that Christ rose again. Wherever the tidings of this event have reached, they have altered the living and thinking of "nations and kindreds and peoples and tongues."

Every "good and perfect gift" of civilization is but a by-product of the Gospel of a living Lord. Emancipation from every form of tyranny, the "four freedoms," and all freedoms, had their origin in the death and resurrection of Jesus Christ. The world may "little note, nor long remember" what He did when He offered up His life a ransom for sinners at the "place of a skull," and when on that first Easter morn He shook off the shackles of death in His borrowed tomb; but it will to the time of the end feel the effects of what He accomplished.

Whether or not one believes in its reality, the resurrection of Christ is of vital consequence to every person on earth. It is the "touchstone of destiny" for all mankind.

But while it is of interest to consider the meaning of the resurrection to the world at large, those of us who believe are more concerned about what the fact that Christ lives signifies to

The Church

The true church, the "called-out ones," composes the body, the bride, the beloved of the Lord Jesus Christ. She is His chief heart interest, not only because, at the fearful price of His own poured-out blood and broken body, He purchased her salvation, but because she is the sole repository and dispenser of His Gospel in this world. Upon her, filled with the Holy Spirit, rests His hope of reaching sinners with the message that by His death and resurrection the Father has been reconciled to, them. The church remains on earth for the specific purpose of beseeching men to be reconciled to God.

No wonder, then, that the Lord surrounded the fact of the resurrection, "the keystone to the arch of the Gospel," with incontrovertible evidence. All of the claims of the Lord Jesus Christ as Saviour and Lord depended upon the historic validity of His rising from the dead. His resurrection was the seal of all His redemptive work and the guarantee of His salvation to everyone who would accept it by faith.

Paul stated it clearly:

"If Christ be not risen, then is our preaching vain . . . . And if Christ be not raised, your faith is vain; ye are yet in your sins. Then they also which are fallen asleep in Christ are perished. If in this life only we have hope in Christ, we are of all men most miserable."

It is an astonishing fact to contemplate that when Jesus died, no one, so far as we can judge from the scriptural records, believed in His resurrection. His disciples had seen Him demonstrate His mastery over death three times, when He brought to life the twelve-year-old maiden, the young man of Nain, and His personal friend, Lazarus. They had heard His plain assertion: "I am the resurrection and the life." They had been told by Him again and again that "the Son of man must be delivered into the hands of sinful men, and be crucified, and the third day rise again." They remembered it all vividly enough after He rose from the dead; but on the day of His burial, not one of them had confidence in Him that He would return to life.

On the eve of His crucifixion, "Then saith Jesus unto them, All ye shall be offended because of me this night: for it is written, I will smite the shepherd, and the sheep of the flock shall be scattered abroad." What a scattering of the sheep there was when they all forsook Him and fled! For their faith too had fled. The darkness that covered the land for the three hours that Jesus hung upon the cross was no blacker than the despair which fell upon the spirits of the disciples when Jesus was laid in Joseph's new rock-hewn tomb. The two disciples on the Emmaus road but expressed the hopeless cry of the entire group: "But we trusted that it had been he which should have redeemed Israel."

Yes, the evidence of Christ's resurrection had to be unmistakable, not only to convince an incredulous, hostile world, but to confirm the faith and restore the confidence of the bewildered little flock. The Lord was well aware that if this band of weak men and women were to carry His Gospel to the ends of the earth, if they were to invade Satan's strongholds and storm the very gates of Hell, they would have to be possessed of, and obsessed with, an unshakable faith in His resurrection. That He was alive was the final, undeniable proof that He was God and not man. His children were not to "follow cunningly devised fables" but to rely upon genuine facts, incidents that actually occurred. For this reason the Lord saw to it that the resurrection was the best attested fact in the evangelical record. It became for the church "the Gibraltar of Christian faith and the Waterloo of infidelity."

Consider the circumstantial evidence of that first Easter: the empty tomb; the orderly graveclothes; the broken Roman seal; the disrupted stone; the fearful earthquake; the angel visitants; the terrified guards; the frightened women; the dumbfounded disciples, and the manifest lies of the enemies of Christ who gave "large money unto the soldiers" to publish the fiction that His disciples had made away with His body.

But that was by no means all. "He showed himself alive after his passion by many infallible proofs, being seen of them forty days, and speaking of the things pertaining to the kingdom of God." Although Jesus was naturally eager to get back Home to His Father, there was so much for Him to do in assuring His children that He was indeed alive—very God of very God—that He was actually delayed on earth forty days! He made seventeen personal appearances, before and after His ascension, to various persons individually and in groups. "He was seen of above five hundred brethren at once." In so short a treatise we cannot even list the numerous details which substantiated His resurrection.

Yes, God multiplied the evidence; and, thank God, the church at last believed it and after Pentecost went forth ecstatically to proclaim it in the power of the Holy Spirit. The book of Acts and the entire missionary enterprise from that time until the present hour were the results. The resurrection of Christ is the central message and the motivating power of the church.

One of the strongest arguments in favor of the literal resurrection of the Lord Jesus Christ is the continuance to this very day of that belief against all opposition and persecution. It has been the most persistent of doctrines. Men were burned at the stake, singing of a living Christ through the flames; frail women were thrown to ravenous beasts, affirming that Jesus was alive. It is not surprising that "their sound went into all the earth and their words unto the ends of the world."

This is the heritage of the church today. We preach not a defeated Jesus, still hanging upon a cross of sin and shame.

The head that once was crowned with thorns
 Is crowned in glory now;
A royal diadem adorns
 The mighty Victor's brow.

We have a risen Saviour! Because He lives, we live also. Because He lives, we are "stedfast, unmoveable, always abounding in the work of the Lord, forasmuch as [we] know that [our] labour is not in vain in the Lord." Because He lives, we "can do all things through Christ which strengtheneth [us]." Because He lives, "we are more than conquerors through him that loved us."

Now the church militant, we suffer, we toil, we sacrifice, "as unknown, and yet well known, as dying, and behold, we live; as chastened, and not killed; as sorrowful, yet always rejoicing; as poor, yet making many rich; as having nothing, and yet possessing all things." Soon we shall be in the church triumphant, in the presence of our living Lord, "a glorious church, not having spot, or wrinkle, or any such thing." And we owe it all to the fact that Jesus not only died for us, but that He also rose again "for our justification"!

But what of the individuals to whom Jesus made personal appearances after His resurrection? We are interested in knowing what the fact that Jesus was alive meant to

Mary of Magdala

How like the grace of God it was that Christ should have made His first post-resurrection appearance to Mary Magdalene! Tender and touching is the tale of His dealings with her. While it cannot be definitely proven that she was "the sinful woman" of Luke's Gospel, there is no question but that she had been a great sinner. Evermore she bore the designation, "Mary Magdalene, out of whom went seven devils." The "seven" would indicate the lowest depths of human depravity.

Apparently she had drunk the vile cup of iniquity to the dregs. The very name of her hometown, Magdala, was synonymous with every heinous sin; and history records that its wickedness finally destroyed it.

Whether or not Mary became acquainted with Jesus at Simon's feast, it is certain that somewhere along her life's way she encountered Him and heard His call to sinners; "Come unto me, all ye that labour, and are heavy laden, and I will give you rest." Ever afterwards she gave evidence that she "loved much."

And why should she not love Christ? He was the only One whose love had not done her harm and the first really worthy Object that ever claimed her worship and affection. He saved her soul, forgave her sins, gave her a new life; and she yielded her heart to Him in complete devotion. As she had gone all the way in sins, so she went all the way with her Lord when she was redeemed.

Imagine, then, Mary's agony over the suffering and death of Jesus. One of the last to leave the scene of horror, she had lingered until Joseph took charge of the body of the Lord, and Nicodemus appeared with his hundred-weight of myrrh and aloes. With a heart breaking under the weight of her woe, Mary hastened home to prepare additional spices that she and the other women might perform the last sad ministrations for Christ. Her faith had suffered a staggering blow. She had believed Jesus to be God, for who but God could have forgiven her sin and changed her life? But could God lie silent and dead, wrapped in the garments of the grave?

Restlessly she hurried back to the tomb while it was still dark. Perhaps a faint hope stirred within her heart that Jesus might do something about His own death as He had done about that of Lazarus, who had been dead longer than He.

Mary "seeth the stone taken away from the sepulcher. Then she runneth, and cometh to Simon Peter, and to the other disciple, whom Jesus loved, and saith unto them, They have taken away the Lord out of the sepulchre, and we know not where they have laid him." When John and Peter heard these tidings, they started off immediately for the tomb and quite likely Mary followed them, for she was there after they returned to their homes.

"But Mary stood without the sepulchre weeping." She wept for the agony of her Lord upon the cross; she wept for the cruel end of such a blessed, holy life; she wept for her own hopelessness and bereavement. Surely the end had come for her and for all of the world He had come to redeem. There was no one to whom to go: He only had the words of eternal life; He only could "bind up the broken hearted." Her Lord was irretrievably gone, and the waves of doubt and sorrow rolled over her and engulfed her soul. Of course, her grief was wrong, because it was the result of unbelief; but that did not make her less pitiable.

But suddenly, in a moment, Mary's mourning was turned into an ecstasy of gladness! Through tear-wet eyes she beheld Jesus, alive! Revealed to her in the mention of her name, since "never man spake like this man"; in an instant her faith in Him as her God was restored, and her burden of sorrow was lifted. She knew it was He because again He met the need of her heart.

It was not alone His familiar outward appearance and the tone of His voice when He called her "Mary," but it was because He was aware of her spiritual difficulty and took care of it at once. Bidding her not to delay Him by clinging to Him since He was already on His way to the Father, He gave her a commission, "Go and tell"; and Mary went singing on her way, a happy, triumphant witness of the resurrection!

We turn from this joyous scene to another eyewitness,

Thomas the Twin

In the make-up of his personality, Thomas Didymus (the twin) was the complete antithesis to impulsive, affectionate Mary of Magdala. His was a thoughtful, inquiring mind. He was the calculating type that wanted to be certain of everything. He did not jump at conclusions; cautious and deliberate, he seldom made mistakes in judgment. Lack of courage was not his weakness, for when Jesus was about to walk into the jaws of death by returning to Judea to raise Lazarus, it was he who proposed: "Let us also go, that we may die with him."

He may not have doubted any more than the others; but because he was so outspoken about it, the record stands against him. They were all guilty of not believing Christ when He stated that He would die and after three days rise again. If they heard Him at all, they must have believed that He was using some theological figure of speech. So obsessed were they with the popular Judaistic, Messianic view of a glorious kingdom to be restored to Israel that they gave no credence at all to His references concerning His passion.

The incredulity of Thomas was reprehensible and not to be passed over lightly. Jesus had once told the Jews, "If ye believe not that I am he, ye shall die in your sins." While God has patience with an honest inquirer, unbelief has no virtue in His eyes. Contrary to the popular atheistic view of our day, skepticism is not an indication of intellectuality, either.

The risen Christ was cognizant of the difficulty of Thomas, of the awful doubt that was shaking his soul, of the violent struggle that was taking place in his heart. "He knew all men, and needed not that any should testify of man: for he knew what was in man." Because He was God, He was aware, too, of those unbelieving words Thomas had spoken so hastily, in the bitterness of his soul, when he believed that all was lost at the crucifixion: "Except I shall see . . . I will not believe."

It is amazing that when eight days later Jesus appeared personally to Thomas, He did not reprove him for his doubts. He had compassion upon him, for He knew how sick at heart Thomas was and He dealt with him as kindly as He had with poor, sorrowing Mary.

"Then saith he to Thomas, Reach hither thy finger, and behold my hands; and reach hither thy hand, and thrust it into my side, and be not faithless, but believing. And Thomas answered . . . My Lord and my God."

Did Thomas touch the wounds of Jesus for proof? Certainly not! The fact that Christ understood his need was enough for "Doubting Thomas," who from that instant became "Believing Thomas." Not only was he transformed into a bright and shining witness for the resurrection, but after the descent of the Holy Spirit on the day of Pentecost, he became a flaming evangel. History records that he gave a good account of himself as a missionary to distant Parthia.

Christ lives! And He is interested in the soul trouble of those who, like Thomas, find it hard to believe in the supernatural. "He that cometh to God must believe that he is, and that he is a rewarder of them that diligently seek him . . . . If any man will do his will, he shall know of the doctrine."

Thus Mary of Magdala became a witness of the resurrection, and so did Thomas the Twin,

"And Peter"

All of us have a fellow feeling for Peter, because in so many ways he resembles most of us. Constructed of the same imperfect material, he was so rash; he made so many mistakes; he talked so much; he so often failed at critical times. But withal he was an interesting and lovable character, irresistible and irrepressible.

It amazes us to note the reaction of Christ to Peter upon their first encounter: "And when Jesus beheld him, he said, Thou art Simon the son of Jona: thou shalt be called Cephas . . . A stone." In the three years that Peter followed Jesus as His disciple, very infrequent were the indications of any rock-like substance in his character. There was a brief glimpse of it when he made the Great Confession: "We believe and are sure that thou art that Christ, the Son of the living God." But on the whole his performance was definitely disappointing and not up to Jesus' estimate of him. But that was before the resurrection!

Peter was a much more direct personality than Thomas; he was an extrovert in every respect, a man of action rather than a man of thought. He was not held back by inhibitions, cursed by an inferiority complex or tortured by a skeptical mind. His was a battle with a dispositional weakness which he attempted to conceal by bluster and bravado: he was a craven coward. No one was better aware of it than he, unless it was his Lord. But Jesus also knew a wonderful secret about Peter: He held the key that could unlock Peter's personality. He holds such a key for the hearts of all of His children!

After the crucifixion, Peter was in deeper soul trouble than even Mary and Thomas. Not only overwhelmed with the awful sense of loss that Mary felt, not only filled with a bitter doubt, as was Thomas; but on top of these experiences of sorrow and unbelief, he was suffering from a gnawing conviction of sin.

No man ever hated himself more than did Peter after the death of Jesus. He remembered with agony his egotistical boasting that he would never forsake Jesus, he who not only deserted with all of the others, leaving Jesus to His enemies in His hour of need, but who "denied with an oath, I do not know the man"!

All four of the Gospel writers tell the shameful story of Peter's treachery. Apparently the Holy Spirit wanted us to know how far the best of men may fall and how high the worst of men may be lifted up by His grace. The heinous sin of Judas seems no worse than Peter's, the only difference being that Peter repented while Judas did away with himself, thus himself shutting the door to God's mercy.

Jesus, when a prisoner in the house of the high priest before His trial, "turned and looked upon Peter . . . and Peter went out and wept bitterly." What was in that look only Christ and Peter knew, for He deals personally and privately with the need of every heart. For the first time in his life, Peter saw himself as he really was, and he felt that he no longer had any claim upon the love and mercy of Christ.

No wonder the angel in the empty tomb declared to Mary of Magdala and the other women: "He is risen; He is not here . . . go your way, tell his disciples and Peter." Can it be that Peter, because of his shameful conduct, no longer even claimed to be a disciple? His faith had been crushed, and he had sunk into the depths of despair and self-incrimination.

If he had only remembered the promise of Jesus to him, he would not have known such utter defeat. "Simon, Simon, behold, Satan hath desired to have you, that he may sift you as wheat: but I have prayed for thee, that thy faith fail not."

So Jesus arranged to be "seen of Cephas" in person after His resurrection. His initial appearance to him with the ten disciples apparently did not accomplish what the Lord wished, nor did the visit to the eleven when He dealt with Thomas. The third appearance to the seven at the Sea of Galilee was for the obvious purpose of restoring His erring Peter.

Since Peter had denied Him thrice, three times Jesus put to him that burning, heart-searching question: "Lovest thou me?" He had to separate Peter forever from his old occupation of fishing which he now probably felt was the only thing he was fit for; He had to draw out of his heart the love of which he was capable. He uncovered the rock. Did Peter believe in the resurrection after this experience? He did, because it was the living Christ who remade his vessel which had been broken upon the wheel of sin. His sin freely forgiven, restored to his place of leadership among the disciples, Peter became one of the greatest preachers of the resurrection ever known on earth.

Hear him on the day of Pentecost: "Him, being delivered by the determinate counsel and foreknowledge of God, ye have taken, and by wicked hands have crucified and slain: Whom God hath raised up." Listen to him in Solomon's porch: "The God of our fathers hath glorified his Son Jesus; whom ye delivered up . . . . And killed the Prince of life, whom God hath raised from the dead; whereof we are witnesses." A prisoner of the Jews, in the presence of Annas and Caiaphas, he declared boldly: "By the name of Jesus Christ of Nazareth, whom ye crucified, whom God raised from the dead, even by him doth this man stand here before you whole."

Peter never stopped preaching the resurrection until the day the enemies of Christ crucified him, head down, a martyr for the Lord Jesus Christ's sake.

Our hearts thrill as we recall these post-resurrection personal appearances of Jesus which brought such a change to the lives of Mary, Thomas, Peter and many others that space does not allow us to mention. Paul, for instance, "man born out of due time," whose meeting with the risen Christ on the Damascus road changed him from a hater to a lover of the Saviour, and transformed him into the greatest missionary this world ever knew. We could follow a great cloud of witnesses down to our day who, although they did not see Jesus bodily, believed and died for the truth of the resurrection.

But the most important thing of all to us is not what the fact that Christ lives meant to them but what it signifies to

You and Me

Does it mean to us, as it did to Mary, that the bitter grief which no one understands has been removed from our hearts; that our Thomas-like doubts are gone; that our personal sin question, like Peter's, has been solved? Has the risen Christ met our own personal needs? If not, then there can be no Easter in our hearts, however fragrant the lilies, and however melodious the hymns of praise. There is no real knowledge at all except experimental knowledge. So what we hear and read and learn about the risen Christ may thrill us, but it is our own personal experiences with Him that will change us.

Are we of this day defrauded because we have not seen Jesus in person? Not at all. Since we have made our appearance so far along the stream of time, of necessity we are forced into the group of those who must believe without seeing. And Jesus says of us, if we accept these things by faith: "Blessed are they that have not seen, and yet have believed." We thus have the advantage over the eyewitnesses. In addition, there is something glorious ahead for us: that is sight. Faith does very well for the present time, but what will it be like to see Jesus and be with Him?

> Jesus, the very thought of Thee
> With sweetness fills the breast;
> But sweeter far Thy face to see
> And in Thy presence rest.

If you are a Christian, think a moment about your own conversion. When you received Jesus as your Saviour, was it because of these infallible proofs of the life and death and resurrection of Jesus Christ in Palestine? I dare say it was not. You were bearing a load of sin and sorrow in your heart; you heard the Gospel; you came to Jesus, and He lifted your burden. You believed, not because of outward evidences, but because He met your interior need. Afterwards, it was a joy to have the truth corroborated, and to know that there was a definite basis of fact for "the things most surely believed among us."

Have you a need today in your Christian life? Remember Christ lives and He can supply it. Trust Him and you will not be disappointed. Christ is experienced in dealing with human hearts. Let Him satisfy the deepest longing of your soul.

And to you, my unsaved friend, the resurrection should mean that there is an all-sufficient Saviour, an almighty living Lord, in Jesus Christ, whom you may know if you will. "If thou shalt confess with thy mouth the Lord Jesus, and shalt believe in thine heart that God hath raised him from the dead, thou shalt be saved."

It is necessary for the salvation of your immortal soul to accept the fact that Christ lives. If He does not live, He is not God; and if He is not God, there is no hope for anyone in earth or Heaven. But He is God and He is alive! And millions of true believers throughout the ages have witnessed to that fact because He met their personal needs.

Will you prove to yourself today that Jesus is alive by letting Him supply the need of your heart and life, by allowing Him to become your Lord and your God? Then you may join with all believers in the song of Easter:

He lives, He lives, Christ Jesus lives today!
He walks with me and talks with me along life's narrow way.
He lives, He lives, salvation to impart!
You ask me how I know He lives?
He lives within my heart.

In the bonds of Death He lay
  Who for our offence was slain;
But the Lord is risen today
  Christ hath brought us life again.
Wherefore let us all rejoice,
  Singing loud, with cheerful voice,
  Hallelujah!

—Martin Luther

Glory Bright! — *He is not here* (Mark 16:6).

Oh, empty tomb of Jesus!
  This holds a glory bright
That fills death's shadowed valley with resurrection light;
Oh, mighty love of Jesus! His feet alone have trod
Earth's heights and hepths of sorrow and made a way to God.

— Annie Johnson Flint

XVIII.

Easter: Is It Wrong for Christians to Observe It?

JOHN R. RICE

You ask, "One thing I wonder about: Why do you use Easter when it is not scriptural. I mean the name and the day set by Rome?"

Again you want to know: "Is it not as important as some other things when we aren't to use heathen gods' names? Yet my dictionary says that Easter is the name of a heathen goddess."

Answer: The *Encyclopedia Britannica* says:

> EASTER, the annual festival observed throughout Christendom in commemoration of the resurrection of Jesus Christ. The name Easter, like the names of the days of the week, is a survival from the old Teutonic mythology. According to Bede *(De Temp. Rat. c.x.v.)* it is derived from *Eostre,* or *Ostara,* the Anglo-Saxon goddess of spring, to whom the month answering to our April, and called *Eosturmonath,* was dedicated. This month, Bede says, was the same as the *mensis paschalis,* "when the old festival was observed with the gladness of a new solemnity."
>
> The root *pasch,* from which so many other names for Easter are derived, is from the Hebrew *pesach* (Passover) from the verb form "he passed over."

The way the observance of Easter came about is somewhat as follows.

The crucifixion of Christ followed the clear pattern laid down in the passover lamb type in the Old Testament. First Corinthians 5:7 says, ". . . For even Christ our passover is sacrificed for us." So, clearly the passover lamb typified Jesus Christ. And just as the Jews, staying inside their houses with the blood of the passover lamb on the doors, were saved from the Death Angel which killed all the firstborn in Egypt, just so, one who has trusted in the blood of Jesus Christ is saved and kept safe by the precious sacrifice of Christ, our Passover.

In John 19:31 we are told that Jesus was crucified on the very day of the preparation, that is, the annual day when the passover lamb was killed and cooked. Christ fulfilled to the letter the type and died on the day when the passover lambs had been slain annually for fifteen hundred years.

At first all the Christians were converted Jews. When they saw the wonderful way in which the passover supper and feast were fulfilled in Jesus Christ, it is natural that this time every year was regarded as a sacred and beautiful time to remember the death and resurrection of the Saviour. So it was the custom, at the Jewish Passover time and just following, to specially remember the death of Christ and His resurrection.

You see, they had been celebrating this time before they were converted, as Jews looking toward the coming of the Messiah. Afterward it was very natural for them still to be reminded of the wonderful fulfillment of this prophecy in type, commanded and observed in Old Testament times by Jews everywhere.

But now there came some trouble. The Passover Day of the 14th of Nisan came at one certain time every year. But Christians had come to feel that the resurrection of Christ from the dead, which pictured our own glorious resurrection yet to come, made every Sunday—the first day of the week—a memorial of Christ's resurrection. Since Jesus rose from the dead on the first day of the week, then Sunday is naturally a memorial to Christ's resurrection.

Now should the Christians keep the Jewish feast of the Passover and celebrate the resurrection of Christ in the month Nisan at a certain time every year, no matter what day of the week it fell on? To do so seemed to them to be staying with unbelieving Jews and following the Jewish ceremonial law. Or would it be better, they asked themselves, to set a certain Sunday every year, and to celebrate annually this resurrection instead of on a week day?

Christians decided to set a Sunday annually for Easter observance. In fact, as the *Encyclopedia Britannica* says,

> Generally speaking, the Western churches kept Easter on the first day of the week, while Eastern churches followed the Jewish rule and kept Easter on the 14th day.

In A. D. 325 the Council of Nicaea decided that Easter should be celebrated on a Sunday. Later when the Gregorian calendar was adopted, the present system of fixing the date of Easter was decided. Now it does not specially matter, but some years ago when there were no electric lights, it was of great importance to have moonlit nights; and for other reasons the movements of the heavenly bodies affected time of festivity or worship or travel or work.

It is true that Catholic officials set the annual time for Easter. But they set up the whole Gregorian calendar also. Am I to refuse to have January because January is named for the Roman god Janus? Must I refuse to call Saturday Saturday because it is named after the heathen god Saturn? Or must I count it a sin to worship on Sunday, named after the sun god? Would it be a sin to live or worship in Manitou Springs, Colorado, when it is named after the great spirit of the Indians, Manitou?

All these names are beside the point. The truth is, Old Testament Jews observed a passover season, a feast period given by the Lord to picture the coming Saviour, our Passover Lamb. New Testament Christians, having this period on their Jewish calendars, used it to worship God and to remember the crucifixion and the resurrection. Out of this came the observance now officially carried on by Catholic and other churches with Palm Sunday, the Passion Week, and Easter Sunday, celebrating the resurrection of Jesus Christ.

Is there any binding obligation on Christians to observe Easter? None at all!

Is Easter a good time to preach on the resurrection of Christ and to remember His resurrection? Indeed it is. Let us thank God that at this time of the year many people are taught to think of Christ's resurrection. Let us thank God that many people go to church on Easter who do not go at other times. Let us thank God that, when some people think about rabbits and Easter hats, Christians can call attention to the death and resurrection of our Saviour.

That is not a matter of law, not a rule of the church, not a requirement; it is simply an opportunity for Christians to happily remember Jesus Christ and rejoice in His glorious resurrection, a chance to preach the Gospel.

It is true that the name for Easter comes from the Anglo-Saxon goddess of spring, *Eostre*, but what matters it about the origin of the word? It means Easter and nothing else, and it would be foolish to make an issue of where we got the name.

Would a Christian be wrong to use the regular names for the planets of our solar system because they were named for heathen gods and goddesses? Is it wrong for a Christian to vulcanize a tire, or to call the process vulcanizing, because it is named for Vulcan, the god of fire?

Names mean simply what they mean. It would be a superstition for

Christians to imagine dark and sinful meanings in every word which comes from some other language into our English language.

The Bible never makes an issue about whether we shall observe Christmas or Easter. Since the Bible makes no issue, it is wrong for Christians to make an issue.

Now if anybody started out to force everybody to observe Easter and Christmas, I would oppose that because it would be contrary to the Bible. Likewise, when one starts out to hinder others' remembering the resurrection or the birth of Christ on certain days, when it is easy to get the attention of many people to these sacred subjects, then I must oppose that, too.

It is wrong to fight over incidentals where the Bible makes no issue. Rather, let us be friendly with all good people who love the Lord and are trying to serve Him, and let us take every occasion we can to get hearers for the Gospel and to get the attention of people on Bible truths.

In the Saviour's name, yours,
John R. Rice

XIX.

Christ's Crucifixion: Friday or Wednesday?

Was Jesus Really Three Days and Three Nights in the Heart of the Earth?

R. A. TORREY

Matthew, in the 12th chapter of his Gospel and verse 40, reports Jesus as saying: 'As Jonah was three days and three nights in the belly of the whale ["sea monster," A.S.V. margin], so shall the Son of man be three days and three nights in the heart of the earth.'

According to the commonly accepted tradition of the church, Jesus was crucified on Friday, dying at 3:00 p.m., or somewhere between 3:00 p.m. and sundown, and was raised from the dead very early in the morning of the following Sunday. Many readers of the Bible are puzzled to know how the interval between late Friday afternoon and early Sunday morning can be figured out to be three days and three nights. It seems rather to be two nights, one day and a very small portion of another day.

The solution of this apparent difficulty proposed by many commentators is the "a day and a night" is simply another way of saying "a day" and that the ancient Jews reckoned a fraction of a day as a whole day; so they say there was a part of Friday (a very small part), or a day and a night; all of Saturday, another day, or a day and a night; part of Sunday (a very small part), another day, or a day and a night.

There are many persons whom this solution does not altogether satisfy, and the writer is free to confess it does not satisfy him at all. It seems to him to be a makeshift, and a very weak makeshift.

Is there any solution that is altogether satisfactory? There is.

The first fact to be noticed in the proper solution is that the Bible nowhere says or implies that Jesus was crucified and died on Friday. It is said that Jesus was crucified on "the day before the sabbath" (Mark 15:42). As the Jewish weekly Sabbath came on Saturday, beginning at sunset the evening before, the conclusion is naturally drawn that as

Jesus was crucified the day before the Sabbath He must have been crucified on Friday. But it is a well-known fact, to which the Bible bears abundant testimony, that the Jews had other Sabbaths beside the weekly Sabbath which fell on Saturday. The first day of the Passover week, no matter upon what day of the week it came, was always a Sabbath (Exod. 12:16; Lev. 23:7; Num. 28:16-18).

The question therefore arises whether the Sabbath that followed Christ's crucifixion was the weekly Sabbath (Saturday) or the Passover Sabbath, falling on the 15th of Nisan, which came that year on Thursday.

Now the Bible does not leave us to speculate in regard to which Sabbath is meant in this instance, for John tells us in so many words, in John 19:14, that the day on which Jesus was tried and crucified was "the preparation *of the Passover*"(A.S.V.), that is, it was not the day before the weekly Sabbath (Friday) but the day before the Passover Sabbath, which came that year on Thursday. That is to say, the day on which Jesus Christ was crucified was Wednesday.

Jesus Crucified on Wednesday

John makes this as clear as day. The Gospel of John was written later than the other Gospels, and scholars have for a long time noticed that in various places there was an evident intention to correct false impressions that one might get from reading the other Gospels. One of these false impressions was that Jesus ate the Passover with His disciples at the regular time of the Passover. To correct this false impression John clearly states that He ate in the evening before and that He Himself died on the cross *at the very moment* the Passover lambs were being slain "between the two evenings" on the 14th Nisan (Exod. 12:6, Heb. and A.S.V. margin). God's real Paschal Lamb—Jesus—of whom all other paschal lambs offered through the centuries were only types, was therefore slain at the very time appointed of God.

Passover Lamb Fulfilled in Jesus

Everything about the Passover lamb was a picture of Jesus: (1) He was a Lamb without blemish and without spot (Exod. 12:5). (2) He was chosen on the 10th day of Nisan (Exod. 12:3), for it was on the 10th day of the month, the preceding Saturday, that the triumphal entry into Jerusalem was made, since they came from Jericho to Bethany six days before the Passover (John 12:1—that would be six days before Thursday, which would be Friday); and it was on the next day that the entry into Jerusalem was made (John 12:12 and following verses), that is, on Saturday, the 10th Nisan. It was also on this same day that Judas went to the chief priests and offered to betray Jesus for thirty pieces of silver (Matt. 26:6-16; Mark 14:3-11). As it was after the supper in the house of Simon the leper, and as the supper occurred late on Friday, that is, after sunset, or early on Saturday, after the supper would necessarily be on the 10th Nisan. This being the price set on Him by the chief priest, it was the buying or taking to them of a lamb which, according to law, must occur on the 10th Nisan. Furthermore, they put the exact value on the lamb that Old Testament prophecy predicted (Matt 26:15, compare Zech. 11:12). (3) Not a bone of Him was broken when He was killed (John 19:36, compare Exod. 12:46; Num. 9.12; Ps. 34:20). (4) And He was killed on the 14th Nisan between the evenings, just before the beginning of the 15th Nisan at sundown (Exod. 12:6, A.S.V. margin).

If we take just exactly what the Bible says, viz., that Jesus was slain before the Passover Sabbath, the type is marvelously fulfilled in every detail; but if we accept the traditional theory that Jesus was crucified on Friday, the type fails at many points.

Furthermore, if we accept the traditional view that Jesus was crucified on Friday and ate the Passover on the regular day of the Passover, then the journey from Jericho to Bethany, which occurred six days before the Passover (John 12:1) would fall on a Saturday, that is, the Jewish Sabbath. Such a journey on the Jewish Sabbath would be contrary to the Jewish law. Of course it was impossible for Jesus to take such a journey on the Jewish Sabbath. In reality His triumphal entry into Jerusalem was on the Jewish Sabbath, Saturday. This was altogether possible, for the Bible elsewhere tells us that Bethany was a Sabbath day's journey from Jerusalem (Acts 1:12; compare Luke 24:50).

Furthermore, it has been figured out by the astronomers that in the year 30 A. D., which is the commonly accepted year of the crucifixion of our Lord, the Passover was kept on Thursday, April 6th, the moon being full that day. The chronologists who have supposed that the crucifixion took place on Friday have been greatly perplexed by this fact that in the year 30 A. D. the Passover occurred on Thursday. One writer, in seeking a solution of the difficulty, suggests that the crucifixion may have been in the year 33 A. D., for although the full moon was on a Thursday that year also, yet as it was within two and a half hours of Friday, he thinks that perhaps the Jews may have kept it that day. But when we accept exactly what the Bible says, namely, that Jesus was not crucified on the Passover day but on "the preparation of the Passover," and that He was to be three days and three nights in the grave, and as "the preparation of the Passover" that year would be Wednesday and His resurrection early on the first day of the week, this allows exactly three days and three nights in the grave.

To sum it all up,

Jesus Died About Sunset on Wednesday

Seventy-two hours later, exactly three days and three nights, at the beginning of the first day of the week (Saturday at sunset), He arose from the grave. When the women visited the tomb just before dawn next morning, they found the grave already empty. So we are not driven to any such makeshift as that any small portion of a day is reckoned as a whole day and night, but we find that the statement of Jesus was literally true. Three days and three nights His body was dead and lay in the sepulchre. While His body lay dead, He Himself being quickened in the spirit (I Pet. 3:18) went into the heart of the earth and preached unto the spirits which were in prison (I Pet. 3:19).

This supposed difficulty solves itself, as do so many other difficulties in the Bible, when we take the Bible as meaning exactly what it says.

It is sometimes objected against the view here advanced that the two on the way to Emmaus early on the first day of the week (that is, Sunday) said to Jesus in speaking of the crucifixion and events accompanying it: "Beside all this, to day is the third day since these things were done" (Luke 24:21), and it is said that if the crucifixion took place on Wednesday, Sunday would be the fourth day since these things were done.

But the answer is very simple. These things were done just as Thursday was beginning at sunset on Wednesday. They were therefore completed on Thursday, and the first day since Thursday would be Friday; the second day since Thursday would be Saturday; and "the third day since" Thursday would be Sunday, the first day of the week. So the supposed objection in reality supports the theory. On the other hand, if the crucifixion took place on Friday, by no manner of reckoning could Sunday be made "the third day since" these things were done.

Many Scriptures Teach This

There are many passages in Scripture that support the theory advanced above and make it necessary to believe that Jesus died late on Wednesday. Some of them are as follows:

"For as Jonas was three days and three nights in the whale's belly; so shall the Son of man be *three days and three nights* in the heart of the earth."—Matt. 12:40.

"This fellow said, I am able to destroy the temple of God, and to build it *in three days*."—Matt. 26:61.

"Thou that destroyest the temple, and buildest it *in three days*, save thyself."—Matt. 27:40.

"Sir, we remember that that deceiver said, while he was yet alive, *After three days* I will rise again."—Matt 27:63.

"The Son of man must suffer many things. . .and be killed, and *after three days rise again*."—Mark 8:31.

"They shall kill him, and when he is killed, *after three days* he shall rise again."—Mark 9:31, A.S.V.

"They shall scourge him, and shall kill him, and *after three days* he shall rise again."—Mark 10:34, A.S.V.

"Destroy this temple that is made with hands, and *in three days* I will build another made without hands."—Mark 14:58, A.S.V.

"Ah, thou that destroyest the temple, and buildest it *in three days*, Save thyself."—Mark 15:29,30.

"Beside all this, to day is *the third day since* these things were done."—Luke 24:21.

"Jesus answered and said unto them, Destroy this temple, and *in three days* I will raise it up. Then said the Jews, Forty and six years was this temple in building, and wilt thou rear it up *in three days?* But he spake of the temple of his body. When therefore he was risen from the dead, his disciples remembered that he had said this. . .and the word which Jesus had said."—John 2:19-22.

There is absolutely nothing in favor of Friday crucifixion, but everything in the Scripture is perfectly harmonized by Wednesday crucifixion. It is remarkable how many prophetical and typical passages of the Old Testament are fulfilled and how many seeming discrepancies in the gospel narratives are straightened out when we once come to understand that Jesus died on Wednesday and not on Friday.

(From DIFFICULTIES IN THE BIBLE. Used by permission. Moody Bible Institute of Chicago.)

For a complete list of books available from the Sword of the Lord, write to Sword of the Lord Publishers, P. O. Box 1099, Murfreesboro, Tennessee 37133.